THE
LANGUAGES
OF
MAGIC

"Combining theoretical insights from linguistics and semiotics with practical applications in magic, and thereby providing a framework for understanding magical practices as fundamentally communicative acts, this book is nothing short of an epiphany. Toby Chappell masterfully connects the dots of 'semiotic manipulation' and leaves you with a very inspiring manual on how to use your own skills. A deep-reaching and very useful book!"

CARL ABRAHAMSSON, AUTHOR OF *OCCULTURE* AND
MEETINGS WITH REMARKABLE MAGICIANS

"*The Languages of Magic* by Toby Chappell is an intriguing study of the building block of magic: language. Delving into the magical power of semiotics, exploring how language and symbols shape our reality, Chappell articulately argues that mastering the art of using the right words and signs is the key to success in magical endeavors. A fascinating and highly recommended book."

DARRAGH MASON,
AUTHOR OF *SONG OF THE DARK MAN*

"What you now hold in your hand is more than a book; *The Languages of Magic* is itself a powerful example of operative magic. This compendium of linguistic and occult wisdom holds the key to transforming the magician, the field of magical studies, and perhaps the world at large. Toby Chappell connects deeply researched concepts in a way that shifts the frame of reference and highlights the immense utility that the understanding of signs and words can offer the magician."

PHILIP H. FARBER, AUTHOR OF *BRAIN MAGICK: EXERCISES IN META-MAGICK AND INVOCATION*

"Speak the universe into existence! *The Languages of Magic* by scholar Toby Chappell provides an overview of magical communication and various schools of semiotics to show that magic is spoken into existence. He tackles a very complex topic from multiple angles and presents the information in a way that is easily understood by nonspecialists. This is required reading for anyone serious about the study and practical application of magical communication."

SCOTT SHELL, PH.D., AUTHOR OF *THE APPLICATION OF PEIRCEAN SEMIOTICS TO THE ELDER FUTHARK TRADITION*

THE
LANGUAGES
✪F
MAGIC

Transform Reality through
Words, Magical Symbols, & Sigils

TOBY CHAPPELL

Destiny Books
Rochester, Vermont

Destiny Books
One Park Street
Rochester, Vermont 05767
www.DestinyBooks.com

Destiny Books is a division of Inner Traditions International

Cataloging-in-Publication Data for this title is available from the Library of Congress

ISBN 979-8-88850-067-5 (print)
ISBN 979-8-88850-068-2 (ebook)

Printed and bound in the United States by Lake Book Manufacturing, LLC

10 9 8 7 6 5 4 3 2 1

Text design and layout by Virginia Scott Bowman
This book was typeset in Garamond Premier Pro and Futura with FMBoylar Rough
used as the display typeface.

To send correspondence to the author of this book, mail a first-class letter to the
author c/o Inner Traditions • Bear & Company, One Park Street, Rochester, VT
05767, and we will forward the communication, or contact the author directly at
semiurgist.com.

Scan the QR code and save 25% at InnerTraditions.com.
Browse over 2,000 titles on spirituality, the occult, ancient
mysteries, new science, holistic health, and natural medicine.

To my high school Latin teacher,
Richard Beaton, who taught me the magic of
language, and to Michael Aquino, who taught
me the language of magic.

CONTENTS

FOREWORD

THE ART OF METACOMMUNICATION   IX
By Stephen E. Flowers, Ph.D.

ACKNOWLEDGMENTS   XIII

✪

PRELUDE

THE MAGIC IS IN THE COMMUNICATION   1

1 WHAT DO LANGUAGE AND SEMIOTICS
  HAVE TO DO WITH MAGIC?   10

2 A SURVEY OF DIFFERENT MODELS OF MAGIC   43

3 A BRIEF HISTORY OF SEMIOTICS   72

4 VIEWING MAGIC THROUGH LINGUISTICS AND
  THE PHILOSOPHY OF LANGUAGE   112

5 LANGUAGE, MYTH, AND MAGIC   147

✪

INTERLUDE

THE METHODOLOGY FOR THE CASE STUDIES   173

6 CASE STUDY I   175
  MEDITERRANEAN MAGIC IN ANTIQUITY

7 CASE STUDY II   209
  RUNES AND SEMIURGY

8 CASE STUDY III   242
MODERN APPROACHES TO SEMIURGY

CONCLUSION   288

✪

AFTERWORD   290
THE WORDS AIM THE ARROW
By Don Webb

APPENDIX A   294
WHY DO MAGICIANS WRITE FICTION?
By Don Webb

APPENDIX B   301
MAGIA LOCI
By Brenda Yagmin

✪

GLOSSARY   306

NOTES   311

BIBLIOGRAPHY   319

INDEX   328

THE ART OF METACOMMUNICATION

Stephen E. Flowers, Ph.D.

What you are about to read represents a breakthrough in the theory of practical magic. Without theoretical understanding—either conscious or unconscious—practical results are impossible. Indeed, without a theoretical framework, results are hard to obtain in any avenue of life. Humans typically have to struggle to gain some sort of theoretical mastery—the Mozarts of this world are few and far between. To facilitate this process, it is essential for most people to have a teacher. A mentor of this sort does not even have to be an intentional or conscious teacher, just a model of thought and action. It is best and most efficient, however, to have a conscious teacher-student relationship on some level. You are lucky to have acquired this book, for in its contents you have access to just such a teacher.

Toby Chappell is a seasoned veteran of two major initiatory schools of magic and has undertaken the study of topics related to the present work at the university level. To teach well, one must first learn and master. Such teachers are to be most trusted, as they do not entirely depend on their ability to "sell" their ideas based on eloquence and charisma—it goes beyond that.

Gaining the kind of experience and knowledge in play here is no easy thing and often subject to the manifestation of luck, or good fortune—the gift of a god, if you will. In my own experience, I found this to be true. My interests coincided with the presence of the right teachers and mentors who were willing to put me in touch with others who had even more to teach in connection with my specific needs. My original advanced work was in connection with runology, although the keys I came to understand were really ones that could be applied to most any symbol system.

Modern magical theories often lag well behind the philosophical realities, both with respect to the underpinning of magic in antiquity and the foundation of current academic understanding of the topic. No longer is "magic" considered erroneous thinking, but rather has come to be understood as a form of metacommunication. The question of *why* people believe magic works is no longer relevant; it has become more a question of just *how* magic does, in fact, work.

Seeking to understand this process through an exploration of the links between categories such as symbols, language, and communication may seem strange at first, since people tend to think of magic in terms of quasi-physical models that suggest flows of energy or chemical reactions. The semiotic theory of magic also takes such concepts into account, as these phenomena are subject to the mechanisms and laws of operative communication: one physical apparatus communicates with another (e.g., a radio transmitter and receiver) according to the same laws of semiotics as do two people speaking with one another in a shared language.

It is worth remembering that our ancestors recognized that language is central to the magical world. One Old Norse saga reveals that kings were charged with mastering three things: runes, languages, and chess—that is, signs, different dialects of language, and strategic thinking. Ancient magicians were often also poets and interpreters of languages. They could translate one language into another and, in the process, came to understand how symbols and signs opened the gateway between two worlds—the world of symbols and that of phenomena. Magic is the translation of signs into events (both objective and subjective). This process is constantly happening in the daily experiences of human beings, but it is hidden from most of us due to its commonplace appearance.

Toby Chappell knows how to seek and find the mysteries of magical communication, make them his own, and pass them on to diligent students. This book will help you open your eye to an awareness of the world of wonders so that you can begin to make use of it in a sound and reliable way. That is saying a lot.

STEPHEN E. FLOWERS, PH.D., studied Germanic and Celtic philology and religious history at the University of Texas at Austin and at the University of Göttingen, West Germany. He received his Ph.D. in 1984 in Germanic languages and medieval studies with a dissertation entitled "Runes and Magic." He is the author of numerous books, including *Original Magic, Icelandic Magic, The Fraternitas Saturni, Revival of the Runes,* and *Gothick Meditations at Midnight.*

ACKNOWLEDGMENTS

Stephen Edred Flowers, Don Webb, and James Fitzsimmons each opened my eyes and ears to different aspects of the inherently communicative foundation of magic. The roots of their ideas support the branches of my own idiosyncratic approach to finding different ways to communicate with what Is To Be. A further thank you goes to Stephen for permission to reproduce several runic tables that have been adapted from his book *Rune Might*.

While I am currently pursuing a degree in linguistics, I am still largely an autodidact in the disciplines of linguistics and semiotics. To ensure my foundation of understanding is sound, I consult with my friends who have studied some of the ideas in this book in a more formal and structured way. Scott Shell, Christopher Merwin, Mark Roblee, and Bo Christiansen have been immensely helpful in fact-checking my writing and suggesting new avenues for exploration in their respective academic fields.

I've enjoyed discussions about these concepts with colleagues and friends, including Thomas Brovelli, Brenda Yagmin, Adam Nox, Kaeti MacNeil, Charles Moore, Joseph Eichenbaum, and Matthew Frederick. These conversations have helped to guide the direction the book took as well as reveal various rabbit holes that I am in the process of exploring (or tricking others into exploring).

The locations where I have found it productive or inspirational to write have been an indispensable part of the creation of this book. This includes Peculier Pub and Think Coffee in Greenwich Village, New

York; the famous Rose Reading Room at the main branch of the New York Public Library; Manuel's Tavern in Atlanta; Fitzrovia, London; and a particular cabin in the Adirondack Mountains of upstate New York.

Finally, I am overjoyed to be working again with all at Inner Traditions. Everyone there who has touched this book in some way has made it better.

THE MAGIC IS IN THE COMMUNICATION

W/*hat is magic?*

This is one of those questions that many people have outdated ideas about, assuming they have any thoughts about it at all. For some, it's just a thing stage magicians do in places like Las Vegas. For others, it's the thing people did before the Abrahamic religions took root and spread beyond their original cultures, calling up visions of shamans and village "witch doctors." For still others, magical thinking is an entirely embarrassing notion in the days of smartphones, cryptocurrency, space exploration, and electric cars—or, in other words, "Who needs magic when we have science?"

Yet science itself can easily become like a religion in the ways people assign to it unlimited powers of explanation; start wars over which branch of science is most correct or useful; or regard anything not sanctioned by their preferred branch of science as evil/primitive/dangerous/ immoral. This is a position known as *scientism*.

The fact of the matter is that humans are not completely rational. We lash out in anger at things that don't matter in any objective sense. We play the lottery—whether by buying a Powerball ticket, jumping out of an airplane, or jaywalking across a busy street in Manhattan. We fall in love, and not always with people who will make good long-term (or even temporary!) companions. We vote for colorful politicians more for their entertainment value than for how well they will represent the best interests of their constituents. As a species, we are remarkably bad at assessing risk and making far-sighted decisions that are in our best interests.

This is why any position that claims that reason alone can entirely explain and guide the human condition seems to be at odds with the actual behavior of real humans. Despite our unique qualities, we are still primates at our core—and this evolutionary heritage influences our behavior and social structures far more than most of us would like to admit. Science is a magnificent and essential tool for explaining *how*; it is wholly inadequate for explaining *why* or assigning meaning.

So where does this leave magic?

In this book I'm going to do a weird thing: use the science of linguistics and the philosophical toolkit called semiotics to talk about the not-always-rational practice of magic. The terminology and analytical techniques may be modern, but I am using them to get back to an understanding of ancient ideas about how we perceive and affect the world by treating it as a partner in communication. The connection between semiotics, language, and magic is the core principle of this book: *the magic is in the communication.*

We've lost touch with the necessity of remaining truly open to the Being of things.* Communication can only happen between equals, or between those who can sufficiently "meet in the middle" of their knowledge and experience to find common ground for communication. By opening ourselves to the Being—the essential qualities that distinguish "this" from "that"—of what we wish to affect, we can communicate more effectively *and thus engage in magic more effectively.*

Hardly anyone would deny that *language* is closely related to communication, but describing magic in terms of communication might at first seem to be a stretch. In fact, the history of magic—whether

---

*"Being" is capitalized here to distinguish the concept or property of Being itself. See the discussion about the ideas of Martin Heidegger in chapter 4.

premodern, postmodern, or anywhere in-between—is replete with tropes and techniques that can be best understood as communication processes. In this book, we'll look at some of those: sigils, spells, invocations, and even situations where writing itself can be regarded as a magical act. We'll also explore the idea of a *text*—a collection of any kind of signs—and how the ideas of cohesiveness and coherence work together to create meaning (and for the magician, thus become a means of changing both the self and the world).

I'm going to be using a lot of relatively recent ideas (late nineteenth century onward) to look at far older things. Throughout this work, I hope to show that while the terminology may be new, the ideas have been lurking behind the actual practice of magic for millennia. Magic-as-communication is a particular conceptual model we can use to understand something essential about magic (and our tendency toward it as a species, even when we try to frame what we are doing in nonmagical terms for social or other reasons). Conceptual models aren't judged by whether they are "true" (because they are not *trying* to convey truth); rather, their effectiveness and analytic/predictive power are the crucial criteria for whether they are useful. Conceptual models are ways of thinking about the assumptions, success criteria, and relevance of the things they are applied to. Thus, I can't prove to you that magic "exists" (whatever that means), but I *can* show you how magical thinking as a conceptual model reveals and suggests useful ways of looking at yourself and the world. We will also examine how this model might help you to escape the limitations you have placed on yourself through overuse of other models that work well enough in their own domains, such as scientific thinking.

But before we get too deep into that, we need to settle on some definitions that put the relationships between these three ideas of magic, semiotics, and linguistics in their proper context. After all, if we're going to work with these ideas in a methodical way, we must use criteria and descriptions that reveal meaningful differences—that is, by having some situations that they definitely *don't* apply to, and supporting that assertion with persuasive reasons, we can then get a better sense of what situations these ideas *do* apply to. We also have to avoid being like Lewis Carroll's Humpty Dumpty, using words like *magic* to mean whatever we want them to mean from one utterance to the next.

I'll expand on these definitions in later chapters, but let's start here.

MAGIC

Magic is a form of operative communication that uses symbolic means to bring about a change in the practitioner (the one doing the magic) and, when necessary, a change in the world outside the practitioner as well.

It's vital to note that magic is often only one step in bringing about the desired change; it must usually be followed up with tangible action in the world. One of the ways that magic functions is as part of a tool-kit for reconfiguring your perception of what is *possible* so that further actions and awareness will align with it. It's usually not enough to just think vivid thoughts to visualize a change you want to see in yourself or the world; we are constantly reframing our view of reality and categorizing possibilities according to their likelihood, desirability, and social implications. We have to fight those voices in the back of our heads—of parents, co-workers, neighbors, authority figures, and others—telling us what we should or shouldn't want or do. This is yet another outcome of our primate heritage: we cooperate to a degree with what those in our circles of interaction and authority want even when we *think*—or want to believe—we are acting entirely of our own volition.

Let's break that definition down.

Operative communication means that we are using communication to *do* something, not just talk *about* something. This is encapsulated in the idea of a *performative utterance*—speech that immediately brings about an effect, like "I now pronounce you man and wife." J. L. Austin has quite a bit to say about performative utterances, and we will look at his ideas closely in chapter 3. Humans obviously do plenty of operative communication in nonmagical contexts; thus, while *operative communication* is a good replacement term for *magic* that avoids some of the latter term's historical baggage, it is not enough—at least without more context.

Symbolic means indicates that the practitioner—the one doing the magic—leverages symbols, whether linguistic or metalinguistic, to call up the right imagery that lets them put the desired change in the right context (or frame of reference). For example, the magician who is doing a bit of wealth magic may include in her ritual various things, objects, or representations that to her symbolize and suggest the type of wealth she is intending to acquire.

A change in the practitioner emphasizes that the person doing the magic is *different* (or at least on the way to being different) in some way following the magical act. They have shifted some part of their self-image, seeing themselves or their possibilities for action or change in new or more coherent ways. Or as my teacher and friend Don Webb says, the secret of magic is to transform the magician. Not all permanent changes in the practitioner will have some corresponding change in the outer world, but many if not most will—the transformed person will reflect those transformations in their behaviors, attitudes, values, and goals.

SEMIOTICS

Semiotics (sometimes called *semiology*) is the formal study of signs. A sign is anything that stands for, refers to, represents, or evokes something else. The related term *semiosis* refers to the capacity shared by *all* living things by which they perceive and interpret signs.

For example, a word refers to the thing we agree it means; smoke points to the existence of a fire; the detection of butyric acid indicates to a tick that a mammal is nearby—the word, the smoke, and the detection of the chemical are all types of signs. Some signs occur naturally, like the smoke or the positioning of a dog's tail. Others are what Aristotle called *conventional* signs—their meaning is arbitrary but established through convention, and we make a decision to employ the sign to communicate something instead of that communication "just happening" on its own as a byproduct of some other action.

A certain kind of sign, called a *symbol* by the American philosopher Charles Sanders Peirce,* has special importance to the theory of magic discussed in this book. Arbitrariness and ever-evolving convention are the key concepts with symbols—there is no inherent connection between the symbol and its meaning; if it in some way looked like the thing or idea it referred to, it would be a different form of sign called an *icon*. The practice of magic uses, in part, the type of signs called symbols to reframe and represent the practitioner's vision of what is possible and desirable; once the inner reality of the magician has fully embraced this new vision, the magician then works to bring about a corresponding change in the outside world.

LANGUAGE

A *language* is a form of spoken, gestured, or written communication that has a quantifiable structure while still allowing for nearly infinite flexibility in what can be expressed.

Human languages use features of the vocal tract and/or gestures primarily made with the hands (as in signed languages, or the gestures that often accompany spoken words). These forms of communication are used for intentionally conveying information (unlike a sneeze or a yawn, which also convey information but are not intentional). Written languages (alphabetic and syllabic ones, at least) generally reflect the spoken forms of a language according to their own rules for recording those sounds. Human languages of any form also share various design features like those described by linguist Charles Hockett, such as *displacement, reflexivity,* and *cultural transmission*. We'll look at these features and more in chapter 3.

---

*Pronounced like "purse."

Linguistics—the study of language—is generally considered to be a subdiscipline *within* semiotics (although many linguists do not use the concepts or techniques of semiotics as part of their work). As mentioned before, words are themselves a certain kind of symbolic sign, and the rules for the use of those words within the context of their language form a semiotic code. That is, the meanings of the individual symbolic signs (words) combine to form phrases and sentences (syntagmata, or collections of signs) which have more complex meaning; this meaning comes not only from the meaning of the individual words themselves, but also from the cultural knowledge and personal experience of the person hearing/reading/seeing them. The way meaning is encoded and then derived through interpretation is of central importance to the study of semiotics and language as essential elements of the practice of magic.

CHAPTER PREVIEW

In chapter 1, we'll look more closely at the concepts of magic, language, semiotics, and communication with a focus on how these ideas can be useful in a magical context.

We'll review some of the history of the study of magic in chapter 2, including the work of anthropologists E. B. Tylor, James Frazer, Claude Lévi-Strauss, and Stanley Tambiah. This examination of older theories of magic, especially the parts of them that have relevance to current anthropological ideas on magic, will set the stage for the theory of magic-as-communication that is central to this book.

Chapters 3 and 4 will take a deep dive into the ideas of some of the key thinkers in linguistics, semiotics, and the philosophy of language. This will include such major figures as Ferdinand de Saussure, Charles Sanders Peirce, Martin Heidegger, J. L. Austin, Ludwig Wittgenstein, Umberto Eco, and Charles Hockett—always with an emphasis on the applicability of their ideas to understanding communication in its context as a magical tool. This chapter will also look at the philosophical school known as German Idealism to introduce the core notion of the Self, which is both the subject and object of any magical act.

In chapter 5, we will examine mythological ideas about language and magic, including gods of divine communication in a variety of cultures and time periods. This chapter also sets the stage for the three "case study" chapters that follow, which will look at different schools and techniques of magic to examine how they use the principles of magical communication we have discussed to that point.

Chapters 6 and 7, containing Case Studies I and II, will explore a few specific historical types/techniques of magic in light of the information about language and semiotics discussed in earlier chapters. These historical applications of magical communication are selections from the Greek Magical Papyri and the Nag Hammadi library (chap. 6) and runes (chap. 7). Each chapter will include a brief overview of the respective types and techniques as well as an analysis of their communicative features and underpinnings.

Chapter 8, containing Case Study III, concludes the main text of the book with an examination of the uses of magic as operative communication in several modern schools of magic, including the practices of Aleister Crowley, Austin Osman Spare and his influence on Chaos Magic, the early Church of Satan (the period 1966–1975), Thee Temple ov Psychick Youth, and the Temple of Set. These important modern schools of magical thought provide the background for tying together both premodern and postmodern ideas of magical communication as something that has been implicit in magic for a long time.

At the end of each chapter, I provide reading lists of some key books that will allow for a deeper study of the themes and concepts discussed. The complete publication information for these books can be found in the bibliography.

My hope with this text is to expand on the ideas of important thinkers in the examination of magic, and to combine my love of linguistics with the practical applications that arise from thinking about magic in linguistic and semiotic terms. While the author is a senior member of a leading school of the Left-Hand Path* (the Temple of Set), care is taken to present the material and ideas in this book in ways that will hopefully be useful to those of *any* magical school or spiritual persuasion.

---

*From my book *Infernal Geometry and the Left-Hand Path* (Inner Traditions, 2019), page 4: "The concept of the Left-Hand Path . . . is the unending pursuit of enhancing and perpetuating the magician's self-aware, psyche-centric existence. In doing so, the individual becomes a more potent actor within the objective universe and seeks to know his or her own positive transformations as reflected by their effects on the outer world."

1

WHAT DO LANGUAGE AND
SEMIOTICS HAVE TO DO
WITH MAGIC?

I first became aware of the idea of magic as a process of communication through chapter two of Stephen E. Flowers's 1984 Ph.D. dissertation *Runes and Magic*. In 1981 to 1982, Flowers was studying in Germany under the eminent runologist Klaus Düwel at the University of Göttingen. Since Flowers was writing his dissertation on magical uses of runes, Düwel advised him to consult with the anthropology faculty to acquire a thorough grounding in current ideas on the nature of magic. Through these discussions, Flowers discovered the work of Jan van Baal and Stanley J. Tambiah; they had combined ideas from philosophers of language like J. L. Austin and Ludwig Wittgenstein with structural anthropology to form models of magical communication.

One of my primary goals with this book is to make certain core concepts of linguistics and semiotics more accessible to nonspecialists. These topics have often been buried within dense, specialized vocabulary in books that can seem intended more to impress than to inform. This approach has its place, especially in terms of the continued development of linguistics and semiotics as sciences (and with all the academic specialization and jargon that this necessarily entails).

However, as I will argue throughout this book, the essential ideas of semiotics and its subdiscipline linguistics can not only be understandable to the layman but also useful for understanding the process and intent of magic. This book is primarily aimed at magicians, as well as those with an interest in the history and theory behind magic. By examining these tools not normally associated with magic in our modern world, the magician can become more effective and powerful. They might even learn a bit about more effective mundane communication too.

Borrowing a term from the French philosopher Jean Baudrillard, I call this approach to magic *semiurgy*: the creation or manipulation of signs, linguistic or otherwise, to cause specific effects within the psyche of the magician. These effects can then be reflected in changes in the world of the Real: that is, the objective universe of matter, physical laws, and other self-aware inhabitants, each of whom seeks to understand and affect their surroundings through language and other systems of signs.

WHAT IS LANGUAGE?

The concept of language is notoriously difficult to define. (In fact, *all* words are ultimately difficult to define; in chapters 3 and 4 we'll spend a lot of time looking at the perception and creation of meaning.) While we must acknowledge that we can never give a comprehensive definition, we can at least provide a working description that will provide a useful starting point for the ideas in this book.

Language is the use of forms of spoken, gestured, or written communication that have a quantifiable structure while still allowing for nearly infinite flexibility in what can be expressed. The use of language is dependent on context for meaning; that is, the circumstances in which we use language always influence—if not determine—the meaning (both what is intended and what is perceived).

Context is vitally important for magic as well. In effect, the practitioner is altering the context in which they communicate so as to shape the meaning—and thus the response—of their words and actions to bring about their desired result.

When Did Language Begin?

As with many questions about the capabilities and behavior of early members of the genus *Homo*, the physical evidence for language capability is sparse and its interpretation speculative. New discoveries can and do completely rewrite significant portions of what we think we know about early humans and their ancestors. The lag before newer information makes it into popular accounts—like this one, as opposed to a scientific journal—makes it even harder for the nonspecialist to stay on top of current ideas. Thus, we will be looking at the question of when language began in broad terms, knowing there will come a point when that information is outdated yet preserved here in fossil form so to speak.

Two features had to be in place in hominids before language as we know it would be possible. One is the behavioral and intellectual capacities that allowed language to become complex and change over time as different early hominid populations spread out and began to evolve independently. The second is the set of physical features (larynx, oral and nasal cavity, tongue shape and dexterity, neck angle) that permit the wide variation and precise control of human sound generation.

Anatomically modern humans appeared in the fossil record two to three hundred thousand years ago, at which point the physical capability for spoken language as we know it was already there. Given how closely coupled the physical capabilities are to the intellectual and behavioral underpinnings of language, it is reasonable to assume that the mental *capability* for language was available by that time as well (even if it was not very developed yet). It is certainly possible if not likely, as Daniel Everett argues, that the gestural and limited vocal capabilities of members of genus *Homo* prior to that (in *Homo erectus*, for example) were used for effective communication; however, they were missing either the physical or intellectual capabilities (or both) for anything approaching the complexities of language in modern humans.[1]

There's another important factor missing before *Homo sapiens* arrives on the scene: the complex culture that could be passed on in part through language. This development would have thrived as part of a feedback loop with culture perpetuating ever more complex language use—combined with language use influencing the creation and preservation of increasingly complex culture. Culture can be broadly broken into four categories:

1. *material* culture—the physical things produced, like buildings, tools, jewelry, pottery
2. *ethnic* culture—the genetic relationships shared by those participating in a given culture
3. *ethical* culture—the ideas and attitudes shared by those participating in a given culture
4. *linguistic* culture—the shared language among members of a particular culture

While language only forms the last category, and thus is not the sole cause of culture, it does greatly influence and aid in the evolution and preservation of the other three categories.

These last two aspects of culture—ethical and linguistic—are for the most part where the understanding and practice of magic can be found. Ethical culture would include magic as a method for understanding and influencing the world and its inhabitants. Linguistic culture provided a means for conceptualizing and communicating the types of changes desired. Even early humans would have observed that their capabilities for complex and precise communication far exceeded those of other animals, and from this they would have inferred that this seemingly unique tool would give them power over the world around them. The use of magic at its most basic level assumes that it is possible to affect and create phenomena within the world, so anything that gives humans a sense of power and control over the world outside themselves is available for use as part of magic.

Why Did Language Begin?

One of humanity's "superpowers" is the way we can extensively imitate and expand on the behaviors and ideas we observe in each other. Other species imitate of course, but not to the extent that imitating and especially elaborating *in a generalized way* are a core component of human behavior and culture. We pick up—often subconsciously—on things like the speech patterns, manner of dress, or likes and dislikes of those around us, and then spread those things further in personalized forms. Early humans copied and passed on things like making fire, communicating by making particular sounds, wearing clothes for protection from the elements, and decorating both their environment and their bodies. These copied behaviors and others became essential to surviving through living and cooperating with each other. Humans are, as psychologist Sue Blackmore termed us, the "meme machine."

A *meme* in its original sense is a concept or behavior that is spread through human culture by imitation (*memesis*), often carrying some symbolic meaning. Whether a particular meme continues to spread or instead to die out, this copying process happens in a manner somewhat analogous to natural selection: if the meme leads to suitability within its selection environment, then it will survive and continue to spread through copying. That is, if the meme creates symbolic or practical significance *within the context in which it is spread*, then it will continue to be copied and/or used. Otherwise, it will die out—it will become "old-fashioned" and lose its relevance (like a fad that has passed), or perhaps it will even be seen as dangerous and thus necessary to suppress.

According to memetic theory, memes function as *secondary replicators* that can shape the spread of symbolic behavior much in the same way that natural selection—the primary replicator—governs evolution through the survival of biological changes that lead to adaptation to a specific environment. Just as with natural selection in evolutionary biology, particular memes don't necessarily survive because they are the *best* ideas or behaviors, but merely because something about them triggered our impulse to copy them again and again. Memes began to coevolve in early hominids along with genes, transforming us both physically and symbolically into ever more effective meme machines.

How do memes relate to self-development and to magic?

As Don Webb tells us in *How to Become a Modern Magus*: "The secret of magic is to transform the magician."[2] Techniques and theories of magic, like any other symbolic behavior, spread memetically. If the techniques prove useful, or the theories have useful explanatory power, the memes encapsulating them survive and continue to spread. The magician is experimenting with whether certain ideas and behaviors are useful to their *own* memeplex* of magical techniques and theories. The concept of the secondary replicator is important for this: by altering your personal selection space—that is, by intentionally putting constraints on yourself through finding your limits and ways to surpass and expand them—you can then mindfully evolve and become a more sovereign and effective actor in both your inner and outer worlds. The first replicator—natural selection—works without any external intelligence driving it toward certain ends; individual species simply evolve (or not) toward abilities and physical characteristics that allow them to survive and pass on their genes to the next generation. Mindful evolution is the creation and use of additional replicators through the ability to reflect on your circumstances and make conscious decisions about adding selection pressures that alter your existence toward desired ends. Just as the athlete must find new ways to challenge their skills and physical abilities, the magician must create situations for transforming their own abilities. They then apply that more potent and powerful self toward changing the world around them to be a supportive environment for further self-transformation.

---

*A memeplex is a collection of memes that are replicated and enhanced together.

The astronomer Gerald Hawkins summed it up perfectly: "A gene pool interacting with the environment shapes the body. A meme pool interacting with the cosmos shapes the mind."[3]

The Acquisition of Language

For a glimpse into why language use is so critical to unlocking the intellectual and behavioral capabilities of modern humans, consider the following.

There is a limited window of development in children, called the *critical period*, when they can fully acquire the ability to use and understand language. While it would be thoroughly unethical to create an experiment to study what happens when a growing person is deprived of this critical period, there have nonetheless been a few isolated incidents due to extreme neglect and/or abuse that confirm its importance. In these incidents, growing children were robbed of the necessary exposure to language that induces the brain to fully develop the capacity for language.

What about the use of human language by nonhuman animals?

Much has been made in recent years of various great apes—typically chimpanzees and bonobos—and their supposed ability to understand and use some features of human language. For our purposes, it is necessary to look at features of language design and use that are—as far as we know—particular to humans; these features are also likely to be the most useful for talking about magic as a tool that arises out of the uniquely human way of understanding and interacting with the world.

A useful framework for discussing different components of language use is the *design features of language* formulated by linguist and anthropologist Charles Hockett. We'll look at more of the list and its implications in chapter 4, but for now will focus on the following:

- *displacement*: the ability to talk about people or objects that are not currently present (in space and/or time)
- *productivity*: the ability to create new sentences of unlimited complexity on any topic

- *reflexivity*: the use of language to talk about itself
- *cultural transmission*: the spread of language through connections between those who are capable of developing and using it; closely related to humanity's memetic propensities

The first two of these features sometimes appear in a limited fashion in the primates most closely related to humans (bonobos and chimpanzees). The other two features are, as far as we are aware, unique to humans. All four of them help us to understand the true potential of language and, in turn, to see how language can illuminate some critical aspects of magical practice.

This entire book is an example of reflexivity: using language to talk *about* language. Other than perhaps the occasional, context-dependent use of a learned sign for "word," there is no evidence of reflexivity in the great apes' limited use of human language. There is a conceptual barrier for folding language back onto itself that the great apes do not show any evidence of possessing or developing. The reasons for this are not entirely clear; we can't really explain why humans *do* have it, which complicates explaining why other animals do *not* have it (despite possessing some linguistic capabilities that are, at times, impressive). In chapter 4 we'll look more closely at how this skill contributes to magical communication.

If humans are meme machines, then one of the most fascinating things those machines build is the wide range of complex cultures seen throughout the world. The same cultural structures we build also have an outsized influence on the transmission and transformation of language; this spans from the individual toddler learning their native language(s) all the way to large-scale shifts in the use of language over time. *Culture and language evolve together.*

One of the primary ways cultural transmission works is through our capacity for imitation. We are hardwired to pick up on the behavior patterns of those around us, and then to incorporate those patterns into our own behaviors (sometimes consciously, but most often subconsciously). Culture also depends on depth and precision of communication; as Daniel Everett notes: "Culture entails symbolic reasoning and projecting meaning on to the world, meaning that is not about things as they are, but as they are interpreted, used and perceived by members of the community that uses them."[4]

Language enables culture to build on a foundation that can be expanded and refined over time. Through language, it is possible to preserve and spread not just the material artifacts of culture—such as tools, buildings, or art—but also the symbolic aspects: the information about "Why?" and "With what meaning or significance?"

In one mundane example of language assisting in the transmission of important knowledge, someone can of course demonstrate the techniques for carving a canoe from a massive tree trunk. However, for creating even more effective canoes, capable of traveling over longer distances, there are certain details that require language for them to be conveyed with precision. These include techniques for effective carving, how to know when the optimal shape of the hull is reached, how to work around certain defects in the wood, and so on. If the person demonstrating the carving makes a mistake, that mistake can be passed on as part of imitating what they are doing. Language adds precision in situations where it matters most. *Language preserves important details that observation cannot; even more importantly, it can explain* why *those details matter.*

The importance of language in preserving and transmitting more symbolic aspects of culture shows up readily in mythology and storytelling, which we will take a closer look at in chapter 5.

HYPERSTITION

Language paves the way for an entire range of new behaviors that are not possible (or perhaps even conceivable) without it. For example, language certainly did not *cause* neolithic British islanders to build Stonehenge, but language was *necessary* for the coordination required to build Stonehenge. A monument of this sort almost certainly could not have been built (or even conceived) as it is without the precise communicative and cooperative power of language.

Let's look at the idea of hyperstition and what it tells us about language's utility in bringing certain things into being. First, a bit of background on a bizarre entry in the sometimes stuffy world of academia.

The Cybernetic Culture Research Unit (CCRU)* was a loosely organized cultural theory collective that existed from 1995 to 2003 at (and later beyond) Warwick University in England. They worked within an experimental, often surreal, type of "theory-fiction" that combined elements of cyberpunk culture, Western occultism, and a healthy dose of the "Weird Tales" genre of fiction typified by H. P. Lovecraft, Clark Ashton Smith, and others.

One of the CCRU's most prominent and enduring ideas is *hyperstition*. Hyperstitions are initially fictional aspirations that take root and spread (and encourage work toward their realization), such that they ultimately become real. A hyperstition stands in contrast to a *superstition*, which is a fictional idea that *remains* fictional (even if it does affect our behavior).

Perhaps you take extra care every Friday the thirteenth, lest you endure some bad luck. Then one such Friday you're walking down the street and trip and sprain your ankle. On an intellectual level, you probably know there's no actual significance to the fact that this was the day you had an accident. But as part of making meaning out of the event—which humans seem compelled to do—the superstition *does* contribute to the meaning you make after the fact. You may even retroactively blame the superstition for causing your fall, or for causing the inattention that led to your fall, and so on. Nonetheless, the idea

---

*Major figures associated with the CCRU include founders Sadie Plant and Nick Land. Land has become a rather divisive figure of late, having created and endorsed a particular philosophy of accelerationism that has been embraced by the so-called alt-right movement. This section is only concerned with Land's earlier ideas as part of the CCRU, not his later political opinions.

of Friday the thirteenth and its effects remains fictional (i.e., without actual causal power). At worst, Friday the thirteenth was a placebo: a story to tell yourself about why you fell. Despite this real effect, there is no causal power involved even if there is—however tenuous—some retroactive explanatory power.

Hyperstitions, however, begin as fictions—fantasies, pipe dreams, "What if?," "Wouldn't it be nice?," "It's our destiny," and so on—but then, through the hold they create on those who are gripped by their possibility, they eventually become actualities.

One commonly cited and cogent example is the idea of space travel: placing humans into vessels that can journey far beyond Earth. Space travel has been part of our speculations and hopes ever since man realized that those features of the night sky were not just part of a dome enclosing the earth but in fact distant stars and worlds. In a sense, the idea—the *meme*—of space travel used humans to make itself real. To reach the moon, it was first necessary that various branches of knowledge—astronomy, physics, technology, politics, economics, and so on—evolved to support the possibility that we could make this kind of space travel feasible. *Hyperstitions rarely follow a linear path toward their realization.*

Hyperstitions can only be recognized as such *retroactively*. Until it becomes real, it's just a fantasy; when it does become real, the inevitability of it becomes more obvious and believable in hindsight. If such fantasies never actualize themselves, they are not yet hyperstitions but merely suppositions about what *may* someday be possible or desirable.

Hyperstitions, when they are pushing toward realization, influence the course taken by cultural evolution. In this sense they are, like memes, secondary replicators. Many processes of cultural evolution are subject to the forces of selection and suitability (languages, memes and other spreading ideas, technology, weaponry, etc.). Replicators respond through feedback cycles to the forces imposed by suitability for further replication—ideas become self-sustaining through their ability to manifest what is possible and desirable (in the context in which they evolve or perish).

Nick Land suggested that hyperstitions function as:[5]

1. an element of effective culture that makes itself real
2. fictional qualities of a future possibility that has not yet come into being
3. coincidence intensifiers
4. a call to the Great Old Ones (a reference to H. P. Lovecraft's fiction; see below)

I'll add a further observation of an apparent commonality shared by all hyperstitions: they seem rather unlikely when first conceived. Through repetition, the formative hyperstition takes on an air of possibility as the possibilities latent in the world evolve. The fact that we can talk about, describe, and capture in communicable form these possibilities for hyperstition helps us to spread them; by the same token we can also refine them and perceive what else is needed to make them real—the same qualities of magic as a progressively refined process of communication.

The first two functions suggested by Land are fairly self-explanatory, but numbers three and four are worth a closer look, especially in our context of magic—bringing inner possibilities into outer form—as a process of communication.

Coincidence intensifiers: Magic—when it is effective—works with perceiving and building connections between synchronicities. That two things appear to occur at about the same point in curved*— conventional—time is largely a function of physics and happenstance. The type and intensity of meaning applied to such coinciding events—a synchronicity—is the purview of the meaning-making capacity of the

---

*Drawing from ideas in Frank Belknap Long's 1929 Cthulhu mythos story "The Hounds of Tindalos," curved time is the way we perceive time according to the natural laws of the material universe. In contrast, angular time is the subjective and fluid perception of time by a sentient being within that material universe. See chapter 1 in my *Infernal Geometry and the Left-Hand Path* for a further exploration of this dichotomy.

psyche. However, the more minds that are aware of a potential hyperstition, the more meaning can be derived from events that seem to point toward that hyperstition's coming into being.

A call to the Great Old Ones: Lovecraft's Great Old Ones are one of the foundational topics of my 2019 book, *Infernal Geometry and the Left-Hand Path*. I will briefly summarize the core ideas here.

While the figure of Cthulhu has gained a significant degree of name-recognition in pop culture, Cthulhu himself only appears prominently in one story with a few passing mentions in a handful of other stories. Although Lovecraft distinguished between different types and ranks of deities and other cosmic entities in his fiction—such as Great Old Ones, Elder Gods, Other Gods, and uncategorized entities such as Yog-Sothoth—in popular usage "Great Old Ones" is often used as a catch-all.

The most prominent such gods and cosmic entities in terms of development and number of mentions in Lovecraft's works are Azathoth, Yog-Sothoth, Nyarlathotep, and Shub-Niggurath. Azathoth—the "crawling chaos"—is the chaotic (unformed, unordered) creator god (and progenitor of most if not all the others). Yog-Sothoth is the all-knowing cosmic entity coterminous with all space and time; this is the principle of order that arises spontaneously from the interactions of the crawling chaos. Nyarlathotep is one of the most interesting and well-developed entities in all of Lovecraft's works; he is known by many names and faces and is the only one who willingly "crosses over" to initiate (instead of just occasionally respond to) contact with humans. As Nyarlathotep has parallels with (earth) gods who also have communicative features such as Hermes, Odin, and Thoth, we will look more at this important figure in chapter 5. Shub-Niggurath—the "goat of a thousand young"—was a fertility figure described more by Lovecraft's successors than by Lovecraft himself; sometimes depicted as female and at other times as male, Shub-Niggurath appears often in incantations.

Taken together, these four gods and entities outline a progression of unfolding understanding from the undifferentiated chaos that forms the background of all creation (Azathoth) to the order that spontaneously arises from interactions within that chaos as the physical laws governing it shape it in certain ways (Yog-Sothoth). Then, as those capable of perceiving this chaos and order—gods, other intelligent beings—place it in the context of their understanding (Nyarlathotep), these burgeoning masters of the cosmos come to realize they can shape that cosmos according to their own designs and desires and bring unlimited new ideas and objects into being (Shub-Niggurath).

The unfolding of these Lovecraftian figures forms a cosmogony—myths describing the creation of the cosmos—but can also be seen for their perspective on the work and creations of individuals. This same progressive emanation from the formless to the fully formed as a jumping off point for further creation reflects the way ideas and other creations come into being. Even our own creations are often mysterious to us: they arise from inspiration as we respond to the impulse to bring about something new, and we are often unaware of where that inspiration comes from. At a larger scale—when many minds seek to bring the same thing into being, something they picked up from other minds and then spread memetically—the force of potential hyperstitions ends up taking on an almost cosmic importance and scale as they consume us with the desire to see them become real. That is, they become mythic yet still with an air of attainability. Looking back at our example of space travel, the desire to see that come about certainly seemed as if it were guided by something bigger than the individual humans who wanted it.

The Lovecraftian gods, other than with the occasional mysterious motives of Nyarlathotep, don't take a direct interest in the affairs of humanity; such benefit as we draw from their formative influence on the cosmos as it unfolded and expanded is not part of any plan. It has proven to be far more important simply that this unknown and unanticipated potential was set in motion, with no grand plan forcing possibilities into predetermined configurations. In this sense, hyperstition can be seen as a culmination of certain configurations of possibility that happen to take hold memetically. When these hyperstitions take hold and then become real retroactively, they have fulfilled this possibility from the Great Old Ones (used here as a general term for the various principles at work in *this* universe that Lovecraft gave names to in *his* universe).

WHAT IS SEMIOTICS?

What is a sign?

In *semiotics*—the formal study of signs—a *sign* is something that stands for, refers to, represents, or evokes something else. For example, as we noted earlier, a word refers to the thing we agree it means, smoke points to the existence of a fire, the detection of butyric acid indicates to a tick that a mammal is nearby—the word, the smoke, and the detected chemical are all examples of different types of signs. We'll further describe the different types of signs in chapter 3.

As you can see, a sign in the semiotic sense is not limited to *visual* signs, although such visual signs—road signs, "no smoking" signs, an icon on your smartphone, an obscene gesture, and so on—*are* particular types of semiotic signs. *To a semiotician,* all *communication is mediated by signs.*

Semiosis is the innate capacity for creating and interpreting signs. At first glance, this might sound like something uniquely human. However, it is shared by *all* living things (even, unfortunately, the aforementioned ticks). For example, birdsong is a sign: it may indicate to other birds of the same species there is one who is ready to mate, or serve as a warning sign that predators are nearby. Other living things (not just the birds they are intended for) pick up on these signs and interpret them according to their own interests or instincts.

Linguistics is a discipline within semiotics—that is, linguistics is a particular application of semiotic ideas—even though not all linguists think of themselves as semioticians or use the terminology and concepts of semiotics. Words are signs, and we combine them into more complicated *sign networks* (collections of interrelated signs); these result in phrases, sentences, novels, and so on that together carry more meaning than the individual, isolated words can. Within these sign networks—or *semiotic webs*—the relationships between their component signs create meaning that combines and sometimes even exceeds the meaning of the component parts. Signs do not stand in isolation; any sign is understood through its relationships with other signs—recall our discussion of context above.

Because of its universality among humans, language is a convenient collection of signs for discussing ideas in semiotics; this is why the first well-known modern attempt at systematizing the study of signs was begun by a linguist, Ferdinand de Saussure. He called his hypothetical science of signs *semiology*, and through this he contributed foundational and highly influential ideas to what became known as *structuralism* in the early and mid-twentieth century. Chapter 3 will discuss both Saussure and structuralism in more detail.

Signs and Meaning

The study of signs creates a deeper understanding of meaning, particularly with how we arrive at the meaning of signs in the context where they are interpreted. This context is hugely important: signs do not have a universal meaning that is independent of context, but rather the context is part of what determines the meaning *in that particular instance*. This is easily observed with language. For example, "pool" means something very different if you're intending to take a swim as opposed to heading to a bar for a game with friends. This contextual dependence extends to nonverbal signs as well: a seductive look from your spouse carries different meaning than the same look from a waitress hoping for a bigger tip.

These are broadly written examples, though, to get across the basic concept about the importance of context. Even with something like a pool, in the context of being an enclosed structure containing water for swimming, there will still be meaning that varies. When you hear any word (or phrase, or sentence, etc.) there will be shades of meaning and understanding you bring to it that are yours and yours alone. All your experience, feelings, fears, and fantasies about pools—as well as when, where, why, and from whom you're hearing about them—affect what comes to mind when you hear the word. The next time you hear the word, the full context will not be exactly the same—and may trigger different memories, experiences, or associations with the concept referred to by the word *pool*. Every time you hear the word it calls to mind meaning and associations that are ever so slightly different—we think of a word as "always meaning the same thing" as a convenient fiction, but it's really an average of all the times we've ever heard that word combined with the particular circumstances in which it is encountered *this* time.

In semiotics, this process of arriving at contextual meaning is called *interpreting the sign*. A sign has no meaning in and of itself; *it is the interpretation that gives the sign meaning*. Recall our definition of a sign as "something that stands for, refers to, represents, or evokes something else"; the sign is *not* the thing itself, but rather the thing that leads to this interpretation. The word "tree" (outside of some artificial arboreal arrangement!) is not an actual tree; the butyric acid sensed by our aforementioned tick is not the mammal that created that chemical. Furthermore, this relationship between the sign and the thing it refers to is not just a simple one-way representation in which *A refers to B*; the thing referred to by *B* is always in all circumstances *also* a sign. This is a vitally important point, which will be introduced below and discussed in more detail in chapter 3 when we look at the ideas of Ferdinand de Saussure and Charles Sanders Peirce.

At a deep conceptual level, imagining a new reality (something we want to change about the world around us, through magic or not) depends on determining appropriate signs for this vision that interrelate with *existing* signs that are part of the reality we desire to change. From there, we modify and add to the existing sign network to rearrange it into a new form; this is true for both mundane communication and change (e.g., deciding to turn on the light in the bedroom) as well as *magical* communication (discussed later in this chapter).

Ultimately, *anything* that we assign meaning to is a sign; in other words, *by interpreting something we treat it as a sign.* Signs are the mechanism through which we accumulate and contextualize meaning, experience, and understanding. Communication would not be possible without signs and without this capacity for semiosis. *In light of this, semiotics is really about how we understand—and alter our perception of—reality, and also how we represent the reality we have perceived or constructed.*

Infinite Semiosis

In the above introduction to the interpretation of signs, I mentioned the (perhaps counterintuitive) idea that the thing to which a sign refers is *also* a sign, which is, in turn, subject to interpretation. A simple explanation of the point is as follows: the perception we have of anything we encounter—revealed through any of the senses or purely based on internal ideas and sensation—is a *representation* of the properties manifested in the things themselves. Moreover, as a representation it is: (a) context-dependent for its meaning in the present time, place, and situation; and (b) subject to further interpretation as itself a sign. This is a crucial point in semiotics, and it will also be relevant to the discussion of German Idealism in chapter 3.

This situation of signs always pointing to other signs is called *infinite semiosis* by semioticians. Charles Sanders Peirce, the founder of semiotics as we know it today, found this idea disturbing especially in his early work; in his later work his stance on it softened as he further developed ideas about how sign networks arise and create an internal cohesion and coherence.

If this *semiotic chain*—that is, a sign leading to its interpretation, leading to another sign to interpret, *ad infinitum*—never ends, how are we able to arrive at an interpretation that, even if not final, is one we can confidently use? Eventually, the interpreter of the semiotic chain just gets a sense of where the interpretation is leading (or accepts their default interpretation of a sign without considering it further) and stops further interpretation. All of this happens nearly instantaneously, which is part of why it's often hard to explain exactly what you were thinking beyond "I felt like this sign meant X in this situation." (This is also why it can be hard to change your interpretation of certain signs, or to accept that a new interpretation is now the more commonly intended one; this chain of interpretation happens quickly and subconsciously, unless you make a concerted effort to stop and carefully consider the interpretation of some part of the chain.)

This also leads to a perhaps startling conclusion: *the meaning—the actionable interpretation—of a sign is* always *found partially outside the sign itself.* Signs can lead us toward certain interpretations deriving from our expectations and sense of what was intended by those signs, but the interpretation that we act on is always ultimately dependent on context. This is another way of stating the design principle (à la Hockett) that words are *arbitrary*; this arbitrariness is applicable to all signs, not just linguistic ones (e.g., individual words). Arbitrariness of linguistic signs refers to the lack of inherent connection between a word and what it refers to, with general meaning being agreed to by convention. This stands in contrast to "arbitrary" in the sense of attempting to change the meaning of words at random, using them to refer to something completely different each time they are uttered.

A Model of Communication

We're getting a little ahead since we haven't talked much yet about magic itself in this chapter (that's in the next section), but I do want to start to integrate the discussion of semiotics into our main topic of magic and communication. For that, we need at least the beginning of a model for *mundane* (nonmagical) communication, which we can then extend through later chapters into a model for operative—that is, magical—communication.

Discussions about semiotics can be dense, arguably pretentious, and often of questionable relevance to the average person's understanding. You obviously don't have to be a semiotician or a linguist to communicate effectively; when we use semiotics and linguistics as part of an explanation for how effective communication happens, these should add to what we *already* implicitly know.

Simplification and relative ease of use are among the reasons for creating and using virtually all tools.* A particular tool abstracts away certain details to make the essential functionality of that technology more broadly accessible and its results easier to recreate. Tools extend what we're able to do; a spear or sharpened rock or a gun are far more effective for certain goals than just using our comparatively weak hands and fingers. To begin to see how semiotics and particularly language can be used in a magical sense, let's take a brief look at how these two tools for communication function in mundane contexts.

A classic model of communication, the *sender-message-receiver* (SMR) model, was popularized by linguist Roman Jakobson. The ultimate roots of this model can be found in the "speech circuit" model of Saussure.

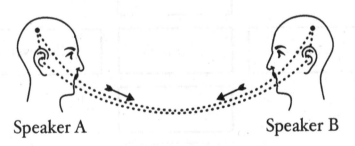

Speaker A   Speaker B

Saussure's speech circuit

In the SMR model, and its predecessors, communication is a form of *telementation*: a method for "transferring" thoughts from the mind

---

*I use the term "tool" broadly here in reference to all that we might lump under this general heading, spanning from early hominid tool use, to writing, to hugely complicated telescopes that we've sent into space. We will further examine the relationship between tools and magic in chapter 4.

of the speaker *A* to the listener *B*, who then as a speaker transmits thoughts back to *A*. The assumption underlying this model is that the language they are using for this mutual "transfer" of thoughts has a *fixed code* and *fixed rules*. That is, the model has embedded assumptions that the language they are using not only is a static thing with unvarying meanings and intent ascribed to its words, but also has rigid rules that govern its correct usage. From there, it's just a simple case of correctly encoding and decoding the messages that are part of the communication. These static, predictable properties are necessary in Jakobson's model to ensure that the message is transferred from brain to brain efficiently and accurately. Thus, the model implicitly ignores— or at least sidesteps—the role that interpretation plays both in whether communication is understood and in what background knowledge is assumed by both parties in the communication.

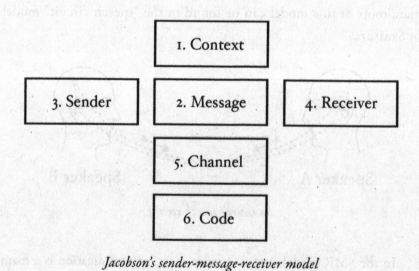

Jacobson's sender-message-receiver model

It is no coincidence that this model, especially Jakobson's version, was beginning to gain traction just as another hyperstition—the computer, in the modern sense of the word—was becoming real after decades of anticipation. It is around this same time (the late 1950s) that cognitive science and its commentary on how humans create and process language began to take hold. This included an implicit (and sometimes explicit) metaphor that the human brain could be understood as a particularly advanced type of computer. Even the increasing controversies about generative artificial intelligence (AI) continue this brain-as-computer metaphor, promising that if we just feed a language-processing AI system enough data it will eventually learn how to create sentences and larger texts that are indistinguishable from those a human might generate in the same situation or context.

While Jakobson's SMR model *does* include context as one factor in communication, its explicit reliance on both fixed code and fixed rules does not leave enough leeway to the parties in a particular communication to freely interpret the communication in terms of their own experiences, preferences, mood, and so forth. In other words, fixed code and fixed rules imply that as long as you follow the rules and only use words in expected ways (i.e., with their so-called literal meanings), the communication will invariably be successful. That is, the other person's understanding will be based on this same code and set of rules. This breaks down, however, on at least two important points: everyone can speak to an experience where communication was not successful *despite* the speaker being convinced they had been very clear and precise; also, a communication model that assumes a fixed code and rules does not leave room for introducing new words or using old words in new ways.

What is needed is a model that more closely lines up with the real experiences of humans attempting to communicate with each other. This is necessary not only for understanding human-to-human communication in a more realistic and flexible way, but also for the creative flexibility needed for using signs and words in novel ways as part of magic to alter the practitioner and/or the world around them.

Conceptual models are just that, though—models. They contain assumptions and assign weight or significance to different factors in an effort to provide explanatory power. Conceptual models are not judged on whether they are true because that is not their function or intent; rather, they are assessed on how well they fit the facts at hand and also how well they form a framework for predicting and analyzing the phenomena they pertain to. They can't be reduced to mathematical formulas. This property of working well enough in some areas but not being sufficient in others can be true for scientific models as well: Newtonian physics explains the motions of objects very accurately until it becomes necessary to use quantum mechanics or general relativity for a better explanation of particular types of problems. This lack of one model that supersedes all others is also true for conceptual models in general, as they attempt to provide a way for understanding certain concepts that arise from the interactions of minds. The conceptual model of signs—both linguistic and nonlinguistic—that we use for understanding *magical* communication will affect the conceptual model of magic itself; this will form the basis for the next section, "What is Magic?"

A model of magical communication that works with underlying tendencies in the language in which it is expressed will generally be more successful than a model that ignores these tendencies. This also suggests that studying other languages, or even other ways of expressing ideas in languages you already know, will open up new possibilities for not only conceptualizing new ideas and desires, but also for communicating them effectively. This is yet another way in which magic depends on first transforming the magician: you must conceive of and be able to describe greater possibilities before you can effectively bring them into being.

WHAT IS MAGIC?

As we will see in chapter 2, the difficulty of defining magic—along with the general skepticism toward the very idea, which goes hand in hand with scientism—has hampered its study as a conceptual model; this difficulty persists despite the model's prominence in the human experience. Magical thinking is one of those things people often do without even being aware of it (or acknowledging it if they do catch a glimpse of it in their own behaviors).

Magical Thinking: Not Just for Ancient Peoples

To the person fully invested in modernist ways of thinking, magic can feel like something that is quaint, disproven, primitive, or perhaps even evil. Or perhaps such a person buys into Arthur C. Clarke's very Frazerian statement: "Any sufficiently advanced magic is indistinguishable from technology."[6]

Magical thinking is a mindset that draws connections between events that cannot otherwise be explained by mundane laws of cause and effect. Magical thinking is part of how we invest meaning into the phenomena that we experience. The limitation of simple cause and effect is that many things happen to, for, or around us that are not explainable in terms of the laws of the physical universe. For example, the concepts and laws of astrophysics can reveal how the moon was formed, how its phases manifest, and how its surface features appear from earth; these same laws are wholly inadequate for explaining the folklore and mythology that are attached to the cultural significance of the moon throughout humanity's history. The human drive toward shaping meaning and significance is where magical thinking can emerge. Meeting and falling in love with your life partner, making sense of the sudden passing of a close friend, or wondering where inspiration comes from in writing a poem—to the extent that causes and effects can be seen in examples such as these, there is still a huge gap in determining significance that is solely up to the person(s) experiencing them.

Many if not most people in the modern world would protest that there is no magical thinking in their understanding of the world. This attitude is analogous to the discussion of mythology we will offer in chapter 5: the progressive—and not always deliberate—disenchantment of the world has conditioned us to want to see our actions and attitudes as rational, scientific, and solely based on facts. Have you ever pleaded "Please start!" to your car while turning the key when you thought you had a dead battery or other mechanical problem, then breathed a sigh of relief and gave your impassioned plea partial credit for causing the car to start against the odds? Perhaps you made a wish before blowing out the candles on your birthday cake, crossed your fingers for good luck, or wore a particular shirt for every big meeting or event. These are all examples of how otherwise rational people think in magical ways, drawing connections outside of normal chains of cause and effect.

The rational and the scientific are *learned* behaviors and thought patterns; they are added on top of our default, natural inclinations. Included in these defaults is magical thinking, which is easy to observe in young children as they learn to map their own behaviors and feelings onto observable phenomena in the world. This is closely related to children's growing comprehension of language and how to do things with words; it is one reason why treating magic as a communication process can be so effective, as it works with existing structures in our comprehension and relationship to the world outside ourselves.

In the introduction, we defined magic as follows: *Magic is a form of operative communication that uses symbolic means to bring about a change in the practitioner (the one doing the magic) and, when necessary, a change in the world outside the practitioner as well.*

Since magic works as part of a conceptual model, there is no single definition that can be used for magic; *the definition is dependent on the model that is being used.* Since this book sets out to describe one particular model—magic as a process of communication—it is important to begin to identify what some of the components of that model are.

The model starts with the concept of the *perceptual world*—the inner world of the magician, based on their worldview and experiences. This perceptual world includes the way the magician sees himself—which may or may not correspond to how others view the magician!—as well as their desires, hopes, fears, and limitations. It also includes the magician's understanding of the world outside himself, including both the physical world but also the people who inhabit and act within that world both individually and collectively. The perceptual world is closely related to the semiotic concepts of the *Umwelt* (from Jakob von Uexküll) and the *phaneron* (from Charles Sanders Peirce), both of which will be covered more thoroughly in chapter 3.

The world outside the magician is the *phenomenal world*. The magician could have a fairly accurate understanding of this world, its physical laws, and its inhabitants. They could also have fanciful, incorrect notions about the phenomenal world. In general, the more closely the perceptual world contains an accurate model of the phenomenal world, the more easily the magician can communicate with the phenomenal world and its inhabitants. No correspondence can be exact, however, since the phenomenal world is always dependent on interpretation through the signs of this world. In other words, the perceptual world affects *itself* as it is also the source of the interpretation of new signs encountered in the phenomenal world. This is why it is a good idea for a magician to have a solid grounding not only in the physical sciences, but also in political science, sociology, economics, and related areas of study; these realms of study provide gateways toward better understanding the phenomena and people that can be encountered. This is the core significance of the Delphic maxim γνῶθι σεαυτόν (*gnothi seautón*, "know thyself"): you must know yourself to know how that self-perception colors your perception of the world. (This is another reason why successful magic first requires that you change *yourself* so that the effects of that inner change can be mapped onto the changes needed in the outer world.)

As noted earlier, *semiosis* is the capacity shared by all living things for perceiving and interpreting signs they encounter in their environment. The creation and interpretation of a particular type of sign, called a *symbol*, is unique to mankind (on this planet at least!). A particular scent or footprint has a significance that is innately tied to those occurrences of signs, but in contrast a symbol *only* has meaning according to the culturally conditioned conventions about those signs. There is nothing in the sign that is the letter "t" that ties it to the sound that letter represents in English (or other languages with the same sound); that association of letter and sound is agreed upon by convention among those who use the Latin alphabet for writing English. The same type of arbitrary convention holds for a "no smoking" sign (a picture of a cigarette, surrounded by a circle and crossed through with a diagonal line). In a more abstract example, in an old Western movie the good guys were always shown with white hats and the bad guys with black hats; you immediately knew the moral alignment of those characters when they appeared on screen because you knew the convention that had become a recognized part of the language of film at the time.

The interpretation of signs is the way that we create meaning in the perceptual world—meaning informed not just by the conventional meaning of symbolic signs but *also* conditioned by our experiences, attitudes, desires, and the context in which we encounter the signs. Recall that individual signs do not stand alone; they are part of a sign network (semiotic web) whose connections and component signs in turn become part of the interpretation of particular signs. Thus, if we examine what it means to change oneself—change the perceptual world—in semiotic terms, introducing new signs or altering the associations of existing signs has a ripple effect throughout the semiotic web that is being created and interpreted. We build new meaning into individual signs and modify the connections we perceive between different signs in our semiotic web; this leads to changes both big and small within the perceptual world of the magician, opening up new possibilities and visions for what may yet come to be. Now equipped with a new conception of the self and its possibilities, the magician can communicate with the phenomenal world in a way that extends the reach of this enriched semiotic web.

Symbolic Communication: An Overview
In semiotics, a *symbol* is a particular type of sign that is:

- *arbitrary*—its meaning is decided by convention, *not* by some concrete relationship (like an image, a distinctive hoof print, a smell) between the sign and what it refers to

- *culturally coded*—in addition to whatever meaning an individual attaches to the sign in their perceptual world, there is meaning commonly associated with the sign that comes from the particular culture (or subculture) in which the sign is found (e.g., the "thumbs up" gesture indicates agreement in the US, but is a highly offensive insult in some parts of the Middle East)

Keep in mind, as we've seen elsewhere in this chapter, that words are also symbolic signs. Their meaning, as with all symbolic signs, can shift over time and in particular contexts. You—or some particular speech community to which you belong*—may have your own private meanings for certain words or other symbolic signs. That is, you have your own idiosyncratic uses that make sense to you but may be confusing to someone else; this happens because they are missing the rest of your semiotic web, which supports that specific meaning for the sign.

Using symbolic communication for magical purposes means that you choose which symbolic signs to add, replace, or alter in the semiotic web that contains the key components of the change you desire. We perceive reality through these networks of signs, networks that contain all the associations, desires, meanings, fears, and limitations that we attach to this particular facet of ourselves and the world we interact with. In order to change our inner reality—which is necessary before attempting to change the reality *outside* ourselves—we must first deconstruct part or perhaps even all of this particular sign network. We can then reconstruct it with the symbols—and thus meaning and significance—that more closely align with our vision. At that point we can, perhaps through using a ritual dedicated to this purpose, reinforce that new network, which will hopefully eventually replace the old one.

---

*A linguistic or speech community is a collection of language users who use language with similar norms and expectations—think about the different manner in which you communicate with coworkers versus your casual friends. You are part of multiple speech communities, depending on the different contexts and people that you communicate with.

Viewing magic as a process of communication through signs helps us to see more clearly that our desires, fears, and limitations are deeply interrelated—these are the very same things that are often the target of self-change aided by magic. Recall that no sign stands on its own; signs are *always* related to the other signs as part of a semiotic web. As linguist Patrick Dunn noted: "The semiotic view of magic recognizes that we do not come to desires out of a vacuum, nor do they come to manifestation in a vacuum."[7] Before dismantling or altering a particular region of the sign network that encompasses your entire perceptual world, it is important to have some idea of why it was configured the way it was to begin with and/or what purpose that particular configuration served. The reason(s) may not be valid or desirable to you anymore, but knowing what advantages such a configuration once offered will help with knowing if and how it should be changed.

Let's say you want to get a new job to make more money and are contemplating how to approach this desire magically in addition to the mundane actions that this entails (resumés, applications, interviews, etc.). As part of sketching out the semiotic web that uncovers the significance and meaning of different aspects of your current situation—evaluating the existing map to understand how or even if it should be modified—you realize that even though you would like a higher salary, you *do* like the short commute and the hours. Connecting this to the map of the desired new situation, you determine that a job that earns the amount of money you're looking for would require both less flexible hours but also more interaction with people. Having sketched out the entire semiotic web for this situation—and you should literally write these down in order to visualize the relationships and relative importance of the signs involved in this network—you can evaluate and weigh the advantages and disadvantages of both the old and potentially new jobs. Keep in mind, this isn't just a standard list of "pros" vs. "cons," but an exploration of what these different aspects *signify* to you. Maybe working fewer hours signifies freedom to fill your time with other things but makes you feel like you're failing to fulfill your deeply ingrained Protestant work ethic. Or maybe the short commute brings a positive feeling about your impact on the environment, but you're bored with your route since there is no other way you could drive to the office. Perhaps contemplating leaving your current job brings up emotions about abandoning your coworkers or the stress of having to adapt to a new situation and new people, and so on.

Maybe you decide you're better off where you're already at—there's no magic needed there (other than perhaps shifting your focus to money magic to fill in the gaps in your financial situation, or perhaps doing magic to add enchantment for overcoming the boredom of your current job situation). Or maybe you decide to modify the sign network of your desired outcome to include a job that doesn't require as much interaction with people or working hours, knowing that it may take longer to achieve.

The point of this not-so-contrived example is to illustrate how magic is not just about the new shiny thing we decide we want, but about uncovering more of the sign networks that inform your perceptual world. These ultimately form the basis for creating effective change within and beyond yourself.

MAGICAL FICTION AND FICTIONAL MAGIC

Fiction has a peculiar knack for becoming real when the right person reconfigures their conceptions of what is possible and impresses that vision on the phenomenal world. The use of handheld, wireless communicators in *Star Trek* inspired aspects of the design of cellphones beginning in the early 1970s. Leo Szilard, who hypothesized a workable mechanism for achieving a nuclear chain reaction—an integral part of both nuclear power plants and nuclear bombs—took inspiration from H. G. Wells's 1914 novel *A World Set Free*. The description of the Church of All Worlds in Robert Heinlein's *Stranger in a Strange Land* led to an actual neo-pagan organization that borrowed the name and some of its ideals and practices.

In the hands of a magician—one who works with a conceptual model that uses symbolic communication for self-transformation and for impressing the results of those changes on the world outside the self—interacting with fiction as both creator and consumer is a powerful set of techniques. Various genres of speculative fiction have included works by authors who considered themselves practitioners of magic, authors such as Arthur Machen, Dion Fortune, Alan Moore, Don Webb, William S. Burroughs, Fritz Leiber, Michael Aquino, and Grant Morrison. They all have embedded magical themes in their work, using fiction to explore their own models of magic and the implications of those models.

The reverse situation, where magicians have taken inspiration from an author who would have been repulsed by the idea of actually practicing magic, is epitomized by H. P. Lovecraft. Lovecraft was a staunch materialist, yet he took immense inspiration from his dreams to create fiction and regarded his dream world as having a reality of its own. One of his most interesting and pervasive characters is Nyarlathotep, the messenger of the various Great Old Ones and Other Gods who first came to him in a dream. Nyarlathotep manifests some familiar characteristics of gods of earth who invent or oversee communication, like Thoth, Hermes, and Odin. His significance in Lovecraft's stories emphasizes the importance of communication between the different levels of reality, from the dream world as a subset of an individual's perceptual world to the phenomenal world that is subject to influences beyond its control (via the Great Old Ones, etc.).

To maintain an air of plausibility, fictional depictions of magic will often borrow from ideas that have been associated with magic throughout recorded history: spoken spells; mysterious, hidden, dangerous, or forbidden books; invocations and evocations for establishing communication with something nonhuman; and signs and images whose very existence causes some sort of change in those who create or encounter them. All of these portray actual tools for operative communication that have been used in various schools and techniques of magic since the dim past. Fantastic (or speculative) fiction as we know it today is really only possible from a modernist perspective—that same disenchanted post-Enlightenment perspective that subjugates as much to scientism as it can get away with. Disenchantment also lessens the willingness of most readers to entertain thoughts of how the ideas in such magical tropes might work in practice. With an effective model for magic—such as the communicative one that is the core idea in this book—"fictional" depictions of magic can become inspirations for actual practices.* After all, even the most mundane change that you desire to make—turning on the light, adjusting your wake-up time, making a fully loaded sandwich exactly like the one you pictured in your mind—was imaginary until you took the initiative and steps to make it real.

This process of turning the imaginary into the real suggests a model for magic that begins with the realization that things could be other than they are, combined with the inspiration to make it so. Inspiration comes from mysterious places; sometimes a word or image will trigger a semiotic chain of thoughts based on the interpretation of these signs, or you see a way to alter a meme that you've copied, or sometimes there is no apparent source at all. Whatever its source in a given instance, inspiration is the seed that is necessary for change, the grain of dust that triggers the formation of a snowflake and, ultimately, the storm that follows. Magic—as operative communication—is a tool for translating this initial inspiration into the changes that are first necessary within the perceptual world. This is followed by altering a particular semiotic web to contain the right symbols that suggest an interpretation that can accommodate your vision. The newly re-spun semiotic web then suggests the effective mode of address for communicating this mindfully

---

*Examples of this include the system of angular magic created by Michael A. Aquino in part from ideas in the fiction of H. P. Lovecraft (see my *Infernal Geometry and the Left-Hand Path*), and Brenda Yagmin's transformation of megapolisomancy (from Fritz Leiber's *Our Lady of Darkness*) into an actual practice of city magic (see Appendix B for more about this practice).

evolved vision to those mechanisms and forces in the phenomenal world that can help to realize your vision.

This chapter offered a glimpse at what language and semiotics are from a magician's perspective, seen as a particular ordering of core concepts and ideas that are part of the development of linguistics and semiotics as distinct disciplines over the last couple of centuries. The conceptual model of magic-as-communication was introduced as well, providing some necessary background as important core ideas of language, semiotics, and magic are expanded on in the following chapters.

The history of magic has undergone varied and unexpected twists and turns over the last couple of centuries. This has happened—not coincidentally—in a timeframe roughly corresponding to the expansion and specialization of different ways for the natural and social sciences to study and explain the human condition. To better understand the foundations of the conceptual model of magic put forth in this book, we now turn to an overview of different models that have been proposed by anthropologists, sociologists, and semioticians.

2

A SURVEY OF
DIFFERENT
MODELS OF MAGIC

Until the nineteenth century, there was very little explicit attention paid to the conceptual models behind magic both among practitioners and from skeptical outsiders like philosophers and anthropologists. Rather than on models, the focus was instead on techniques: generally repeatable spells and symbolic signs passed on clandestinely from one practitioner to another, sometimes combined with lists or tables of entities (or other "intelligences") as in Goetia, the angelic magic of John Dee and Edward Kelley, or the planetary magic of Agrippa.

Why then the sudden interest in models and theory of magic in the mid-nineteenth century? One of the intellectual legacies of the Enlightenment was the tendency toward analysis and categorization, especially in those areas of knowledge that up to that point had largely resisted being reconceptualized as sciences. Two such areas of study most pertinent to this book are anthropology and linguistics.

Linguistics was developed most thoroughly during this period in the German-speaking areas of Europe, which had largely rejected the ideals and worldviews of the Enlightenment in lieu of their idiosyncratic brand of Romanticism.* Pioneered by figures like Jacob Grimm (of Brothers Grimm fame), linguistics became part of the German search for identity and went hand in hand with the nationalistic furor sweeping Europe in the mid-nineteenth century. Different lands that previously were only loosely grouped together by common language, ethnicity, and culture became more conscious of their unity. They then formed formal nations to complete this compartmentalization (with explicit borders that often became the subject of conflict). Recall from our brief discussion of the four major divisions of culture in chapter 1 that *linguistic culture*—those aspects of culture that are preserved, modified, and passed on through language—forms one key component of cultural identity alongside those other aspects of culture that tie a group of people together. So, it's not surprising that the study of language became part of this search for identity and ultimately nationality.

The parallel development of modern anthropology as a distinct science followed a different path, albeit one also driven by the zeitgeist and attitudes of its time. The first prominent anthropologists emerged in those areas of Western Europe that were both industrialized and major colonial powers, especially England. The game-changing efficiency of industrialization increased the general technology and wealth gaps between those countries that had become industrialized and those that had not; the colonial holdings of those same countries grew even further behind by those same metrics. Anthropology in part emerged as a way of studying and attempting to understand the vast differences in mindset and worldview of the Western European "haves" and the "have-nots" of the lands they exploited. As in the case of linguistics in the soon-to-be-unified Germany, the cultural differences catego-

---

*Romanticism as a transcultural phenomenon was in large part a reaction to the Enlightenment—an attempt to rediscover and regain what was lost in the latter's focus on rationality, scientific materialism, classical art forms, and cosmopolitanism. Furthermore, there was a growing realization that the Enlightenment had not resulted in the society it had promised but had come closer to doing the opposite: witness the bloody terror of the French Revolution and its rippling effects into other parts of Europe.

rized and described by anthropology also became part of the search for national identity in England, France, the Netherlands, and other colonial powers.

Anthropology of the mid to late nineteenth century focused on an evolutionary model of mankind's cultural development, especially regarding magic and religion. This is not surprising given the dominant influence that the concept of evolution had in the West at the time. The idea that natural selection—gradual change over time as a function of suitability for a given environment—governed the development of many types of systems was also a key influence on fields of study as diverse as linguistics and Karl Marx's dialectical materialism. Herbert Spencer (1820–1903) was a British philosopher, biologist, and anthropologist; he coined the expression "survival of the fittest" to describe the process of evolution through natural selection. The popularity of his writings among the general public was a significant gateway for his ideas about evolution, which also influenced a variety of scientific disciplines.

British anthropologists also bought into the idea—as would nearly any educated Victorian of the day—that British culture was the pinnacle of humanity due to its wealth, technological superiority, and worldwide presence. Thus, any evolution of cultural ideas and norms was "clearly" destined to lead to the inevitable outcome of the proper, rational, cultured English gentleman.

NINETEENTH-CENTURY BRITISH ANTHROPOLOGY AND MAGIC

Herbert Spencer applied his understanding of evolution to social issues, including the first description of magic as a form of proto-religion. He did not see religion as something that replaced magic; rather, his concept was that religion arose from the transference of worship from ancestors (the agents of magic in Spencer's view) to divine figures. In other words, religion didn't supersede magic as such as absorb it and give it a more transcendent focus.

Spencer's rival E. B. Tylor (1832–1917), however, used his position as the first professor of anthropology at Oxford to elevate the study of magic to the status of a major topic in anthropology. His study of magic was firmly rooted in evolutionary models: magic began as an extension of animism, religion arose alongside the recognition of humans as the only creatures with souls, and eventually polytheistic religion evolved into monotheism. Tylor regarded this "discovery" as confirmation of the applicability of Darwin's ideas to the culture of humans just as Darwin himself applied them to biology.

Tylor introduced the strict, mutually exclusive division between religion and science: in religion (which to him encompassed myth as well) events unfold according to the will of the gods; in science, events are subject only to physical laws and occasionally the choices of humans. Due to this explicitly scientific bias, Tylor had a very dim view of cultures—both ancient and current—that practiced magic. He coined the term *pseudo-science* specifically to describe magic. He also condemned magic as "one of the most pernicious delusions that ever vexed mankind,"[1] and ridiculed cultures that practiced it as being like children who needed guidance and education to overcome their "primitive" ideas.

James Frazer (1845–1941) popularized Tylor's evolutionary model far beyond the realm of academia with his encyclopedic work *The Golden Bough*. Frazer's work influenced authors, poets, mythologists, and philosophers such as H. P. Lovecraft, James Joyce, T. S. Eliot, Robert Graves, and Ludwig Wittgenstein. Whereas Tylor saw magic and religion as two aspects of the same broad set of ideas, Frazer separated out magic as an explicit precursor to religion. Also, like Tylor, Frazer was skeptical about the efficacy and validity of magic and could only see it as "erroneous" thinking—that is, thinking that could be "corrected" by advancing first to religion then to science as the dominant conceptual model within a culture.

However, rather than simply completely dismissing it outright due to its supposedly erroneous nature, Frazer did attempt to understand how magic was thought to work within cultures where it was practiced. He formulated two laws to explain the workings and conceptual model of magic, both of which continue to be quite useful in a semiotic-focused concept of magic.

The *law of sympathy* (also called *sympathetic magic* or *imitative magic*) states that magic works with images or objects that are *similar* to the intended target or result of the magical operation. Altering, mutilating, or destroying the image—or doll or effigy—is intended to create a corresponding effect on the real target. The semiotic analogue to the law of sympathy is the type of sign known as an *icon*—a sign that in some way resembles the thing it refers to. This is also part of a type of analogical thinking called *metonymy*: the use of some object or visual image that is closely associated with a thing being used to represent that thing (like saying *the White House* instead of *the President*, or *the press* instead of *journalists*).

Sympathetic magic is probably the most widespread bit of magical thinking that people engage in without even realizing it or appreciating its significance. The stereotypical example of the law of sympathy is the voodoo doll (which has virtually nothing to do with actual voodoo practices). The image is a "good enough" representation of the target, and harming or mutilating a part of the doll is intended to bring about an analogous effect on the corresponding body part of the victim. However, this example sells short how widespread this type of magical thinking really is, and how blurry the lines can be between magic and religion. You can see variations of the law of sympathy in examples as wide-ranging as a Christian wearing a cross—creating a sympathetic association with Christ's suffering as a cornerstone of that religion—to signaling allegiance with a sports team by wearing its uniforms or other emblems. Both of these connect the wearer's aims and sense of identity with the target of that particular adornment, while at the same time creating a magical conduit for influencing and being influenced by that target.

The *law of contagion* suggests that once one object has been in touch with another, a connection continues to exist between those objects that can be utilized for magical purposes. In this view, magic can be done with one object or person as the target through the manipulation of the other object that retains a magical connection to the first: a curse can be transferred to another person through an object they once owned, or the magic power of a saint can be summoned through one of their relics, and so on. The semiotic correspondence to the law of contagion is the type of sign known as an *index*—a sign whose existence points to or connects to the existence of something else (e.g., a hoof print that reveals the nearby or recent presence of a deer).

Despite their towering influence on the early years of anthropology as a formal science, the ideas of Tylor and Frazer were not immune from criticism even in their day. Their definitions of magic and religion—for example, Frazer defined *religion* as a belief in powers higher than man and an attempt to propitiate or please them—were fairly simplistic and the evolutionary model suggested a timeline that has little explanatory or predictive power. However, Frazer's two laws have continued to be useful as foundational elements for understanding magical thinking. His laws will be discussed more thoroughly in chapter 3 when we look at the semiotic ideas of Charles Sanders Peirce.

Further critique of both Tylor and Frazer came from the pioneering sociologist Émile Durkheim (1858–1917). Durkheim rejected their notion of religion as being exclusively concerned with gods and other spiritual entities, focusing instead on interactions with the sacred as the basis for religion. Durkheim further redefined religion as being social in nature—something that binds communities together—with magic being more focused on the individual. This is an important distinction for our purposes, as it opens up the idea that magic works to realize the *individual* will of the magician instead of the *collective* will of the society the magician lives in (reinforcing the common notion of the magician as outsider or at least someone who accomplishes things through unconventional means). The distinction also fits in with Durkheim's idea of the cult of the individual: the notion that the changing relationship between an individual and their society is a necessary and beneficial outgrowth of population density (and of the increased interactions between individuals that this density entails).

Durkheim's approach to magic can be described as *symbolist*: magic is an expression of desire through symbolic means, and magical rituals are not to be interpreted literally but rather as a form of created meaning. This creation of meaning through symbolic means is akin to the same meaning-making we create through the symbols called words in language. *The perception—and modification—of reality depends on the symbols used to describe it or interact with it.*

THE TWENTIETH CENTURY: ANTHROPOLOGY EVOLVES

In the twentieth century, anthropologists continued to refine their views of magic as a cultural phenomenon, now generally focusing more on contemporary usage of magic than their counterparts of the previous century. The influence on anthropology from other fields of study, including linguistics and semiotics, has led to theories and models of magic like the one developed in the present text.

The sociologist and anthropologist Marcel Mauss (1872–1950), a nephew of Émile Durkheim, continued to develop the French symbolist view of magic alongside his collaborator Henri Hubert (1872–1927). Mauss and Hubert argued that the use and meaning of sympathy (similarity) and contagion in magic reflected societal conventions;[2] that is, their meaning is at least partially conventionalized much in the same way that the meaning of language is (along with other symbolic signs). To Mauss and Hubert, "magical actions are recognizable by their ritual structure containing noncausal relations between action and reaction based on an iterative sequence of conventionally specified actions."[3]

Max Weber (1864–1920) gave a name to what he called the *Entzauberung der Welt*, usually rendered in English as the "disenchantment of the world." Weber used this phrase to describe what he saw as the separation of magic from religion in the advent of modernity, and ultimately toward the elimination of magic—which he regarded as ignorant and ineffective—from any chance of being confused with religion. Then religion could function unimpeded by magic and embrace rationality—sort of a blending of the second and third phases of Frazer's evolutionary model. Weber regarded the Protestant Reformation as an essential milestone in this evolution, as it began to chip away at what he saw as the blending of religion and magic in Roman Catholic ritual and accelerate the disenchantment. The Enlightenment a couple of centuries later hastened the disenchantment even further.

Bronisław Malinowski (1884–1942) spent most of his career working with the inhabitants of the Trobriand Islands of Papua New Guinea. His work was part of a larger trend in anthropological studies of magic toward focusing on social attitudes toward magic. This shift also represented a change in focus from dismissing magic as an aberration of so-called primitive peoples toward starting from the assumption that magic *does* work within a particular cultural context. This then leads to explaining *why* it works (or at least why its practitioners treat it as if it works).

In the case of Malinowski's field research, he formulated the theory that magic provided an emotional release and feeling of control over events where someone would normally feel powerless or inadequate. Magic also provided, according to his observations, the impetus for alternative solutions when other knowledge was lacking (including, but not limited to, gaps in the scientific knowledge about the physical processes of the world). This was an important turning point: magic was now, according to a Western scientist, *useful* and served an actual purpose other than to blind its practitioners from the truths of modern science and/or religion.

The other major turning point in anthropology brought on by Malinowski's theories about magic was the acknowledgment of the magical power of words. His attempts at translating the Trobriand islanders' magical formulae made him realize that for them "words were *actions* that achieved practical effects."[4] While Malinowski did still hold magic to be irrational and ultimately a delusion, his conclusion was that it was nonetheless regarded as effective *in the cultural context in which it was practiced*. This shift from a question like "Why do they mistakenly think that magic works?" to "How does their worldview provide a framework that makes magic a meaningful practice?" was an important one. Malinowski's work was a significant influence on Stanley Tambiah's approach to magic (more on which below).

Claude Lévi-Strauss (1908–2009) was a pioneer of structural anthropology. Structuralism was a broadly defined movement in the social sciences that drew on ideas from linguist Ferdinand de Saussure (see chap. 3). Structuralism holds that thought arises from specific classifications—particularly, taxonomies of opposites—that are projected on the world and provide evidence of the underlying human-created thought structures at play.

Lévi-Strauss's analysis of certain shamanic healing rituals led him to suggest that this particular form of magic worked on three levels: (1) the psychological states undergone by the shaman; (2) the sick person who is the recipient, perhaps skeptically, of the shaman's attempt at healing; and (3) the audience for the healing ritual who also actively reinforce the attitudes of both the shaman and the one who ails. As an essential part of his training and initiation, the shaman would have himself undergone some sort of sickness or crisis.

Lévi-Strauss stated that all humans have two modes of thought: a "normal" and logical mode that is limited in the meaning it can ascribe to all phenomena, and a "pathological" mode of thought that is overripe with meaning.[5] The patient represents the former type of thought, the shaman the latter. The shaman's "pathological" (i.e., rich with meaning) mode of thought enables him to ascribe symbolic importance to the patient's malady and thus apply further symbolic means to magically heal the patient. The audience serves as a mediator between these two modes of thought (and their contradictions)—they are in effect the communication medium between the two otherwise dissimilar modes of thought. Their magical thinking helps to shift the frame of reference for the patient to enable his "logical" mind to accept the meaning imposed by the "pathological" mind of the shaman.

A SEMIOTIC TURN

By the mid-twentieth century, structuralism had become the dominant paradigm within the social sciences, perhaps most prominently in linguistics and anthropology. One of structuralism's underlying dichotomies—the relationship between *signifier* (that which refers) and *signified* (what is referred to), together constituting a (linguistic) sign—formed the basis of Ferdinand de Saussure's proposed science of semiology. We will take a deeper look at Saussure's ideas in chapter 3.

The "structures" that are at the core of structuralism are those evident in the creations of human beings: dichotomies, hierarchies, and symbolic behavior coalescing as identifiable culture that can be transmitted and preserved. As language is one of those behaviors that is uniquely human (at least in the extent to which humans have developed it), it stands to reason that the structures created through language will be reflected in human culture. With the importance of the linguistic sign—Saussure's signifier and signified in a feedback loop—firmly established within structuralist anthropology, analysis of language and its effects began to be seen as one of the key components of anthropological research.

The first explicitly semiotic analysis of magic—and conception of a semiotic model of magic—was developed by the Norwegian folklorist Ronald Grambo (b. 1928). He conceived magic as "a means of conveying messages."[6] Effective use of magic according to this model requires that the recipient—a god or other "unusual addressee,"* the phenomenal world, a neighbor or adversary one wishes to influence, and so on—understand to some extent the message conveyed through magic.

---

*An unusual addressee is a god or a spirit who would presumably carry out the magical act on behalf of the magician. The term originated with Jakobson.

Thus, the words and other signs that accompany the actions of magic are meaningful both for the magician and the recipient of their magic.

Grambo also introduced the importance of the *frame of reference* to the operation of magic. The frame of reference is not only the context in which the magical act is undertaken, but also (a) those factors of the worldview of the magician and the culture within which they work, and (b) the semiotic web the magician perceives and modifies through the magical act.

The desired phenomena—the intended outcome(s) of the magic—constitute a grammar; that is, the phenomena themselves suggest the shape and components of the communication designed to bring about those phenomena. Grambo characterized this as a *system of syntagms.* A *syntagm* or *syntagma** in linguistics is a set of words ordered in a certain way and which comprise a unit of meaning; this can be as simple as a phrase or be built into more complex *syntagmata* (sentences, paragraphs, etc.). In short, a syntagma is the accumulation of individual units of language into ever more complex units. Applied to magic from a semiotic perspective, syntagmata are formulas: units of significance that are combined and manipulated to change the sign networks that the magician uses to relate to the phenomena they desire to affect. Grambo characterizes these as variables and constants, both of which have meaning conditioned by the frame of reference understood by the magician.[7]

In Grambo's semiotic model, the magic (i.e., the message) is encoded in a symbolic or semiotic form comprehensible to both the sender (the magician) and the receiver. (The receiver is the phenomenal world that will manifest the desired result from the magic, or the unusual addressee that will carry out the intention of the magic.) The recipient in turn encodes and sends the return message—the result of the magical operation—in a form intelligible or perceptible by the original sender. This should be very reminiscent of the sender-message-receiver model

---

*Grambo uses the British spelling of syntagm, pl. syntagms. In the present book we will use the more common spelling of syntagma, pl. syntagmata.

discussed in chapter 1, along with the same limitations. Nonetheless, Grambo's semiotic model applied to *magic* was a groundbreaking but unfortunately little-noticed contribution to the more comprehensive semiotic models of magic explored here.

The Innovations of Tambiah and van Baal

Stanley Tambiah (1929–2014) took Malinowski's ideas about the magical use of language and combined them with linguistic insights from J. L. Austin and Ludwig Wittgenstein. This led to Tambiah's formulation of a linguistic model of magic, forming a key influence on the semiotic model that underlies the present book.

Tambiah was a social anthropologist, working within that branch of anthropology that focuses on the study of patterns of human behavior as they create social structure. He rejected the distinction between magic and religion as developed by Tylor and Frazer, seeing these concepts as intertwined manifestations of the same basic impulse.

The central idea that Tambiah took from Malinowski was that, in cultures that recognize the magical power of words, the "uttering of words itself is a ritual."[8] Ritual is composed of both words and deeds, each having significant weight in the execution and success of the ritual. This model opens a profound door: words themselves, in all the ways they can be structured and used, have an effect that results in the transformation of the magician, the world outside the magician, or both.

The practical effect of words was not a new idea. The category of speech called *performative utterances*, conceptualized by J. L. Austin in the 1950s, illustrates this potential for practical effect. A performative utterance is a speech act that by the very fact of being spoken in the correct circumstances causes something to change. For example, the phrase "I now pronounce you husband and wife," spoken in the right situation by a person with the authority to do so, creates this particular union of marriage *through the utterance itself.* Tambiah's insight, inspired by Malinowski's ideas, was that this same union of word and deed—when accompanied by other aspects of ritual—could have a similar magical effect.

The use of language in ritual is related to, but separate from, the mundane use of language for profane communication. That is, language in this context still creates and conveys meaning, however the communication is not primarily between people. Rather, meaning in magical communication arises from the effects the words have on the participants but more importantly on the perspective of the world that people construct through language. This arises from the nearly universal notion of the creative power of the word; in many creation myths, words are responsible for creating the cosmos itself or are the vehicle through which the gods create and rule. Tambiah summarizes this as follows:

> The Vedic hymns speculated on *vāc* (the word) and asserted that the gods ruled the world through magical formulae; the Parsi religion states that in the battle between good and evil it was through the spoken word that chaos was transformed into cosmos; ancient Egypt believed in a god of the Word; the Semites and the Sumerians have held that the world and its objects were created by the word of God; and the Greek doctrine of *logos* postulated that the soul or essence of things resided in their names.[9]

In chapter 5 we will discuss in more detail the importance of myth and storytelling. They are still vitally important even to modern humans in industrialized societies, even though those people may be less aware of it due to the disenchantment of the world spoken of by Weber. One way to participate in the stories and myths that govern our view of the world is to reenact them. The followers of a god may mimic his actions in order to bring about analogous results. For example, Odin won knowledge of the runes after undergoing an ordeal (see chap. 7), then used his understanding of the runes for magical purposes and for gaining further self-knowledge. By working with runes, a modern-day runer, or rune magician, is reenacting those actions of Odin in order to bring about results meaningful and applicable *to them*. In a similar vein, using words to create or alter our external world also resonates with these myths in which words create the cosmos as we know it. Magic is nothing if not a reshaping of the world, whether it is the inner world of the magician or the outer world as experienced through five (or more) senses and three (or more) dimensions.

Owing to his background in structural anthropology, Tambiah ultimately followed Saussure in equating *words* with *signs*. Thus, Tambiah's well-developed views of magic fulfilled some of the promise of Grambo's speculations on a *semiotic model* of magic.

Similarly to his incorporation of ideas from J. L. Austin, Tambiah also realized the applicability to magic of some observations by the philosopher Ludwig Wittgenstein. Wittgenstein heavily criticized Frazer's characterization of magic as false science; he understood it rather as primarily working with *symbolic* expression of certain desires.[10]

Within Tambiah's model of magic as a combination of—symbolic as well as practical—word and deed, magic is not an ill-informed attempt at science but rather a rhetorical art that orders reality according to the will of the magician. This follows from his understanding of Wittgenstein's contention that the *meaning* of words was a function of their *use*. Malinowski intuited that particular way of understanding words in the rituals of the Trobriand islanders; their words—even if the largely the same as words they used in a profane setting—took on certain meanings in ritual acts that could not be understood outside of that context. Tambiah incorporated Wittgenstein's suggestion that magic connects the different aspects of the worldview of a culture by giving those aspects symbolic importance;[11] the words used as part of magic give presence to the targets and aims of magic, since "magic always rests on the idea of symbolism and of language."[12]

Jan van Baal (1909–1992) was a Dutch anthropologist who, like Malinowski, also spent a significant portion of his career engaged in field work in Papua New Guinea. Like Tambiah, van Baal's theories of magic and religion emphasized the use of signs that humans use to communicate with their universe according to their particular frame of reference.

While van Baal's work is not rooted in a particular school of semiotics, he does follow the generalized understanding of semiotics that is characteristic of structural anthropology. Van Baal separated *signs* into *symbols* and *signals*. These signs are distinguished by signals belonging to specific situations where they are only meaningful within that context, while symbols can be meaningfully used outside of the situation;[13] thus, symbols derive from and adapt to context. This distinction emphasizes that "owing to the use of symbols, man is no longer situation-bound. Using symbols, he creates a distance with his world, which is the reason why he can be active in his world."[14] Since humans are able to conceive of themselves in contrast to the universe around them, yet at the same time live and act within it, there is an implicit solitude that can be overcome through repairing this divide through the use of symbols. Symbols give meaning to the universe and to the relationship between individuals and the universe.[15]

Central to van Baal's theories is the ability of humans to think *ascriptively*; that is, they assign meaning to the phenomena they experience. Through the creation and use of symbols the phenomenal world becomes a partner in communication (both linguistically and metalinguistically). In this model, the magician chooses and arranges the symbols—linguistic or otherwise—appropriate to his desire; he then uses these symbols to engage in communication with the unmanifest according to what he perceives to be the correct mode of address. The magician (the *subject*) encodes desire through this mode of address (the *direct object*) and communicates with the "other reality" he wishes to affect (the *indirect object*). The response is the *subject* in a return communication, with the result—the desired phenomenon—now being the *indirect object*. Stephen Flowers illustrated van Baal's model of magical communication as follows:

subject ⟶ direct object ⟶ indirect object
(man)   (symbol-symbolized)   ("other reality")

                                              ↓

indirect object ⟵ (phenomenon) ⟵ subject
(ultimate aim of operation)

Magical communication according to van Baal's model

According to van Baal, the communication model for the fulfillment of desire can be understood in this way:

> In this discourse man feels addressed or singled out by his universe,
> and he endeavors to address it in turn, trying to discover the kind
> of address to which his universe will be willing to answer, that is,
> willing to show itself communicable. The formula he finally discov-
> ers in answer to his quest is not really man's discovery but a gift,
> a revelation bestowed upon him by the universe. The formula is
> the outcome of an act of communication in which man's universe
> reveals to him the secret of how it should be addressed in this or
> that circumstance, a secret which is at the same time a revelation of
> its hidden essence in that particular field.[16]

COGNITIVE MODELS OF MAGIC

Starting in the 1970s, anthropologists began to move away from the
study of magic. One of the reasons behind this was the transition away
from structuralism as the dominant paradigm in anthropology; post-
structuralism, cultural relativism, and postmodernism began to hold
even more sway. As a result, the study of magic as a phenomenon started
to emerge in other disciplines which had new methods—and biases—
for characterizing and describing it.

One such emergence is in cognitive science, a field that did not
pay much attention to magic in its first few decades. Cognitive science

is an interdisciplinary field, drawing not only from anthropology but also from psychology, neuroscience, computer science, and linguistics. The focus is on cognition, or how the mental and physiological systems in humans process, represent, and act on both internal and external information.

Jesper Sørensen (b. 1968) approaches magic from two normally opposed aspects of cognitive science. From the viewpoint of cognitive psychology, he studies constraints on the human ability to create and work with categories; these limitations reveal universal patterns of culture that can then explain some commonalities in the ways different cultures understand and work with magic. From the viewpoint of cognitive semantics, Sørensen looks at how we create meaning as part of working with magic. The combination of these approaches recognizes both the underlying forms of magic that manifest across cultures, and also how the universal quest for meaning builds culturally specific significance on top of those underlying forms.[17] The emphasis in these perspectives on magic is on the thought processes behind magic, with special attention to what those thought processes reveal about different forms of magic and the ends to which they are directed.

From this perspective, magic is a particular *cognitive model*—a way of ordering and working with information and perception based on an approximation of the underlying cognitive processes at work. Cognitive models are descriptions of the processes they attempt to illuminate, rather than striving to reduce the behavior and its cognitive processes to simple one-size-fits-all explanations. In the case of magic as a concept or model for interacting with the world, a wide range of behavior is in evidence—a variety of cognitive, behavioral, semiotic, and communicative theories can explain *some* aspect of magic, but none can encompass everything that falls under the umbrella of magical thinking. Sørensen's view of magic is not limited to cognitive explanations, however; instead, magic is:

> a synthetic concept that covers a broad range of cognitive, cultural and social phenomena. . . . The challenge for the scholar, then, is to

construct a comprehensive model that links these different explanatory levels.[18]

Just as semiotics is largely about the relationships between signs, cognitive models of magic seek to connect different thought processes and
understand the relationships between them.

FURTHER DEVELOPMENTS IN THE
SEMIOTICS OF MAGIC

Codes and Maps

In *Magic, Power, Language, Symbol*, the linguist Patrick Dunn describes
magic as a way of perceiving, controlling, and manipulating codes. A
code is a "framework into which we place our symbols."[19]

Let's look at codes in general before digging into Dunn's use of them
in his magical theories. Codes are a fundamental construct in structuralist models of semiotics;[20] they don't determine meaning by themselves,
but they *do* collect conventions or rules for interpreting signs into models that normalize the ways that meaning is produced in specific contexts. For example, there are codes that govern sexual practices (what's
permissible and what is considered transgressive or perverted), food
(what counts as acceptable food and means of preparing/consuming it),
social norms in various situations, and so forth. Much of this happens
beneath the surface of our active awareness; we behave and interpret the
behavior of others in terms of the conventions that are part of our host
culture (or which signal "in group" or "out group" status regarding what
we do or don't want to be associated with). We may not notice when
someone conforms to a code applicable to a particular situation, but we
definitely notice when they violate that code. *Since codes are set according to the accumulated expectations and norms of a culture, learning how
not only to notice the codes but also how to transcend them is an especially
powerful tool for a magician.* We must be wary, however, about adopting alternate codes solely because they are associated with rebellion or

individualism; it is part of the nature of codes that ones that begin as transgressing against prevailing norms often become a *new* norm that is eventually accepted among the broader codes deemed permissible within a culture.*

Dunn points out that since we know the world through the symbols that we attach to it, and thus, by extension, we know the world through the codes we use (whether consciously or not), *these codes then become the conduit for changing that same reality*:

> Changing those codes makes it more likely that we will get what we desire, not just because we will see things in a new and more productive way, but also because reality itself will be affected by our changed codes, bringing new symbols in contact with us.[21]

The codes you work with predispose you to discern the world around you in certain ways. Changing yourself—and the world—through magic begins with changing your perception and visualizing new possibilities that can be reinforced through a variety of means.

Now we will explore ideas about semiotics and magic from two scholars of Germanic culture, Stephen E. Flowers and Scott Shell, both of whom have formal advanced training in linguistics. In between them, we'll also take a short detour through semiotician Winfried Nöth's attempt to describe magical semiosis.

Flowers and Shell also have in common the unfortunate obstacle that the field of interest of their research—academic runology—has

---

*One particular trope here, almost a cliché, is "normal" middle-aged, often affluent, adults adopting what was considered rebellious in their youth: lawyers riding Harleys, white collar professionals playing in heavy metal bands on the weekends, and so forth. On the surface, such behaviors seem to be deviations from social codes (i.e., people with this level of affluence and maturity "just don't do" those things), whereas in reality they have become permissible or even tacitly encouraged pseudo-deviations from expected norms—and thereby are neutralized by being absorbed into the ever-evolving code for acceptable behavior in the West.

in recent decades become increasingly skeptical about whether runes were sometimes used in magical ways in ancient times. Their models of magic, however, are applicable to more than just runes. They both point out that when you decline to attempt to define *magic*—as is widespread in the literature of academic runology—it's easy to dismiss the very idea of magic out of hand. A methodical or scientific study of the potential magical uses of runes requires a model and definition of magic to measure against; otherwise, we're just back to Humpty Dumpty and his ever-shifting meanings of words to suit whatever he required of them at the time. Semiotics stresses that meaning is not just about the signs or words used, but also derives from the worldview (the code) in which they are used; thus, it's not possible, at least from a semiotic perspective, to judge the magical intent or effectiveness of an inscription based *solely* on the inscription itself. This principle has implications far beyond just the question whether runes were used historically as part of magical operations.

Runes and Magic

Stephen Edred Flowers (b. 1953) is uniquely qualified to integrate concepts from language and semiotics into a model of magic. In addition to his formal training in Germanic linguistics, he—alongside his academic studies beginning in the mid-1970s—immersed himself in the experimental practice of magic using what he was able to reconstruct of the runic tradition. As a result of writing about both his academic and practical work (often in the same books), he has been one of the central figures in the runic revival outside the academic world from the mid-1980s onward. His first book, *Futhark*, appeared in 1984.

Flowers's works targeted at the general public (some of which are published under the pen name Edred Thorsson) are always firmly grounded in both the academic and the initiatory. This stands in contrast to other writers on runic topics who have sometimes ignored well-established academic info about runes in favor of their personal, ungrounded speculations.

In the same year that *Futhark* was published, Flowers completed and defended his doctoral thesis titled *Runes and Magic*. This work expanded on the ideas of Ronald Grambo, Jan van Baal, and Stanley Tambiah to develop their suggestions of a semiotic/communicative model of magic and apply it to inscriptions in the original form of the runes known as the Elder Futhark (see chap. 7).

When discussing Flowers's contributions to the semiotic theory of magic, the first thing we must do is actually to discard the word *magic*!* Just as we discussed in the introduction, a huge part of the problem in defining and conceptualizing magic is that it has been used to mean so many different things in so many different contexts. The word can only be used effectively when accompanied by exhaustive explanations about how it is to be understood in the given context. Flowers suggests that a less loaded term would be *operative communication*,[22] which of course emphasizes the semiotic properties of magic as well.† In operative communication "symbolic acts are often responded to in phenomenological ways."[23]

According to Flowers, operative communication is created by meaningful, real communication between a normally relatively powerless operator and members (or the essence) of a supersensible realm.[24] It is significant that in multiple places in the Eddas‡ and various Elder

---

*Flowers does write about magic using the word "magic" in many of his works, although he always defines it precisely at the outset, so as to limit distortion of his ideas (i.e., he avoids the usual approach of tacitly encouraging the reader to have it mean whatever they want it to mean).

†Flowers also follows Egyptologist Herman te Velde's description of magic as practical theology (see chap. 5), although he notes that many forms of magic—especially those that are animistic in nature—do not necessarily depend on any idea of working with, on behalf of, or using the tools of divine figures.

‡The *Poetic Edda* and the *Prose Edda* are two significant collections of lore and mythology about the Germanic peoples in what is now Scandinavia and Iceland. The anonymous *Poetic Edda* was likely compiled and written down in the thirteenth century although the material in it is from several centuries earlier. The *Prose Edda* was written by Icelandic scholar Snorri Sturluson in the early thirteenth century; it was written largely as a reference for poets wishing to compose new poems drawing from Norse mythology.

Futhark inscriptions the runes are explicitly said to be of divine origin. This view of magic as operative communication is thus precisely the same kind of communication with the divine realm that is well-recognized in the ancient Mediterranean cultures. As we'll discuss in chapter 7, there is strong circumstantial evidence that early runemasters were exposed to Greek and Roman ideas about magic alongside their exposure to writing as capable of both mundane and magical uses.

Flowers builds his model of communication with the supersensible realm on these two requirements:

- *Mutual intelligibility* between the operator and their partner in communication. That is, they must be speaking "the same language": using or creating shared meaning that gives their communication significance. This in turn is predicated on a certain degree of similarity between these partners in communication.
- *Similarity* requires that the operator must, at least temporarily, become enough like the divine figures that they call upon or work with to be able to communicate as near equals.

In the runic corpus, this requirement of similarity manifests most often in so-called runemaster formulas. In these, the operator takes on a divine name or persona that acknowledges the divine origin of the runes alongside claiming the knowledge and state of being that entitles them to use runes in this manner.

One famous runemaster formula is the *ek erilaR** formula, found among other places on the well-known Lindholm amulet (see chap. 8). The word *erilaR* is of somewhat uncertain origin, but it is widely accepted among runologists to be a title indicating a runemaster (an Eril). The Lindholm inscription continues as *ek erilaR sā wīlagaR*

---

*The *-R* is the conventional way for transcribing a Proto-Nordic sound found only at the end of words, which was in the process of transitioning between the sounds [z] and [r]. In some sources you will see the letter *z* used.

ha(i)teka; this has typically been read as "I 'the eril' am called the crafty one." The ritual formula of the form "I [—] am called [—]" is a common one associated with the god Óðinn (Odin), the patron of runes and of magic. By claiming the knowledge and initiation necessary to use the runes, the operator is in effect claiming kinship and understanding with Óðinn and as a result is empowered to do things with runes that Óðinn would do.

Further to the goal of creating similarity between the operator and Óðinn, Elmer Antonsen notes that the etymology of *erilaR* likely derives from a Proto-Indo-European verb meaning "to set in motion; to rise up".[25] here, the operator "rises up" through knowing how to assert the runemaster formula, elevating their state of being to one alike to Óðinn, thus enabling communication (and the sharing of ability and skill).

Flowers draws parallels to well-established ancient Greek magical formulas where the practitioner asserts mutual identity with the god Hermes—another figure like Óðinn, Thoth, and even Lovecraft's Nyarlathotep who are explicitly associated with writing and/or language in magical contexts.[26] These formulas in the Greek Magical Papyri (see chap. 6) show a strong influence from Egyptian techniques and concepts of magic, specifically the process *pḥ-nṯr*: "to reach a god" or "to employ the magical powers of a god."[27] The magician is not doing this to beseech the god to act on his behalf, but rather instead to "himself *employ the magical powers of a god.*"[28]

It should be clear by this point that Flowers's conceptual model of magic—with or without that problematic term in the description—is explicitly and nearly exclusively about communication. Yet, while it *is* a semiotic model in the sense that words are signs—rooted in ideas from structural anthropology—it is not a model that many semioticians today would necessarily claim as one of their own (due to the dominant Peircean influence in current semiotics). For that we need to look at the study of magical communication through the eyes of semioticians who have incorporated it into their theories of sign-based communication.

Acts of Magical Semiosis

Winfried Nöth's *Handbook of Semiotics* is an indispensable and comprehensive source for presenting the history, theory, and various applications of semiotics. In this book, Nöth builds on the sender-message-receiver (SMR) communication model of Roman Jakobson in order to briefly examine what he refers to as *acts of magical semiosis*. Like Jakobson, he assumes such magical semiosis would always involve communication with an unusual addressee who would carry out the magical operation on behalf of the magician—this limits his model to only certain types and forms of magic. A curse formula, for example, is typically addressed to someone of *this* world, so Nöth's (and Jakobson's) theories are unable to explain how such formulas might work in practice. Unfortunately, Nöth falls into the same trap as Frazer, Tylor, and others by describing magic only to dismiss it as superstitious nonsense—even after presenting a semiotic model that acknowledges the apparent effects of magic within a particular world-view! Nonetheless, Nöth's work does definitively demonstrate—from within the perspective of the discipline of semiotics itself—that the principles of semiosis *can* be applied to the study of magic although his actual model of magical semiosis is limited in its scope and explanatory power.

With regard to runes, however, Nöth's theories support the approach taken in this book toward the power of writing in otherwise illiterate societies. Indeed, he confirms that the etymological evidence supports the inherent connection between magical practices and the very idea of writing:

> The English word *spell* still means both 'to name or print in order the letters of (a word)' and 'a spoken word believed to have magical power'. . . . Another interesting case is the etymology of *glamor*, in the original sense of 'a magic spell', 'bewitchment'. This word is a derivation from the word *grammar*, from the popular association of semiotic erudition with occult practices. The etymology of the

German word *Bild* ('image') also contains a magic element, namely, the Germanic etymon **bil-* 'miraculous sign'.[29]

Nöth reminds us of some connections that might be surprising to those who have only ever considered literacy as a mundane and commonplace phenomenon. Writing and grammatical structure (as objects of study) were from their very beginnings innately linked with magical practices. The fact we are so jaded about literacy now in the West, with it being a basic and mundane skill that can be assumed for the majority of people, has made it harder to see what these things meant in terms of prestige and power when they were new. This point is discussed further in the context of the early Germanic peoples in chapter 7.

A Peircean Approach to Rune Magic

Scott Shell combines formal training in both Peircean semiotics* and Germanic linguistics to create a model of operative communication—magic—that builds on current insights in semiotics with regard to how meaning and significance are created.

The central development in Shell's semiotic approach to magic—focused specifically on runes—is encapsulated in his *law of magical semiosis*. His goal with this law was not to create a comprehensive semiotic model of magical communication, but rather to counteract an unfortunate tendency in academic runology that dismisses any possibility of magical uses of runes *without ever defining magic or presenting a model of magic to measure against.*

Shell is quite explicit that since "not every runic inscription has magic as its most salient quality, not all runic inscriptions are magical."[30] He can support the claim that *some* inscriptions are magical and some are not because he has taken the question out of the realm of

---

*This refers to semiotics based in the theories of Charles Sanders Peirce, whom we will be discussing in great detail in chapter 3. Shell studied with the semiotician Irmengard Rauch, who is a notable exponent of the Peircean school.

personal whim and bias, replacing these with a conceptual framework through which a measured judgment can be made and supported.

His law of magical semiosis begins:

> While operating within an *Umwelt* where we assume magic is a *phaneron* in the *Weltanschauung* of the Runemaster, he or she intentionally manipulates signs and sign-relations within a sign-network by the use of icons (like produces like), indices (contagious properties) and/or symbols (learned conceptual properties). While there will be more than one sign within the sign-network, it is the "magical" sign which is the most salient when working with such an object.[31]

Obviously, we're going to need to break that down a bit and briefly explain a few terms. As Shell is firmly in the school of Peircean semiotics, much of the specialized terminology in his law derives from that specific perspective. Here we will provide an introduction to this nomenclature, but we'll revisit some of these terms in more detail in the next chapter in the discussion of Peirce and his ideas.

The *Umwelt*—the perceptual or subjective world that an organism models out of signs in its environment—was a central component of the theories of Jakob von Uexküll, the father of biosemiotics. Peirce coined the term *phaneron** to indicate "all that is present to the mind in any sense or in any way whatsoever, regardless of whether it be fact or figment."[32] A *Weltanschauung* is simply a worldview: the values, assumptions, goals, taboos, and so forth that govern how an individual thinks the world "works" from the perspective of their given culture. What Shell is in effect doing with this constellation of ideas is extending von Uexküll's *Umwelt*, which originally was focused on nonhuman life forms, to include the effects and possibilities of both higher cognition and its cultural effects. In Peircean terms, the signs within a human *Umwelt* now account for not only icons and indices, but also symbols.

---

*From Ancient Greek φανερός (*phanerós*, "visible," "manifest").

Shell's work focuses on the semiotic analysis of runic inscriptions *in their full context* to determine whether they are the product of a *Weltanschauung* that includes a conceptual model of magic. To do this, he relies on the identification and decipherment of sign networks—semiotic webs—such as we discussed in chapter 1. Within a sign network showing the relationships between the most prominent signs associated with an inscription, it is necessary to determine which is the most *salient*—significant, conspicuous, central—sign. If this most salient sign is highly marked* with features associated with magical communication, then this sign dominates—stands out most prominently within—the entire sign network. Due to the interrelations among signs in a sign network, the *entire network* should now be considered a product of the creator's magical *Weltanschauung*. This is a further application of Frazer's law of sympathy: the magical sign "touches" all other signs within the network, bringing them into a sympathetic relationship where they share in that sign's magical intent and especially the communication of that intent.

Let's look at a brief example from Shell's work: the Björketorp runestone in southern Sweden. The stone itself has an inscription, and it is also set as one point of a triangle along with two other plain stones. There is no grave beneath (or within the triangle of) any of the stones, but there was a nearby grave field that has since been destroyed. The consensus about the site is that the stones were set first to mark the area as sacred, alongside other smaller stones arranged to form a circle and a square, and the alliterating runic inscription on the Björketorp stone itself was added later to further sanctify and protect the site. The generally accepted reading of the inscription is that it is a curse upon any who would disturb this memorial,† and Shell argues that the memorial is not just the inscribed stone but the *entire* complex and that this

---

*A linguistic sign—a phoneme, a word, an inscription—is said to be marked if it contains distinguishing features that dominate all other likely understandings of the sign.
†Whether any such curse befell those who destroyed the graves—accidentally, I should add, while harvesting stone for gravel—is unknown.

affects the scope of curse (i.e., it was intended to protect not only the stone but the larger vicinity against disturbance).

The reading that the curse applies to the entire complex strengthens the argument that the inscription was fundamentally magical in intent, since it expands the sign network and the relations within it. This emphasizes the highly marked nature of the inscription due to the scope of what it applies to. The curse is not a simple memorial inscription but also alliterates, which places it in the realm of poetry and emphasizes the relation to Óðinn (a god who uses magical communication) already implied by the use of runes for a sacred purpose. Curses of this type are a classic example of Frazer's law of contagion; their target is anyone who comes into contact with the curse, so the magic comes from proximity instead of being targeted at a particular person. The entire ritual landscape is *itself* a sign, which if "disturbed and rendered profane, . . . will impact the network and trigger the other signs within the system."[33] The inscription is prefaced with a statement that the runes themselves come from the gods, a point about the divine origin of the runes that appears in many contexts in the Germanic world. Thus, the runemaster used the tools of the gods—Óðinn specifically in this case—to do magic like the gods.

This is a necessarily brief look at Scott Shell's approach to magical communication through signs. While his focus was on Elder Futhark runic inscriptions, many of the ideas he advocates (and provides a methodology for) are potentially applicable to analyzing other forms of magical practices. Most importantly, Shell shows how Peirce's classification of signs can be applied *directly* to questions about operative communication, thus opening the doors to using other tools from the vast field of modern semiotics.

In this chapter we looked at a variety of theories and models of magic as they have evolved since the mid-nineteenth century. Because ideas from some of these schools of thought have entered popular awareness, they often form the background of the basic—and frequently disproven or outdated—understanding of those who have not made a serious study of the concept of magic. Thus, it is important to place these ideas in a broad historical perspective so that the reader has sufficient context to understand why semiotic and linguistic ideas applied to magic represent such a significant and game-changing innovation.

In the next chapter, we will look at the theories and concepts of various significant figures in the history of language and semiotics. Since this is ultimately a book about magic, not language and semiosis, we will tie these ideas back to components of many of the models of magic described in this chapter.

FURTHER READING

A Cognitive Theory of Magic by Jesper Sørensen
Defining Magic: A Reader, edited by Bernd-Christian Otto and Michael Strausberg
Magic: A Very Short Introduction by Owen Davies
Runes and Magic by Stephen E. Flowers
The Application of Peircean Semiotics to the Elder Futhark Tradition by Scott Shell
The End of Magic by Ariel Glucklich

3

A BRIEF HISTORY
OF SEMIOTICS

I n the last chapter, we looked at anthropological, linguistic, and semiotic theories of magic from the mid-nineteenth century to the present. This was intended to accomplish two things: (1), to give us a firm footing in the history of ideas in order to appreciate the innovations of an explicitly semiotic approach to magic; and (2), to show the origin of certain ideas about what magic is and isn't—ideas that have, especially through popular and influential accounts like Frazer's *The Golden Bough*, seeped into the awareness of the general public too. As should hopefully be clear by this point, the history of magic as an object of study is complex and there are numerous models that each capture something essential about what it is. Some of these models are used to explain how it works in a given context, and others are simply used to dismiss magic in service of the bias of the theorist.

Even though the last chapter included an introduction to certain semiotic ideas and their applicability to magic, now we must look deeper at the history of ideas in semiotics.

THE DEVELOPMENT OF SEMIOTICS UNTIL THE NINETEENTH CENTURY

Before we dive in, recall that a *sign* is something that stands for, refers to, represents, or evokes something else. For example, words refer to objects (or feelings, or states, etc.); a photograph represents an object; a hoof print indicates the recent or nearby presence of a particular type of animal; the carnivorous Venus flytrap perceives how many of its trap hairs have been triggered to know when something of sufficient size is worth being trapped and digested. All of these are types of signs.

Semiosis is the innate capacity for creating and interpreting signs. This is not something uniquely human but is, in fact, shared by *all* living things as they perceive, respond to, create, and act upon signs in their environment.

The study of semiotics in the West began with the formalized study of medicine by Hippocrates in the fifth century BCE. He was the first to explore the study of signs, specifically medical ones. A particular type of sign, called a symptom both then and now, is at the core of diagnostic medicine. The symptom is *not* the affliction itself, but points to some underlying condition that causes the symptom to manifest. This could be visible as in an x-ray image or the observation of external bleeding, or a report like "I'm having chest pain."

Roger Bacon (ca. 1214–ca. 1293) was hugely influential in semiotics as it was understood in the Middle Ages; his *De Signis* (On Signs) introduced the idea of a linguistic sign and emphasized the *relationships* between signs as a key contributor to their meaning. This foreshadows Saussure's core idea about how meaning propagates through a collection of interrelated linguistic signs.

John Locke (1632–1704) introduced the formal study of signs into philosophy, even using the term *semiotics* for the first time in print, as part of his empiricist toolkit for distinguishing between representation and knowledge. To the extent he was approaching this goal through a semiotic lens, Locke was primarily focused on the use of linguistic signs "to communicate our Thoughts to one another, as well as record them for our own use."[1]

A FORK IN THE SEMIOTIC ROAD

The founders of the two primary schools of semiotics are the American polymath Charles Sanders Peirce (1839–1914) and the Swiss linguist Ferdinand de Saussure (1857–1913). Their ideas are referred to as the Peircean and the structural (semiological or Saussurean) approaches, respectively. The structural approach to semiotics dominated the social sciences from roughly the 1950s to the 1970s, with many of its ideas being developed well after Saussure's untimely death.

These two main approaches to semiotics are not completely incompatible, although they do focus on different things and so semioticians often work primarily (or exclusively) within one school or the other. (Some current semioticians, such as Tyler James Bennett, are in fact engaged in projects to "confront the gulf between semiotics and semiology."[2]) My goal with this book is to pull ideas from both schools (as well as from linguistics) to show different approaches to understanding the communicative properties built into magic.

FERDINAND DE SAUSSURE AND STRUCTURAL SEMIOTICS

Saussure is most famous for a book he did not actually write. The book attributed to him, *Cours de linguistique générale* (Course in General Linguistics), was published after his death. The *Cours* was compiled and edited by former students Charles Bally and Albert Sechehaye, based on lecture notes from Saussure's courses—in some cases courses that neither Bally nor Sechehaye participated in. Thus, an enduring question in the scholarship of Saussure and his ideas has been to what extent "his" book accurately reflects his ideas. There are multiple statements in the book that cannot be found in the notes that were used to compile the book; these are generally regarded as editorializing on the part of the compilers and in some cases contradict other ideas brought out in the book.

The *Course in General Linguistics* holds a vitally important place in the history of linguistics and structural semiotics. Saussure introduced many ideas that are still discussed, debated, and applied today, like the distinctions between *langue* and *parole*, between paradigm and syntagm(a), and between diachronic and synchronic linguistics.* We will look at the first two dichotomies, as well his model of the sign as a *signifier* combined with a *signified*, below.

Bear in mind throughout the discussion of Saussure that for him signs were almost exclusively *linguistic* signs (not just words, but also metacommunicative features of language as well, like body language and other parts of context).

Langue versus Parole

The fundamental dichotomy in language, according to Saussure, is between *langue* and *parole*. *Langue* (a "language") is a French term referring to the abstract rules and representations of a system of linguistic signs; think of it as description of a language (such as English or French) that is an idealized and rigid concept of a signifying communication system, such as you would see in a grammar book. A *langue* is independent of any particular speaker of that *langue*.

Keep in mind, though, that *langue* is descriptive not prescriptive; people "break the rules" all the time in the ways they use words, grammar, and context. One of the reasons these "rules" of grammar and word formation—linguistic codes—can only be guidelines and abstractions instead of rigid laws goes back to our discussion of memes and replicators from chapter 1. Just as with the primary biological replicator

---

*The distinction between diachronic and synchronic linguistics, which we will not discuss in any detail, concerns the ways that languages change over time as opposed to their state at a given point in time, respectively.

where copies of DNA sequences are created with fairly high accuracy but are nevertheless not *quite* perfect all the time, the way we learn and use language by copying others' uses of it also varies a bit individual to individual. And just like in nature—where if the copying were always exactly perfect then evolution could not, well, evolve through the persistence of advantageous variations—the little differences in the pronunciation and usage of words lead each person to have their own version of the *langue* that broadly describes the language(s) they speak.

This individual version of a *langue* is *parole* ("speech"): the patterns of speech for a particular person that include their own conception of the meanings of the words they use. The *langue/parole* dichotomy applies generally to nonlinguistic signs as well; each of us has our own memories, experiences, and expectations that influence the meaning we hold for signs of *all* types.

How we do recognize that an individual's idiosyncratic *parole* is a well-formed subset of the *langue* it derives from? Several concepts in structural linguistics—which developed from Saussure's theories—illustrate this quite well. A *text* is any collection of signs from a *parole*—whether linguistic or symbolic signs, regardless of their method of encoding or transmission. Reading a text is not only engaging in semiosis to interpret the individual signs; it is also deriving meaning from grouping those signs into larger and more complex structures (called *syntagms* or *syntagmata*).

For a text—a collection of *any* kind of signs—to have meaning enabling an interpretation that makes any sense, it must have two important properties: cohesion and coherence.

Cohesion is the set of formal ties that exist within a text. Think of cohesion as a structure that roughly conforms to the rules—also known as grammar—within a *langue*. This does *not* guarantee the text makes any sense, merely that it is well-formed enough that you can begin to attempt to interpret it.

Cohesion is a property of the text itself—it is an assessment that the text generally conforms to whatever set of rules is taken to govern the production of such texts. In language, this means the text has more or less followed the commonly understood rules of syntax, grammar, and word formation so that it can be recognized as representative of that language. *A cohesive text does not necessarily succeed at conveying meaning.* For example, a toddler can utter a grammatically correct (i.e., cohesive) sentence that is nonsense—this is true whether or not the toddler *thinks* they said something meaningful, true, or profound.

Whereas cohesion is a property of the text itself, coherence lies *outside* the text. *Coherence* is a statement about whether meaning can be derived from the text by anyone other than its creator (it is *not* a statement about whatever meaning the author of the text may have intended to incorporate into the text).

The meaning is thus not found in the text but is instead found in our ability to interpret the text and to find the most likely bit of coherence. Meaning therefore exists *outside* of the text, which requires us to bring our own personal understanding of the signs (words, figures of speech, etc.) to any interpretation of the text.

Cohesion and coherence govern the differentiation of a *parole* from a *langue*. Think of cohesion in this context as how far afield from the "accepted" rules *parole* can stray before it is not understandable, and coherence as whether the structure of *langue* is maintained but the actual utterances expressed through *parole* are nonsense. That is, you might be speaking something that *sounds* like English, in that it uses some of the grammar, syntax, and word meanings associated with English, but what is said is not comprehensible. Colorless green ideas sleep furiously.

Let's explore what this means for magical communication, beginning with another look at Saussure's famous speech circuit diagram:

The feedback loop illustrated here reveals some critical things about how Saussure perceived language. In this model, meaning arises from the interactions that are part of the feedback loop shown. Meaning is not determined solely by one or the other party to the communication, but rather only exists only as a social phenomenon within the speech

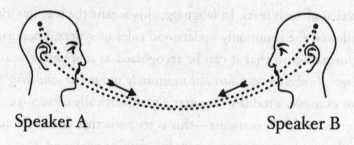

Speaker A   Speaker B

Saussure's speech circuit

community using language in this way. If people start to use certain words in different ways, then the meaning changes. This idea that *meaning is use* becomes important to philosopher of language Ludwig Wittgenstein as well (see chap. 4).

The crucial thing that is missing from Saussure's feedback loop is context. In linguistics and semiotics, *context* is everything about a given situation that can influence meaning: who is speaking; when, where, and why they are speaking; the speakers' backgrounds and understanding of the language they are speaking; social factors; and so forth. The model has an implicit assumption that meaning is static. This arises out of Saussure's distinction between synchronic and diachronic linguistics. At a given moment in a particular context, meaning manifests in a particular way, but this does not tell us anything about what meaning would be at a different time in a different context. With these limitations in scope, however, we can still see that this model represents the *parole* of each speaker manifesting as a subset of the *langue* that forms the basis of their communication.

It's easy to see the influence on Saussure's model on Jan van Baal's communication model for the fulfillment of desire (see chap. 2):

> In this discourse Man feels addressed or singled out by his universe and he endeavors to address it in turn trying to discover the kind of address to which his universe will be willing to answer; that is, willing to show itself communicable.[3]

In other words, the magician seeks a *langue* that the phenomenal world understands and will respond to (the response being the results he seeks). Through this, using his own *parole*—context-specific, personal usage of this *langue*—he attempts to communicate in a way that is meaningful both to him and to his abstract partner in communication. Even if he is using some elements of everyday speech, the context in which he communicates—possibly some sort of ritual or ceremony, but certainly a situation with magical intent—influences the meaning both in the way he expresses it *and* in the way it is understood by the phenomenal world.

Paradigm versus Syntagma

Another important dichotomy in Saussure's conception of linguistics is the relationship between *paradigm* and *syntagma*.* A basic example of a paradigm is what we learned in elementary school as the parts of speech. Nouns, verbs, and other word classes are all broad paradigms that can be drawn upon within a given sentence structure and context while still yielding a grammatically correct and plausible sentence. In the sentence "The girl threw the ball," *the girl* is from the paradigm "nouns capable of throwing things" and *the ball* is from the paradigm "nouns capable of being thrown." Depending on who is throwing what, we can substitute a number of throwers and throwees and still have a sentence that makes sense.

The important part here is—again—context. We couldn't, for example, say (with a straight face at least), "The amoeba threw the ball." *Amoeba* is a noun of course, but we have contextual information that lies *outside* the sentence itself that tells us that amoebas cannot throw balls; the same extra-sentence understanding also tells us that "the girl threw the boulder" is equally implausible. In other words, these nonsensical sentences are cohesive (grammatically correct), but they aren't coherent (containing plausible meaning, as judged by factors within and beyond the utterances themselves).*

---

*From Ancient Greek σύνταγμα (*súntagma*, "ordered arrangement").

A syntagma at its basic level is the specific arrangement of words chosen from a given paradigm—this echoes the distinction between *langue* (the set of possibilities in a language) and *parole* (the context-dependent particulars chosen from those possibilities). But there's something far more interesting going on with syntagmata (plural of *syntagma*).

Syntagmata are the building blocks of meaning; this is the case whether we are constructing a meaningful sentence or combining words and other signs to create an effective ritual. A word, or other sign, does not have meaning in its possibility, but in its application. Even if we consistently use a word or sign in the same way, we know from the principle of arbitrariness—the lack of static, immutable relationship between a sign and its meaning—that we are *still* recreating the word's meaning each time it is used. By building a specific syntagma—unit of meaning—out of the paradigm that fits a given context, we (re)create the meaning of the signs within that given context.

Syntagmata are not just the particular signs—linguistic or otherwise—that are chosen from a paradigm: the process repeats and builds on itself. Think about the way that words are combined into phrases, which are then combined into clauses, which are further combined into sentences, paragraphs, and so on. At each stage, more meaning is created that goes beyond just that contained in the individual components—the more complex the text, the more information from outside the text itself is needed to judge its coherence and interpret its meaning. The process of building ever more complex syntagmata (and their resultant complexities in meaning) is an example of *emergent complexity*: properties and behaviors that are not present within individual components arise from the interactions of those components within a greater whole. The sentence "the girl threw the ball" has far more

---

*Even these statements about noncoherence are context-dependent. We could be describing something happening in a cartoon, or the girl could be throwing a boulder on Pluto's moon Charon (where gravity is 1/34 the strength of that on Earth).

meaning than each of the individual words or phrases that make up the sentence; taken together those words represent a specific action that no individual word in the sentence can capture or even suggest. The interactions between the words, ordered in a particular way and adding new meaning at each level of complexity, create something that even the same words in a different order would not have.

This is an immensely helpful idea for *semiurgy*—operative magical communication—as well. Building syntagmata and the relationships between them is a core component of how we invest meaning into magical acts: meaning that can then be interpreted by our partner in communication, whether that partner is the self, the phenomenal world, or the numinous realm.

In a magical act you are expanding your sign network—your semiotic web—to reinforce a new vision of reality and help it come into being through altering various pathways of your awareness of the goal (without obsessing on the goal itself). *Ritual at its core is a mythic narrative, a story you participate in.* Effective storytelling always requires calling up the right imagery, the memories of previous times a similar story has been told, and connecting your actions with those of mythic and cosmic importance. You are creating syntagmata that *add* to the story and make it more effective in getting across the core idea: the desired result of the magic act(s).

Signifier and Signified

In Saussure's theory of signs ("semiology"), a *sign* is composed of a *signifier* (French *signifiant*) and what is *signified* (French *signifié*). The signified is not the thing itself being referred to, but is instead the concept that the linguistic sign calls up. Roland Barthes noted that the meaning of the Saussurean sign arises from the process of binding together "the signifier and the signified, an act whose product is the sign."[4]

For Saussure, the linguistic sign does not represent reality but instead forms a relational system of signs, which in turn represent *thoughts* about reality. The sign is "not a thing but the notion of a thing."[5] Signs do not represent their objects but instead call to mind our *impressions* of their objects—signs are always subject to interpretation in light of our experiences and prejudices. While Saussure's model of the sign only has these two constituents—signifier and signified—his speech circuit model does imply a third element: the speaker or listener who intends or infers meaning, respectively. This contrasts with Peirce's model (discussed later in this chapter), where a third element—called the *interpretant*—is always part of the sign itself. Nonetheless, Saussure's linguistic sign is intersubjective, mediating the understanding of individuals through their social interactions. Signs receive their meaning in a specific, context-bound situation as part of a network of signs.

The contextual, social nature of signs leads to one of the most essential ideas in semiotics, independent of the specific school: signs *always* depend on other signs for their meaning. That is, signs do not exist in isolation but are "part of an abstract, trans-individual system"[6]—a larger code that shapes their meaning in context as nodes within a network. This is easy to see within a sentence: for example, if the only linguistic sign I give you out of a longer sentence is the word *threw*, you can only have a generic and vague notion of what could be meant. We understand the concept of "throwing" but that is only potential; it is only when we know who threw something (and what they threw) that we can know what this particular use of the word reveals about the situation being described.

This interdependence is harder to see in a larger semiotic context, however, since it messes with our common-sense notion about a more direct relationship between words and objects in the world. When you pick up a mug, you probably don't think about its social significance, how the word for it relates to other linguistic signs, or where to find the exact dividing line between whether something is a mug or a cup. We understand that the first person who crafted a mug likely did so without having given it a name. Nonetheless, language structures our understanding of the world, not the other way around. Saussure reminds us of this when he points out that if words were simply labels attached to concepts that already existed and had their own innate structure, then the exact meaning of words would not vary from language to language (only the labels themselves).[7] Anyone who has spent time trying to translate from one language to another knows that there are often nuances of meaning that simply cannot be translated.

Let's consider signifiers, signifieds, and the interrelatedness of signs in terms of operative communication (or semiurgy).

Despite its idealist underpinnings, with a focus on what is in the mind (or minds), Saussure's semiology does not deny the reality of the objective, physical world. What he *does* observe is that our perception of that physical world is mediated through linguistic signs and the ways we organize and correlate those signs; this is the foundation for the semiotic codes we discussed in the last chapter.

In chapter 1, we looked at a definition of magic as using symbolic means to bring about a change in the practitioner. Symbolic—semiotic—associations are a powerful tool for the magician, as they provide a means to play with shifting personal meaning toward shared meaning and vice versa.

When we carve out a ritual space—whether it's a room, a portion of a room, someplace outside, or wherever—we are marking it as standing apart from the mundane world (even when it is still physically in the mundane world). We perceive it in a new way; that is, we have made a subtle alteration to the semiotic code we use to give meaning to the space, so that it is no longer *just* a room, *just* a clearing in the woods, *just* a crossroads. This shift in perception doesn't depend on a physical alteration of the place—while the mediation of signs often happens below the surface of awareness, we can also *choose* to interpret a sign or signs in specific ways in addition to or even as a contradiction to our senses. Signs are "not proxy for their objects but are vehicles for the conception of objects."[8] Linguistic signs influence our behavior toward the conceptions we associated with those signs, and this further affirms the signifier we attach to a given signified. Thus, each time you use the space for this purpose—whether it remains permanently dedicated or is constructed anew for each use—you reinforce the accumulated meaning as perceived through the signs in use. The sacred nature of the space doesn't create the signifier; rather, the signifier creates the space as sacred according to the meaning it evokes in us.

If you incorporate a bell as part of the opening and/or closing for ritual work, the peal of the bell is itself a signifier. But *what* that exactly signifies—whether banishing or focusing the attention away from the profane world, or perhaps clearing or purifying the air—arises from the personal experiences and other associations *you* bring to it as a magician. There is nothing about the ringing of the bell that inherently possesses these associations; they are agreed to by convention, which is then personalized by whatever meaning *you* bring to this signified.

If you utilize some sort of sacred fire, you are working with a symbol that has held rich meaning perhaps as far back as our distant ancestor *Homo erectus*. Fire has been used for survival, protection, cooking, illumination, and manipulating time by extending light into nighttime (thus enabling activities that would otherwise not be possible in the dark). These experiences create deep cultural associations that are part of how we see and interpret the symbolism of fire.

All these aspects of ritual have meanings we derive from a semiotic code that we are familiar with prior to the ritual. We also expand the code by personalizing and adding associations that are particular to the tradition or school we are working within. *Semiotic codes are always partially shared and partially our own.*

Tying the use of semiotic codes back to our overall thesis about magic as a process of communication, we express intent through the use of signs (linguistic and otherwise) in a way that is meaningful to us. These can't be *too* idiosyncratic, otherwise we risk our partner in communication—the phenomenal world, the numinous world—not being able to understand it. We build up changes to our understanding of these codes through repetition, through investing them with additional meaning again and again. Meaning is use—and more use leads to more firmly entrenched meaning.

From Saussure to Peirce

Saussure's speculations about a potential science of signs—semiology—first came to fruition as part of structuralism (see chap. 2). Structuralism was based as much on Saussure's ideas about the inherent dichotomies in human thought patterns—*langue* vs. *parole*, signifier vs. signified, and so forth—as it was on his theory of linguistic signs in itself. Nonetheless, structuralism became the dominant paradigm in most social sciences in the mid-twentieth century, although by the late 1960s this dominance began to wane. Beginning in the 1940s, the publication of many of Charles Sanders Peirce's papers—an ongoing project even today—finally brought his ideas on a great many topics out of obscurity. This led to an appreciation of Peirce's more finely nuanced model of signs, which also addressed what by the 1960s were regarded as shortcomings in Saussure's model and its resulting semiology.

Saussure's semiology has not been completely superseded by Peirce's semiotics; on the contrary, in many disciplines in the social sciences Saussure's essential model of the sign as a signifier and a signified is still the dominant one. But even this is changing as Peirce's philosophies about signs are being studied more than ever before.

PEIRCEAN SEMIOTICS

Charles Sanders Peirce is one of the three most influential American philosophers, alongside William James (1842–1910) and John Dewey (1859–1952). The three collectively are the founders of the philosophical school called *pragmatism*, which focuses on thoughts and words primarily as tools for action rather than as tools for reflection and representation. Peirce is often called the father of pragmatism and is known for his maxim: "Consider the practical effects of the objects of your conception. Then, your conception of those effects is the whole of your conception of the object."[9] In other words, it's not what you think with it, it's what you do with it. This is sage advice for magicians as well;

magic is far more than just saying the right words in the dark while wearing the right outfit.

Despite his importance to the pragmatic school of philosophy, however, Peirce considered semiotics (or *semiotic/semeiotic*, as he sometimes styled it) to be the fundamental core of his work:

> It has never been in my power to study anything—mathematics, ethics, metaphysics, gravitation, thermodynamics, optics, chemistry, comparative anatomy, astronomy, psychology, phonetics, economics, the history of science, whist, men and women, wine, meteorology, except as a study of semiotic.[10]

Peirce and Signs

So how did Peirce define a sign, and what does this help us to understand about signs that Saussure's definition did not? Peirce offered many definitions at different points in the development of his philosophy as he refined his theories. One of his more fundamental and commonly cited definitions is:

> I define a sign as anything which is so determined by something else, called its Object, and so determines an effect upon a person, which effect I call its interpretant, that the latter is thereby mediately determined by the former.[11]

Here we see the three parts of a Peircean sign, as opposed to the signifier/signified dichotomy of Saussure:

1. the *sign* (more or less equivalent to Saussure's signifier)
2. the *object*, what is determined or referred to by the sign (more or less equivalent to Saussure's signified)
3. the *interpretant*, the effect that interpretation has on a person perceiving a sign

Recognizing that using the term *sign* for both the whole and one of its parts would lead to confusion, Peirce later limited the use of the word *sign* to the entire trio of parts. *Representamen* then became his preferred term for the sign component that is analogous to Saussure's signifier. Thus, Peirce's model is explicitly triadic and requires as its third part the interpretant: the effect caused by the sign through its interpretation. (Note that the interpretant is *not* the person, animal, insect, cell, or whatever is doing the interpretation, but rather the effect that the interpretation has.)

Recall that in Saussure's model, signs are dependent on their relationship to other signs for their meaning and in effect only derive their meaning through being what other signs are not (and by evoking through interpretation what other signs do not). Peirce's conception of signs posits a different relationship between signs: the interpretant of a sign in turn becomes *another* sign, composed of another representamen, object, and interpretant. This leads to the phenomenon of *infinite semiosis* that we introduced in chapter 1. It's worth noting that while he could not eliminate the necessity for it through logic, the idea of infinite semiosis always bothered Peirce. In fact, in later accounts of his theory of signs he found ways around it through revising his definitions specifically to eliminate it. Nonetheless, later interpretations of Peirce have been more welcoming to the idea of infinite semiosis, and it is today generally regarded as an essential and useful component of Peirce's overall theory of signs.

Peirce's Categories of Signs

There are three basic types of signs, seen in relation to the objects they refer to, in Peirce's system of semiotics:

- *icon*, a sign that resembles what it refers to in some way (examples: a photograph, a stick figure, an onomatopoeic word such as "bark" or "meow")
- *index*, a sign that points to or indicates the thing it refers to (examples: a street sign showing the direction for a one-way street,

a hoof print in the snow, the ringing of a bell indicating that a
bell is nearby)

- *symbol*, a sign whose meaning is created by convention (also called
  an *unmotivated sign*) (examples: the letters you're reading right
  now *and* the words they call up in your mind, a "no smoking"
  image showing a cigarette plus circle with a diagonal line, the
  Statue of Liberty, the ringing of a bell in a magical ritual)

Different types can be combined within a single sign. The rune
fehu (see chap. 7) has a name that means "cattle" in Proto-Germanic* (a
symbolic association); the meaning "cattle" is also a symbolic sign suggesting "movable wealth." The rune shape ᚠ is generally agreed to be a
simplified version of a cow's horns, making the same sign *iconic* in the
way it resembles the thing it refers to but also including other *symbolic*
signs as part of the same sign complex.

The basic qualities of signs in Peirce's system are called by him
Firstness, *Secondness*, and *Thirdness*; these refer to the types or degrees
of meaning that a sign can call up within us as we interpret it. *Firstness*
is the possibility within the sign[12]—its virtues and qualities. *Secondness*
refers to concrete actions (or facts)[13]—the existential realities that are
part of the sign. *Thirdness* refers to laws[14]—conventional associations
for the sign that have become so ingrained they are widely known and
are the assumed default meaning of the sign. These assumed default
meanings for symbolic signs are also heavily colored by the understanding, experience, and worldview of the person doing the interpreting. The key notion here is that our interpretation of the sign looks at
different parts of the sign and its relationships to itself, to its object,
and to the interpretant—these relationships arise, beneath the level of
active awareness and logic, as we interpret the meaning of the sign *in*

---

*Proto-Germanic is the hypothesized common ancestor of all Germanic languages both
ancient (Old Norse, Old English, Gothic, etc.) and modern (English, German, Dutch,
Icelandic, Norwegian, Swedish, Danish, etc.).

the context in which we encounter it. Because of the way that Firstness, Secondness, and Thirdness feed into each other, Peirce in his later writings became skeptical of the idea of a purely iconic or indexical sign, at least as they are encountered and interpreted by humans. As the symbolic species, humans have a consistent tendency to bring Thirdness to everything they perceive, which we will talk about further below.

The triad of Firstness, Secondness, and Thirdness is a powerful one; these three perspectives can be applied to each of the three components of the sign, and together they help us to understand how signs influence our perception and the meaning we create out of encounters with signs.

Peirce coined new names for the types of signs that are the various combinations of qualities—Firstness, et cetera—and signs in relation to their representamen, object, and interpretant. The good news is we don't have to employ this fairly obtuse terminology in order to get something useful from Peirce's system and its application to magical communication. The most important things to take away are the core object relations of *icon*, *index*, and *symbol*, and the qualities of *Firstness*, *Secondness*, and *Thirdness*. Indeed, these three numbered qualities are crucial for understanding the way we come to know ourselves through both internally and externally encountered signs, and they can be used to reconstruct nearly the entirety of Peirce's theory of signs.

The Accumulated Experience of Signs

The terminology of semiotics can be useful for categorizing and analyzing the apprehension of signs, out of which we build the perception of ourselves and the world around us. Now we will look at the qualities of signs—Firstness, Secondness, and Thirdness—and what these teach us about the accumulation of experience and understanding as we interpret the signs we encounter. Keep in mind that these qualities apply *independently* to each part of the sign: representamen, object, and interpretant. That is, you could perceive the dominant quality of a sign's representamen as Thirdness, the dominant quality of its object as Secondness, and the dominant quality of its interpretant as Firstness.

When we say that the dominant quality of some part of a sign is its Secondness or Thirdness, we have also encountered the qualities prior to those as well—that is, Secondness also implies Firstness, and Thirdness also implies Secondness.

Some of these reflections on Firstness, Secondness, and Thirdness may go beyond what Peirce intended, but they are presented in the spirit of the quest for widely applicable explanatory power that Peirce strove for—a pursuit that consumed him throughout his lifelong development of a comprehensive system of signs.

Firstness is what is immediate—demanding or at least attracting our attention *now*. It is the perception that something *is*: something has Being. When we encounter Being in this way, we can't help but see some aspect of our own being in its reflection. The Firstness of a sign contains its potential, a potential that can be unlocked and enacted through the interpretation of the sign and connecting the sign to *your own* sign network and semiotic codes. Applied to operative magical communication—semiurgy—Firstness is that initial feeling of inspiration, which we ponder and then translate into a concrete desire: I feel the need to change something about myself or the world around me, but *what*? Firstness reveals the feelings we have about something before we start asking questions to refine our understanding. There is something mysterious and spontaneous about Firstness—we initially can't explain why something draws our attention, because once it leaves the realms of immediacy and indeterminacy it has progressed *beyond* Firstness into Secondness. Firstness—by definition, the inaugural encounter with a sign—is potential waiting for other forces to interact with it, to lead it toward what it might become. When we are struck by the Firstness of a sign, we are drawn into a new facet of our never-ending dialogue with Mystery.

If our interaction with a sign in relation to its object only rises to the level of Firstness, the sign is an *icon*. It resembles its object in some way but doesn't tell us anything about the object beyond some subset of its appearance or initial impression. For example, a photograph in and of itself tells you nothing about the subject of the photograph. If other clues within the photograph form an impression, those are *additional* signs (not necessarily icons) that are embedded in the iconic sign that is the photograph—that is, the iconic sign is only one component of the sign network we have encountered through the photograph.

Secondness begins to reveal and bring into the realm of the real the potential that is latent within Firstness. One of the core properties of Secondness corresponds to an essential principle in Saussure's more specialized focus on linguistic signs: Secondness begins to identify the *differences* between signs that lead to an understanding of their meaning. As Peirce described it: "The idea of other, of not, becomes a very pivot of thought. To this element I give the name of Secondness."[15] Secondness helps us to see the distance between our own perception and the sign, but by revealing this distance we start to close the gap by beginning to understand *what* the sign is (beyond the notion of Firstness, which only lets us see *that* it is). The Mystery that Firstness draws our attention to now begins to give up some of its secrets as we distinguish between appearance and reality—and between sign and object—through the revelations provided by contemplating the sign.

Thirdness arises in part from our expectations about the Secondness of the sign; this is where we either reinforce those expectations (based on previously known facts about signs referring to the same object), or find those expectations violated and thus encounter *another* sign that we must interpret. Thirdness depends on Secondness, which quantifies the differences between the objects of signs; both of these give clarity and shape to the uncreated potential that draws us to Firstness. Semiotic codes are created out of Thirdness; they show us ways to organize our perceptions and expectations, but it is easy to lose sight of the fact that since they are created, they can be changed. Thirdness appears stable—we treat it as a "law" according to Peirce— but it is in fact malleable as consensus about the significance and meaning of particular symbolic signs changes. We lose sight of this at our peril, and as magicians we must always look for where Thirdness can change through guiding interpretations to a new consensus.

To summarize these qualities, Firstness is spontaneity and the encounter with a mystery to be pondered; it is presence but also uncertainty—a feeling that can't (yet) be quantified. Secondness is the factuality of the sign's object, perceived through its conceptual distance from the one experiencing it (and also in its contrast with the objects of other signs). Thirdness is significance and continuity; Peirce's description of Thirdness as "law" describes the recognition of patterns that arise from potentiality (Firstness) leading to actuality (Secondness), such that expectations become our understanding of a sign's object (supplanting the Firstness and Secondness of our perception of the object).

Determining whether our interactions with the components of a sign manifest as Firstness, Secondness, or Thirdness is part of a conversation with the sign. The sign reveals certain things to us, but we also project our own meaning and experience onto the sign as conditioned through the context in which we become aware of the sign.

German Idealism

Now we need to take a brief detour through a profoundly influential yet loosely connected school of philosophy from the late eighteenth and early nineteenth centuries: German idealism. The reason behind the detour is that this particular strain of idealism shaped some of Peirce's ideas as well, especially regarding the way that signs affect our knowledge of objects. This knowledge in turn affects the way semiotic codes are created and become a major part of the background against which we do magic.

Many influential philosophers were grouped under the wide umbrella of German idealism, including Immanuel Kant (1724–1804), J. G. Fichte (1762–1814), Friedrich Schelling (1775–1854), and Georg W. F. Hegel (1770–1831). In this section, we will examine some of the core ideas from Kant, Fichte, and Hegel.

The basic idea loosely connecting these German idealists is that the perception of reality depends on our ability to think rationally. The perception we have of things in the world outside the Self is a representation based upon—*but not identical to*—the properties manifested by things themselves. This perception varies in accuracy and clarity depending on how we observe—and affect!—our own process of perception. For this to work, and not just lead to solipsistic fantasy, there must be some point of connecting overlap between the individual and the object of perception; without this point of overlap, there couldn't be any interaction or perception of things in the world by subjective minds. We perceive this thing-in-itself through our senses and through our thoughts about it—thoughts that can also *change* how we perceive it.

Immanuel Kant's seminal version of idealism—which he called *transcendental idealism*—says that we can only know with certainty those things within the world that we can approach empirically (i.e., through experimentation and experience). Any experiences we have of things in the world come through perception and contemplation: our knowledge of them is thus *ideal*—that is, based on ideas—and not *real*. Note throughout this description that Kant never denies the reality of the objects we perceive; he merely denies that we can know them independently of how we are perceiving them (i.e., via perception that necessarily colors and limits what we can know about them).

Through our ability to perceive objects within the world, however, we also gain conscious awareness of *ourselves*. We become the object—or what is affected—of the subject that perceives and thinks about objects in the world. In other words, we become aware of our ability to see ourselves as distinct from those objects in the world outside ourselves. Our inner experiences change in response to our experiences of these outer objects, and they change in ways *not possible without the encounter with these objects*.

Our experiences are not completely random, however. We combine and order them, trying to build a coherent understanding of the world that we experience—while at the same time our fantasies, misunderstandings, biases, and unspoken assumptions interfere with the accuracy of that understanding. We do this through the creation and use of *categories* for organizing our experiences and their relationships to other experiences. Humans are hardwired to see order even where it doesn't exist; this can lead to cognitive models containing intricate philosophical systems and knowledge of physical processes of the universe—or it can lead to conspiracy theories and imaginative ideas about who is really running things behind the scenes. All things considered, in most situations we do a pretty effective job at filtering, categorizing, organizing, and synthesizing the often disconnected or unpredictable input we receive through our interactions with the world. We make meaning, because that is what we *must* do to survive in a world that has been partially shaped by the preferences, assumptions, and biases of other humans.

This tendency toward order and meaning-making suggests that our perception of the world around us conforms to our minds, instead of the reverse: *we perceive the world in a way that makes it easier for us to make sense of it* (i.e., to create meaning out of it). In other words, we have a strong tendency to discard or ignore what doesn't "make sense." This filtering can make it quite difficult to change our ideas about the world, but we must learn how to see and alter the filtering if we want to change the world itself through magical means. *The realization that you are in control of how you create meaning and significance underpins all effective magic* (and opens even more potent doors for the magician who understands the semiotics implicit in all magic).

The Self is at the center of all this: it is the perceiver, the organizer, and—using magic (or semiurgy)—even the intentional alterer of both the Self and what's beyond the Self.

J. G. Fichte took Kant's ideas about transcendental realism as a starting point and developed them further to ground his system in pure subjectivity, what he called the "pure I"—a position often described as *subjective idealism*. "Subjective" here doesn't signify something that is arbitrary or based on opinion/preference, but rather emphasizes the subject—the doer—as the center of attention and action. This is a far more radical position than Kant's, but it is important to keep in mind that Fichte also did not deny the existence of the real world—he just acknowledges that there are hard limits on what we can know about such objects and concepts in the real world. Fichte approached his view of the primacy of subjectivity primarily from the perspective of freedom, asking: *What philosophical position maximizes the freedom of the individual to chart their own path through existence?* His own designation for his philosophical system was the *Wissenschaftslehre* ("Science of Knowledge"), and he spent the entirety of his life and career refining it and responding to criticisms it received.

The first principle of the Science of Knowledge is: *Das Ich ist, und es setzt sein Sein, vermöge seines bloßen Seins* ("The 'I' is and posits its being by asserting its bare existence."). In other words, the *Ich* (the "I") with its most fundamental act attempts to posit—or claim existence for—itself without any reliance on actions outside of its own activity or perception of itself. Fichte was not trying to suggest some ex-nihilo creation of the *Ich* by itself, but rather he drew attention to the same organizing principle of the mind that was assumed in Kant's transcendental idealism. However, Fichte emphasized *action* as that which creates the *Ich*—through acting on that inherent freedom, Selves come into being as Selves. In other words, the *Ich* must act in order to realize and maintain its *Ich*-ness. In semiotic terms, we would say that the *Ich* must perceive and interpret symbolic signs in order to know it is an *Ich* and to continue to act on that knowledge by encountering and interpreting further signs.

This theory of the "I" stands in contrast to Descartes's famous *Cogito, ergo sum* ("I think, therefore I am"). Fichte did not accept thought as a preexisting given, but rather deduced how a person could come to know that they are a sovereign, individual subject through the effects of the act of thinking. Thinking by itself doesn't create the *Ich*; the "I" arises from the actions that result from thinking.

The *Ich* for Fichte does not exist in isolation; rather, it comes to reflect on itself through interactions with *other* self-conscious beings (other "I"s). By seeing something of itself in others—arriving at a theory of mind that realizes others engage in the same sort of activities through thought—the *Ich* is really *inter*-subjective through what Fichte calls a *summons*. This summons places a limit on the *Ich*'s own conscious self-awareness and at the same time acknowledges that other self-conscious beings exist. A limit on the absolute freedom of the *Ich* leads to knowing that an *Ich* must be limited—know a finite existence—in order to posit itself.

Bringing these ideas from idealism forward into semiotics, we can see several hints of this philosophical underpinning in the way Peirce describes signs and the qualities of Firstness, Secondness, and Thirdness. The transitions between these qualities of a sign are an integral part of the recognition of categories that give structure to the objects of our experiences.

The encounter with Firstness—the confrontation with something that arrests our attention but is not yet known—is the beginning of representation. We only suspect that the *Ding an sich*—the thing in itself—exists to the extent that it makes an impression on our senses. We have had no thoughts about it yet, but our thoughts have been drawn to it. Secondness is relation; as we gain an understanding of what it is we have encountered, we begin to file it away into the conceptual categories that seem to fit it (or to create provisional categories for those previously unknown properties or facts about the sign). Thirdness is what pulls these categories together into something coherent; through this, we find out (or create!) what matters about the sign and the categories we have attached to it. Thinking creates a new understanding of the thing in itself and gives it a reality that is not identical to what reality it possesses on its own (but which is still resonant with what we can perceive of its reality).

I'm bringing in these ideas from German idealism—and tracing how echoes of them can be seen in Peirce's work—not to torture the reader, but to go deeper into the philosophical background he was working both with and against.

Before we leave this foray into German idealism, we must look into some parts of Georg F. W. Hegel's philosophy as well. As with all nineteenth-century philosophers, Hegel began in Kant's shadow; like his fellow idealists Fichte and Schelling, he sought to solve what he saw as the essential problems in Kant's transcendental idealism (and to avoid the pitfalls that these issues led to). Hegel is also important to us here as he is a direct precursor to the pragmatism of Dewey, James, and especially Peirce.

Hegel occasionally referred to his philosophy as *absolute idealism* (a phrase at the time more associated with his contemporary, Schelling). His later followers would expand on absolute idealism as an essential part of Hegel's philosophy. However, the idea that Hegel himself considered the core of his philosophy is *Geist*, which we will look at now.

Geist is usually translated into English as "spirit" or sometimes "mind." Neither of those, however, fully captures what Hegel intended (nor does the English cognate for *Geist*, "ghost"). For Hegel, *Geist* was all that is *not* nature (i.e., all that is not exclusively matter or otherwise physical). While *Geist* does apply to the individual consciousness, Hegel was more focused on the *collective Geist* of humanity, which is the sum total of all the individual *Geists* that have existed throughout humanity's history. This is, in a sense, the "soul" of humanity, combining what is intellectual, rational, and nonmaterial in humans, both individually and collectively. As such, according to Hegel, the *Geist* of humanity follows a similar pattern of development as the *Geist* of any individual. In this, he somewhat foreshadows the evolutionary view of human culture as formulated by E. B. Tylor and popularized by James Frazer: phases of development in humanity as a whole mirror the type of intellectual development present in individuals.

Hegel is generally more concerned about humanity and its patterns than with individuals (although certain individuals embody *Geist* to the extent that they can intentionally alter the course of world history). With all the difficulties of translating *Geist* into English without losing the nuance that Hegel attached to it, it might be most helpful to think of it as signifying "culture." We looked at culture in chapters 1 and 2 as behavior patterns that coalesce into specific semiotic codes for understanding the actions and attitudes of people. Culture is the collective product of minds, manifesting as an identifiable code, and cultures evolve in their form and the way they are understood just as individuals advance their own intellectual growth in response to their experiences and encounters with signs (and with other minds). Thus, looking at the way the *Geist* of humanity unfolds over the entire length of history—in analogous ways to the *Geist* of the individual humans who participate in it—is essentially a look at cultural change over time. A magician must understand this if they are to be able to affect that emergence in any meaningful way.

Hegel may not have much to say that enlightens us as to how signs are experienced and interpreted, but he does suggest much about the way semiotic codes arise out of the collective action and thought of humanity.

The Phaneron

> *Any fact becomes important when it's connected to another.*
> UMBERTO ECO, *FOUCAULT'S PENDULUM*[16]

The influence that Charles Sanders Peirce took from the German idealists fed into one of his most significant yet often-overlooked ideas: the phaneron.

Peirce's connection to German idealism can be clearly seen in his claim that "logic is the science of representations in general, whether mental or material."[17] As he developed his theory of signs, he defined a representation as "anything which is supposed to stand for another and which might express that other to a mind which truly could understand it."[18] This is essentially an early term for what he later classed as a sign. Further connecting idealism with signs, he also notes that "whatever *is* is a representation"[19] and "all is representative."[20]

For Peirce, the phaneron meant "all that is present to the mind in any sense or in any way whatsoever, regardless of whether it be fact or figment."[21] The collective total of things present in the mind consists entirely of signs. Keep in mind that German idealism—and its varieties and descendants—does not deny the existence of the objective universe (the material world and its laws). It does, however, assert that even where we have direct contact with the objective universe, that contact is mediated in part by our perception of it. Or as Peirce would argue, even something that on the surface is purely physical, like touch, still kicks off a process of semiosis. Through this the meaning and significance of what it is we are touching is processed and categorized—this is essentially an update of Kant's ideas on perception and categorization, even though Peirce himself would not have thought of it in those terms.

Recall our earlier discussion of the infinite semiosis that arises from the interpretant of any sign also *itself* becoming an additional sign that must now be interpreted. The phaneron is the component of your consciousness where this infinite semiosis unfolds, in effect becoming a sign network that encompasses everything within your awareness, experience, and understanding (this includes other signs that are part of the network which you have either forgotten about or not yet interpreted!). Within the phaneron, you contextualize an encountered sign in relation to other signs you've already processed, and this sign in turn has the potential to influence the interpretation of *other* signs you may yet encounter.

Everything that enters the phaneron has the potential to affect everything else that has or could enter the phaneron, and certain signs that the phaneron encompasses—symbols—can change in meaning over time. Thus, the phaneron itself changes over time as new signs enter it and are processed. Certain signs become more persistent and dominant in the way the phaneron is used to interpret other signs—that is, they function as selection pressure on how other signs are interpreted. This is another way to understand the creation and function of semiotic codes—the phaneron is the sum total of *your* semiotic code (which may encompass all or parts of other semiotic codes that guide your interactions with other people and the products of minds).

Recall some of our discussions about cohesion and coherence earlier in this chapter; cohesiveness in the phaneron arises from the connections built between signs. Cohesiveness, however, is not meaning. It is a valueless judgment on whether signs within the phaneron have—*or have been made to have*—connections. Coherence is about whether that cohesiveness can be combined to form more and more complex meaning. You may be able to retrace all your clicks down the Wikipedia rabbit hole last night, but that just gives them cohesiveness and not necessarily coherence.

There's a catch with coherence, though.

H. P. Lovecraft famously observed: "The most merciful thing in the world, I think, is the inability of the human mind to correlate all its contents."[22]

Some coherence is good and necessary, and the actions based on that coherence of signs and interpretations of signs lead to actions that coexist well with the coherent thoughts and actions of other minds. In this level of coherence, there is room for change and growth. Too much coherence—that is, only interpreting signs in ways that fit preconceived notions of what those signs "should" mean—limits the flexibility and potential of the phaneron. This in turn limits the possibilities for semiurgy because there is not enough behavioral and conceptual flexibility for effecting far-reaching change within and beyond the self. Achieving and maintaining too much coherence takes Mystery out of the equation as well, because there's not enough room left for things that don't fit the prearranged narrative.

The phaneron brings us back full circle to our characterization of magic as a form of operative communication using symbolic means to bring about change within and beyond the magician. The phaneron is the entire sign network of the individual, and it forms the backdrop against which all new encounters with signs—whether from the inner world or the outer—will be interpreted. Whether you are encountering a new sign in the phenomenal world, or wielding signs to create a new semiotic web to encode a desire that you will leverage through magic, the phaneron is involved and itself undergoes change as part of these encounters with signs.

The importance of the phaneron opens the door to semiurgy, providing a model for how signs are not only processed but also intentionally utilized to shape communication and metacommunication toward specific ends that transcend mundane communication.

Peirce and Semiurgy

As we discussed in chapter 2, while James Frazer's views of cultural history being guided by a linear evolution from magic to science to religion have not stood the test of time, his laws of sympathetic magic have remained helpful for understanding various magical models. In fact, the two main components of this law, usually called the laws of *similarity* and *contagion*, mesh quite effectively with Peircean approaches to magic.

Recall that in Peirce's taxonomy of signs (specifically, signs in relation to their objects) an icon is a sign that resembles its object in some way. This could be anything from a photograph to a stick figure, from a drawing of the moon to its reflection in a body of water. Humans are hardwired to look for patterns in their environment and to fill in the gaps to create coherence out of the signs they encounter. This is why an iconic sign doesn't need to be that precise or detailed to evoke the object it resembles. We can leverage this pattern-making, gap-filling tendency in semiurgy. For example, the appearance of the rune *ingwaz* (◊) is generally understood to represent a seed that is planted. While it does entail symbolic meaning outside the strictly agricultural perspective on a seed—like the metaphor of planting seeds in young minds so that they grow into effective thinkers—it also bears an explicit, deliberate resemblance to a seed. The iconic sign of the rune invokes the various senses of the word and concept "seed." This connection also reinforces the understanding in Peirce's later writing that *purely* iconic (or indexical) signs are rare—if they exist at all (even the most precise resemblance of an iconic sign to its referent *still* evokes additional symbolic meaning as we interpret the sign).

Frazer's other law, that of *contagion*, describes a relationship created by touch or proximity that can then become part of a magical operation. M. R. James's classic story "Casting the Runes" illustrates the law of contagion perfectly. A curse is written on a piece of paper, which is given to the intended victim, but through unexpected circumstances it comes into the possession of someone else who *then* becomes the unfortunate actual recipient of the curse. The curse was imprinted on the paper and remained in contact with the paper as its carrier (its sign!) until activated.

This is an *indexical* relationship, another of the three types of signs in Peirce's taxonomy as understood in relation to their object (or referent). In our fictional example, the paper points to and maintains a connection with the curse itself and gives it an avenue for taking effect. Indexical signs point to the existence of something else that is not present in either the current time or place.

Peirce's phaneron provides another avenue for understanding semiurgy. The phaneron—the all-encompassing semiotic web for the individual—cannot be accessible in its entirety all at once; this is Lovecraft's "inability of the human mind to correlate all its contents." We are limited in the scope of our attention (through training, however, our attention can be expanded to focus on more information and connections at once). As magicians—and especially as semiurgists—we must be aware of this limitation while at the same time exploiting it to provide focus and clarity to our magical operations. Frazer's law of contagion operates within the phaneron as well, since as with any sign network, each sign in the phaneron is in touch with all the other signs in it (whether directly or indirectly).

This emphasizes the importance of context in magical work. We may choose particular places in which to work our magic because of their historical importance or other factors that draw us to them (inspiration—Firstness in relation to what we desire to bring into being—is a significant portion of all magical work). However, while we may be focusing on one specific aspect of the place (i.e., on Thirdness—the symbolic associations we have for the place), the entire context is always there even if it is outside our current awareness or attention.

Context and codes go hand in hand. The context is the entirety of signs to be interpreted in a given location and/or place; there are always more signs present than we can actually focus on and process. The code determines which signs we acknowledge and how we interpret those signs.

The context and its related codes and sign networks are not just something that we read or interpret. They are also what we inject our own shades of meaning and significance into as part of magical operations designed to alter those contexts and codes—whether only for ourselves or potentially for others as well. If meaning is use—as we will see in the next chapter in the context of Ludwig Wittgenstein's philosophy of language—then by using signs in new ways in particular contexts we also create new meaning within those contexts.

OTHER PERSPECTIVES ON SEMIOTICS

Now let us look beyond the foundations of Saussure and Peirce to discuss newer directions in semiotics that developed from structuralism onward; these will help to further illuminate our understanding of magic as a process of communication. First, we will look at the biosemiotics of Jakob von Uexküll, which was developed independently of Peirce and Saussure but has since been integrated into both schools to create theories of the physiology behind semiosis in living things.

Jakob von Uexküll (1864–1944) was an Estonian biologist and pioneer of *biosemiotics*—a field combining biology and semiotics to study the prelinguistic production and interpretation of signs and codes. Biosemiotics is not primarily concerned with signs created and used by humans, but rather focuses on those aspects of semiosis that are common to all life forms.

A key concept in biosemiotics is the *Umwelt*, a German word variously translated as the "subjective universe," "subjective environment," or "self-world." The *Umwelt* is the conceptual map that an organism has made of itself and its world—a map created through encounters with signs in the environment. Von Uexküll approached the *Umwelt* from an evolutionary perspective: only those signs that somehow affect the survival and perpetuation of the organism are part of its awareness and hold a place in its *Umwelt*. When those signs no longer contribute to fitness within a particular environment the species will either adapt to the new signs or become extinct.

Within humans the *Umwelt* takes on additional importance. The signs contributing to the formation of the *Umwelt* are more than just those that contribute to survival in some way. Any living thing capable of semiosis can experience Firstness and Secondness with signs (and incorporate those interpretations of signs into its *Umwelt*). But when Thirdness—perception conditioned by symbolic thought and behavior—is within the conceptual capabilities of an organism, the possibilities for the *Umwelt* are transformed as well.

Sensory input is limited in what an organism can detect and process: for example, the electromagnetic spectrum is only perceptible within a certain species-specific range; only sounds within certain frequency ranges can be heard; and so on. Thus, any sensory input is already mediated through physical or conceptual limitations that shape what can be processed or interpreted. *We perceive the world in a way that makes it easier for us to make sense of it.*

This immediately leads us into Kantian territory, where any organism's parameters of ability to perceive the signs in the physical world affects what it can know about that physical world. For Kant, there is no pure experience of the phenomenal world, and this in turn determines the limits of what information from the physical world can be part of an organism's *Umwelt*. This is why the *Umwelt* is a model or map: it can only represent those features that are within the perceptual capabilities of the organism.

We introduced the notion of conceptual models in chapter 1. These are mental models for how certain processes work in the world; they shape our behaviors and expectations, and if these models don't prove effective, we can modify them or discard them in favor of other models. Conceptual models are representations of the inner workings of the behaviors or mechanisms they model, and like all representations they can vary in accuracy and usefulness. The *Umwelt* is our overall conceptual model of the world around us, which in turn contains other conceptual models for specific behaviors or phenomena.

We don't use the *Umwelt* itself to do magic, but our individual *Umwelt* must include a conceptual model called "magical thinking": bringing meaning to and seeing connections between events that cannot otherwise be explained by mundane laws of cause and effect. The use of the magical concepts within the *Umwelt* in semiurgy derives from the way the map that is the *Umwelt* determines behavior. The possibilities of the *Umwelt* affect the possibilities for actions—constraints on what the magician regards as within their power to influence through symbolic means. This has profound implications, suggesting that it is in your power to affect whatever can be expressed within the sign network that is the *Umwelt*. That must be tempered, however, with what Anton LaVey called the "balance factor":[23] know your capabilities and what is reasonably able to be affected through the reach of your abilities. Likewise, if you've not committed to doing the nonmagical work that is also necessary to create a certain change in your life, don't expect magic alone to bring it to you no matter how vivid the conception is within your mind's eye.

Umberto Eco and Signs That Lie

Umberto Eco (1932–2016) was an Italian medievalist, novelist, cultural theorist, and semiotician. He was also a professor of semiotics at the University of Bologna; he often explored semiotic ideas in his bestselling novels, and blended concepts from both Saussure and Peirce in his own semiotic theories.

Eco wrote many books and essays on topics related to semiotics and cultural criticism, and due to his fame as an author of fiction these nonfiction works are widely read as well. His contributions to the theory and practice of semiotics are centered around his seminal 1976 text, *A Theory of Semiotics*. In it, he introduces a definition of semiotics that, while perhaps partially tongue-in-cheek, leads to some interesting implications for our theories of semiurgy:

> A sign is everything which can be taken as significantly substituting for something else. This something else does not necessarily have to exist or to actually be somewhere at the moment in which a sign stands for it. Thus *semiotics is in principle the discipline studying everything which can be used in order to lie*. If something cannot be used to tell a lie, conversely it cannot be used to tell the truth: it cannot in fact be used "to tell" at all.[24]

This is a novel way of drawing attention to the arbitrary nature of symbolic signs, while at the same time emphasizing how we are able to comprehend and even embrace fiction alongside reality while blending (and sometimes confusing) the two. Since different semiotic codes examine and carve up concepts and categories in different ways, Eco reminds us that we "live in what can be called an 'artifactual' world of our own making."[25] The same ways that lies can be described—as falsifications, inventions, or fictions—*also* apply to signs. Lying is a form of discourse and dialogue, just like telling the truth; thus, it is subject to all the same rules and processes of using signs for communication. In short, a sign is something that is capable of conveying a variety of truths and untruths.

From the perspective of magical communication, looking at semiotics in terms of the capacity for lying reveals that the desired results of our magic are—in the strictest sense—initially untruths in that they do not *yet* match reality. We assert that something is so as if it had already come to pass or will inevitably do so, and then we reinforce it with other signs to complete the semiotic web and follow it up with appropriate magical action. We change the meaning and significance of the overall sign network in order to replace a lie with the truth—to turn fantasy into reality.

Eco's semiotic theories are not limited to the notions of lying and authenticity, however. He emphasizes sign *functions*—the processes of sign production and interpretation—over signs themselves. This derives in part from the lack of emphasis on sign referents—actual objects in the world—in his theories due to his prioritization of the *cultural* origin and content of signs. In other words, the meaning of a sign in a particular context is more influenced by cultural factors than by any potential referent (object) for the sign itself. This leads to another definition he offers for a sign as "an instruction for interpretation"[26] where this instruction is provided through the culturally influenced code that governs the context in which the sign is encountered.

This forms the basis for his preference for focusing on the process of signification rather than on signs themselves. The emphasis on signs in motion opens the door for additional potential for semiurgy as well.

All people are both consumers and modifiers of the semiotic codes that arise from the different cultural contexts they participate in. Most changes in these codes arise slowly from the accumulated individual interpretations of such codes; over time enough people change their interpretation of one part of it so that this new interpretation becomes the default (also known as the *ground*). This doesn't require intention, it just requires us to be humans—humans with their own experiences, biases, and motives, all of which serve to provide individual, idiosyncratic understandings of the codes. However, the magician—and especially the semiurgist, who knows how semiotic codes pervade everything we encounter—can *intentionally* inject certain changes into these codes. As with the memes we discussed way back in chapter 1, finding the right alterations in the code that will "stick" and spread is the key. This will happen on its own haphazardly, but we can be more precise by deliberate putting certain changes to the codes in motion. The codes in effect carry our magic, like a vast network that connects people as individual nodes bound together by the codes in which they participate, both consciously and unconsciously.

This idea of magic as hacking semiotic codes leads us into territory explored by Roland Barthes in both his structuralist and post-structuralist periods.

The Demythologizer

Roland Barthes (1915–1980) was a French cultural critic and semiotician. His earlier work was firmly rooted in structuralist semiotics—based on Saussure's model of signs—while his later work rejected many tenets of structuralism (as well as his earlier Marxism), and he became one of the most important proponents of post-structuralism. Throughout his writings, there is an acerbic wit and a tendency to look at the world from strange angles. This often makes them as entertaining as they are thought-provoking.

Barthes's central project was the *demythologizing* of various cultural phenomena: identifying those areas where a preestablished truth is assumed and finding hidden hypocrisies that lead to hidden coercions. He was not pursuing this as part of some nihilistic quest for the destruction of culture, but rather was attempting to show new paths to freedom. In other words, Barthes's work reveals ways in which people have been subject to limitations on their freedom of expression and choice and have been accepting those limitations as rigid instead of malleable. His work attempts to decode the semiotic codes that are "hiding in plain sight" and to discover their hidden messages (and determine who is generating these messages and for what purpose). He started out approaching this from a Marxist perspective—finding the codes that result from a rather Hegelian view of the unfolding of history—but decisively broke with that later. Ultimately, his goal was to liberate people from the tyranny of mass-produced thought and to help them become more individuated with a true understanding of their desires and motivations. Where this has the potential for failure is most people do not *want* to take full responsibility for their desires and motivations, and after finding this type of liberation they will drift aimlessly looking for new codes and new masters while still thinking of themselves as "free."

Barthes's semiotic approach to demythologizing was initially a variation on Kant's ideas that we actively construct our perception of the world. As a result, we are awash in the constructions of others as they coalesce into the semiotic codes that influence our interactions, behaviors, and expectations about the world and its inhabitants. Barthes, however, is far more radical than Kant; his desire was to liberate the self from preconceived, mass-produced identities that include arbitrary limitations on human activity. Ultimately, he goes so far with the liberating, demythologizing project that he turns these tools on semiotics, structuralism, and Marxism *themselves* to uncover the ways in which they are *also* myths with hidden agendas. In other words, the demythologizer demythologized demythologizing itself. In peeling back the surface layer of myth he did not find reality but instead found just additional layers of myth—sometimes it really is turtles all the way down. This does *not* mean, however, that there is no reality and no truth, but simply reveals, definitively, that truth and reality are ultimately known from within the individual and not solely based on external codes.

His 1957 essay collection *Mythologies* is the most well-known example of these attempts at demythologizing. The essays focus on unmasking media and advertising as tools for social control and semiotic code enforcement. For each topic drawn from cultural artifacts of the 1950s, he emphasizes how its exemplars first appear to say one thing, but there is a second, hidden layer of meaning that reveals the *actual* intent. His goal is to identify and examine this hidden layer, which he calls *myth*. His primary toolkit is semiotics of the Saussurean variety—sign networks composed of signifiers and signifieds—which he uses to look at the inner coherence and interrelations between signs. He contends that signs don't mimic—represent—the world through their relationships with their referents in the world; rather, the *interrelations* between signs create our view of reality and the world. These semiotic webs—codes—

can only be judged to be true based on their coherence, *not* on how their components relate to the world. Looking back on our brief discussion of cognitive views of magic in chapter 2, it should be clear now that semiotic codes and cognitive models are essentially one and the same in terms of their implications for understanding and action.

Another of the essential points Barthes makes is that we do this type of semiotic analysis and evaluation of code coherence all the time without thinking about it. This is the brilliance of his application of these techniques to everyday, commonplace things, from the depiction of various cultures and periods of history in films, to ads for detergent, to astrology, to professional wrestling, to political image-making. Perhaps more than anyone else in the twentieth century, Barthes took semiotics out of the rarefied realm of academia and showed its relevance to all aspects of human culture—culture that arises from the very semiotic codes he sought to dissect.

Barthes's work puts an entirely new spin on magic as a process of semiotic communication. His techniques are powerful tools especially in acts of semiurgy designed to affect others' perceptions. Many of the core techniques of modern advertising—one of Barthes's favorite targets for analysis—are so well known at this point as to no longer seem magical. However, there is still plenty of opportunity for the semiurgist to leverage Barthes's ideas when identifying the sign relationships that can be manipulated toward specific outcomes. The same approach can be utilized to discover when crude semiotic magic is being used on you to cast a myth that attempts to blind you to its real intent.

In this chapter we have taken a detailed look at many core concepts in semiotics and the semioticians behind them. The modern schools of semiotics have continued to develop in far-reaching ways, having adapted to help us better understand a wide variety of features in culture, art, science, and language. We paid special attention to the founders of the two main schools of semiotics, Ferdinand de Saussure and Charles Sanders Peirce, since their perspectives on the nature and implications of signs directly or indirectly form the foundations for virtually all other approaches since the early twentieth century.

All of these theories about signs and meaning aid us in the understanding and practice of magic as well—the material from this chapter reveals key components of the foundations of the semiotic approaches to magic discussed toward the end of chapter 2. In the next chapter we will focus on how the study of language—which we must always remember is, at its core, a system of signs—helps to further sharpen our understanding of the innately human phenomenon of magic.

FURTHER READING

A Theory of Semiotics by Umberto Eco
Course in General Linguistics by Ferdinand de Saussure (Roy Harris
    translation)
Mythologies by Roland Barthes
Peirce on Signs edited by James Hoopes
Semiosis in the Postmodern Age by Floyd Merrell
Semiotics: The Basics by Daniel Chandler
Signs: An Introduction by Thomas Sebeok

4

VIEWING MAGIC THROUGH
LINGUISTICS AND
THE PHILOSOPHY
OF LANGUAGE

I n the last chapter we took a close look at important ideas in the development of semiotics from Ancient Greece until the present. We focused on the two most significant figures in the development of modern semiotics, Swiss linguist Ferdinand de Saussure and American philosopher Charles Sanders Peirce. Linguistics is generally considered to be a specific discipline *within* semiotics, although it should be noted that many linguists do not think of themselves as semioticians or use its terminology. Nonetheless, the study of linguistics is inherently connected with semiotics due in part to the foundational influence of Saussure. In this chapter, we will look at a broad survey of the history of linguistics since the late eighteenth century, with an eye toward those ideas that illuminate our understanding of magical communication. We'll conclude with a survey of relevant ideas from the philosophy of language.

THE BEGINNINGS
OF MODERN LINGUISTICS

Modern linguistics as a distinct discipline begins with the realization that, based on similarities between most European languages that are too consistent to be the result of chance or borrowing alone, there must be a language that is the hypothetical ancestor of the majority of languages spoken in Europe and as far east as the Indian subcontinent. Prior to the discovery of the ancient relationships that led to recognition of the Indo-European language family,* it was already understood that the Romance languages (French, Spanish, Italian, Portuguese, Romanian, etc.) were ultimately derived from Latin. This was known because of the well-understood history of the remnants of the Roman Empire in regions where those languages were spoken. The revelation of the much bigger Indo-European family of languages, which includes those Romance languages, was more about scope.

The Brothers Grimm
The brothers Jacob (1785–1863) and Wilhelm (1786–1859) Grimm are best known to the general public as collectors of fairy tales. Jacob was also a pivotal figure in the development of linguistics and the application of the comparative method† to the study and reconstruction of languages. The Grimms were working during a period when the independent Germanic city-states and principalities were reeling from the Napoleonic invasions and seeking a national identity. Historical linguistics—the study of how different languages change and diverge

---

*The Indo-European language family includes most of the languages spoken in Europe and parts of northern and western Asia, with many of those languages (such as English and Spanish) also now spoken in places far from where they originated.

†The comparative method is used to determine the relationships between languages that are suspected to derive from a common ancestor language. This is done through comparing various features of the languages (grammar, sound patterns, vocabulary, etc.) and using that information to work backward toward the common source.

over time—became a major area of study in the German-speaking lands. This was one of the tools used for understanding the origins of the Germanic tribes—a search for identity, which, in turn, contributed to the nationalist fervor that led to the unification of Germany in 1871 and set the stage for Germany's role in the two world wars.

Saussure and Structural Linguistics

We've already discussed many core ideas from Saussure that continue to have influence today. While the previous examination of Saussure focused on semiotics (or semiology, as he called it), here we will look at some of his specifically linguistic ideas. Saussure was working during a time when linguistics was still a relatively new discipline. His systematic thinking was crucial in giving linguistics a precision—in both terminology and methodology—that helped it to fully develop as a scientific discipline.

Many of Saussure's ideas come in pairs of opposites. We've already seen how his definition of a (linguistic) sign—a *signifier* paired with a *signified*—also noted that signs take their meaning not in an absolute sense but only in their relations to other signs. In other words, a sign is distinct to the extent that it is *not* other signs.

This notion that opposites interact, and the relationships build upon each other to create more complex structures, is an old one in human thought. We naturally group things into opposing pairs: up vs. down, dark vs. light, left vs. right, moving vs. static, known vs. unknown. Perhaps it comes from our own bilateral symmetry (two arms, two legs, two ears, two eyes, etc.) and is something we project onto our view of the world because it is so fundamental to our understanding of ourselves via our bodies. This common cognitive practice can be seen in mythology as well, in its function as a repository of a given culture's ideal arrangements of the cosmos and its divine and nondivine inhabitants. Mount Olympus contrasts with Hades; heaven with hell; Tiamat with Apsu. Odin's true nature is polarian, oscillating between poles of extremes always in the pursuit of knowledge. (We will look more closely at Tiamat, Apsu, and Odin in chap. 5.)

All this is to say that Saussure's work was, consciously or not, helping linguistics to find its place as an expression of fundamental ideas about the arrangement of the cosmos and humanity's place within it. Let's take a brief look at a few of these fundamental oppositions.

Saussure's Dichotomies

The primary division that Saussure introduced is between *diachronic* (changing over time) and *synchronic* (existing at a particular point in time) linguistics. The study of diachronic linguistics corresponds to historical linguistics: the study of how languages change over time. Synchronic linguistics, on the other hand, focuses on the state of a language at a given point in time (perhaps now, perhaps an older time). Despite his earlier work in historical linguistics (in which he made some crucial discoveries about Proto-Indo-European* and its descendent languages), by the time he became a professor at the University of Geneva his primary focus was on synchronic linguistics—he even suggested that this was the *only* appropriate focus of linguistics.

The next fundamental division in Saussure's concept of linguistics is between *langue* (a particular language) and *parole* (speech using that language). *Langue* is an abstraction, a statement about what is grammatically, phonetically, or conceptually acceptable within a language. This can't be a static thing, otherwise a language could not change with respect to either its sounds or the meanings of its words. Since languages are undeniably always in flux, *langue* is an approximation of a language at a particular moment in time, yet it still cannot capture all that is possible within a language.

If we can never fully describe or understand a particular *langue*, then how is it a useful concept (especially for semiurgy or magical communication)? A *langue* is in effect a semiotic code in another disguise. As with all semiotic codes, building new connections and meanings

---

*Proto-Indo-European is the hypothetical reconstructed language that is the source of all other languages in the Indo-European language family.

within the unbounded possibilities of a *langue* creates a potent way to impress your intent on the world.

A third essential dichotomy in Saussure's conception of linguistics is the contrast between *paradigm* and *syntagma*. As we looked at those in the last chapter, they will only be briefly recounted here. A paradigm is a set of possibilities appropriate to a given context; a syntagma is a specific set of such possibilities assembled and given cohesion within that context. *Syntagmata* (plural of syntagma) are assembled in ever more complex combinations to create and convey meaning. For example, words combine to form phrases, which combine to form sentences, which combine to form paragraphs, chapters, books, and so on. Always keep in mind that interplay between paradigms and syntagmata is the basic mechanism of deriving and creating meaning in signs of *all* kinds, not just linguistic signs. This same interplay—assembling the right symbols out of what is available to work with—is the core of semiurgy as well.

Syntagmatic Analysis

Signs—linguistic or otherwise—gain meaning from their differences with other signs *and* in the way they are built into syntagmata. Since signs rely on *other* signs for their meaning, the full meaning of the syntagma (and of syntagmata within the syntagma!) is *deferred* as additional signs added to the syntagma modify that meaning.

Take, for example, the syntagma that is the first line in the so-called Headless Ritual (later to be significantly reworked and popularized by Aleister Crowley as the "Bornless Ritual" or *Liber Samekh*; see chaps. 6 and 8 for discussion of the two versions, respectively).

> *I summon you, Headless One, who created earth and heaven, who created night and day, you who created light and darkness.*[1]

As we assemble this syntagma to create meaning while the line progresses, "I summon" leads from the question "I summon who/what?" to the answer "I summon *you*." Meaning is deferred *again* until the referent "you" is revealed as "the Headless One." At this point, we have redeemed part of the deferral and *retroactively* supplied more meaning to the beginning of the syntagma, but the syntagma doesn't yet tell us who the Headless One is or for what purpose it has been summoned. The syntagma "I summon you, Headless One" is then supplemented by a formula that is repeated: "who created" combined with three pairs of opposites. *Created* is a transitive verb—one that requires one or more objects to act on—and again defers its full meaning until we encounter its object(s).

There are two specific techniques embedded in this pair of formulas, likely intentionally, and this situation again highlights that meaning *always* pulls from what is known outside just the text itself. The first technique is that the ritual formula "who created . . ." is repeated; this repetition not only reinforces the importance of the syntagma being repeated but also retroactively creates more meaning in the previous syntagma. In other words, we now know this is some sort of creator deity. The repetition sets this invocation apart from everyday speech; it is *marked* speech, using a marker—the repetition—to signal that it is being used for more than just mundane purposes. The second technique is that the things the Headless One is said to have created are opposites with cosmic importance: heaven and earth (and presumably everything in between), and night and day (and presumably everything in between), and so on. The Headless One doesn't just create something within the cosmos, it creates the cosmos itself and places boundaries on it.

By this time everyone who has heard or read this invocation before is already anticipating the next lines—beginning with *another* repetition of the "you created . . ." formula (this time, the opposites of "light and darkness"). The syntagmata that have already been created in this instance of the invocation anticipate the rest and defer the meaning of the entire text. They *also* carry remnants of the other uses of this invocation and even anticipate other performances that have not yet been said! This only adds to the reinforcement through repetition that was hinted at in the "you created . . ." formulas—the meaning and significance of this instance of the invocation join with the syntagma that defers part of its meaning until the *next* performance.

This brings the importance of sign networks into clearer focus, and it gives some insight into how they are built and reinforced. It also emphasizes the power of choice when intentionally building a semiotic map to facilitate a magical act: your choices of what to include—or not to include!—affect the meaning you are creating. *Operative communication is a way to prefigure outcomes by connecting them to the chain of deferred meaning that you are constructing.*

HOCKETT AND DESIGN FEATURES

Charles Hockett (1916–2000) was an American linguist who was influential in the development of structural linguistics in the mid-twentieth century. He is most known today for his *design features of language*; we briefly introduced these in chapter 1 in the context of assessing the linguistic capabilities of humans in contrast to other animals. Now we will look at these important features in more detail; whenever we look at cognitive abilities that are unique to humans, we're also looking at symbolic behavior and its usefulness in magical practices. Hockett's design features are a set of capabilities—some physical, some cognitive—that must be present for the full manifestation of human language as we know it.[2] Some animals possess some of these capacities, but according to Hockett only humans possess all sixteen. The full list of features is as follows (the ones marked with an asterisk are, according to Hockett, unique to humans):

1. *Vocal-Auditory Channel*: The ability to create and hear vocal sounds within specific ranges.

2. *Broadcast Transmission and Directional Reception*: The ability to hear nearby sounds created by another human or animal; this includes the capability for determining the direction of the source of a sound.

3. *Rapid Fading (Transitoriness)*: Sound waves dissipate quickly so that they are no longer audible; prior to the invention of sound recording devices, this required that the hearer be near to the source of the sound.

4. *Interchangeability*: A speaker can both speak and hear the same sounds.

5. *Total Feedback*: Speakers can hear themselves speak.

6. *Specialization*: The sounds produced are specialized for the purpose of communication and are intentionally created.

7. *Semanticity*: Particular auditory signals have meanings in a given context.

8. *Arbitrariness*: There is no inherent connection between auditory signals and their meaning (even onomatopoeic words like "meow" are arbitrary in that they reflect the sound system of their speaker's language).

9. *Discreteness*: Sounds can be distinguished as distinct phonemes (individual sounds that are used to convey meaning; for example, *pin* and *bin* are distinct words in English, only distinguished by whether the vocal cords vibrate as part of creating their initial sounds).

10. *Displacement*: Language can be used to refer to things not present in the current time and/or place.

11. *Productivity*: Language can be used to create unlimited new utterances of unlimited complexity.

12. **Traditional (aka Cultural) Transmission*: Language spreads through connections between those who are capable of developing and using it. Languages are not innate but must be learned. According to Hockett, this design feature is unique to humans, as are the remaining four design features.

13. **Duality of Patterning*: Meaningless sounds (phonemes) combine to create meaningful words, and then combine to form more complex units. This is essentially the concept of the *syntagma*, starting from the component sounds and building up from there.

14. *Prevarication*: Speech can be used to communicate falsehoods and other meaningless statements (as we saw in chap. 3, this is a critical feature of Umberto Eco's theory of signs as well).
15. *Reflexivity*: Language can be used to talk about itself.
16. *Learnability*: Speakers of one language can choose to learn another.

Let's look at the features claimed to be unique to humans—cultural transmission, duality of patterning, prevarication, reflexivity, and learnability—in the context of magical communication or semiurgy.

Cultural transmission is closely related to semiotic codes. As we saw in chapter 2, codes convey what is significant and what is expected in a given cultural context. Codes are spread through communication, whether that is done with language or with other metacommunicative concepts like art and advertising. We imitate to some extent what we see (or hear) others like us doing or saying. Codes, like languages, spread through the memes we copy from others (see chap. 1). Codes endure to the extent they are "sticky" enough to continue being copied because they create symbolic or practical significance within their particular context. So, essentially everything that contributes to the spread of memes within a culture applies to language as well. This also applies to different techniques for magical communication; any tool—physical or mental—that "works" (has suitability and effectiveness in some context) will be copied and adapted. There is no one universal approach; the cookbook-style approach can be helpful for learning in the early stages of developing your craft, but just as each person's cultural and personal semiotic codes are unique, you must ultimately find your own way of doing magic that resonates with the codes you find useful or significant.

Duality of patterning gives us another way to look at the cognitive processes behind syntagmata. Keep in mind that Hockett was a structural linguist, meaning he worked within the framework derived from Saussure's work, including of course the dichotomy between paradigm and syntagma. This design principle reinforces the idea that creating and combining syntagmata is a fundamental cognitive process that enables the full complexity of human thought. As such, it is a key component in magical communication as we leverage symbolic elements to express intent and, more importantly, *communicate* that intent effectively to bring about its realization.

Prevarication is not just about lying; it is also about communicating things that are not true or actual *yet*, but which could be made to come into being. We talked about this in a broad sense in the section on hyperstition in chapter one. Magic by its very conception reveals a pathway for making fantasy into reality, for bringing hyperstition into the realm of the actual. Seen in this way, magic is a way of taking certain hypotheticals that *could* be true and bending reality to match the potential (rather than eliminating the potential because it does not currently line up with reality). Prevarication is related to *displacement*: displacement refers to what is not present in the current time or place; prevarication refers to what does not line up with the real as understood within the applicable semiotic code. The code itself—the very thing that prevarication is measured against—is then leveraged as part of the magical communication that turns prevarication into validation.

Reflexivity describes the way language can be used to talk about language—this entire book is an exercise in reflexivity. To do this, we have to be able to "step outside" language and its concepts: we look at language from the perspective of an outside observer and use language itself to understand what language is doing (or is capable of doing). Without reflexivity, we could not speak of magic as a communication process because we could not understand or predict the effects of language—we could only experience those effects. We are also using reflexivity when we talk about the object of desire that we seek to realize with magic. Any thoughts about objects—whether physical, conceptual, or hypothetical—are only possible when we can perceive a separation between ourselves and those objects. *Language bridges the gap between self and not-self.* With reflexivity, we can look not only at this object of desire on its own terms but also look more deeply into the semiotic codes and language constructs that are part of our conception (and categorization) of that object. In other words, we come to understand the object in large part through the way we describe it in language and other semiotic codes.

Learnability is another of Hockett's design features that applies to semiotic codes in general. The conceptual artifacts of culture are never static for long: they spread, expand, and change in response to the way actual people use those codes and subtly modify them as they are copied and adapted for certain uses. We can choose to learn a language just as we choose to obey (or work within) the semiotic codes we encounter in different contexts; humans are infinitely adaptable, able to accept and adopt even the strangest alternatives to their current ways of thinking. This of course also applies to the semiotic codes that we call systems of magic. For example, the principles behind sigil magic (see chap. 8) are not exactly the same as those underlying magical uses of runes. They will have certain things in common because they arise in part from the way that humans conceive symbolic systems, but they will have their unique aspects as well. Just as a baby of Chinese ethnicity but raised from birth by Spanish-speaking parents will learn Spanish as their native language, but can then choose later to learn French, a magician whose underlying magical outlook was originally shaped by their Indigenous shamanic practices in Siberia can also choose to learn and work with Enochian.

LANGUAGE IS A VIRUS

We seem to be almost afraid of silence at times, filling the air with directionless chatter while engaged in the mundane. Language has to be about more than mere communication, because we use it even when we have nothing useful to say. One of the many theories about how language arose is that it is related to grooming and social maintenance, helping us feel connected to other humans. According to this theory, once the ability for spoken language had become part of early hominid behavior along with physiological adaptions that supported it, the language capacity was subject to what humans do with nearly everything they encounter: they consciously adapt it for their own uses, ascribe significance to it, and incorporate it into their semiotic codes.

The Beat writer and magician William S. Burroughs took a view of language that provides useful commentary on magical communication:

> My general theory since 1971 has been that the Word is literally a virus, and that it has not been recognized as such because it has achieved a state of relatively stable symbiosis with its human host; that is to say, the Word Virus (the Other Half) has established itself so firmly as an accepted part of the human organism that it can now sneer at gangster viruses like smallpox and turn them in to the Pasteur Institute. But the Word clearly bears the single identifying feature of virus: it is an organism with no internal function other than to replicate itself.[3]

Seen from this perspective, human thought has been hijacked by language and spreads above all to preserve *itself.* In chapter 1 we talked about memes as concepts or behaviors that spread throughout human culture by a process of imitation (and then undergo competition for determining what will continue to be copied and spread). Language as a behavior is itself a collection of memes—recall the discussion of Hockett's principle of cultural transmission earlier in this chapter—and language is also a vehicle for *spreading* memes. In both cases, the transmission medium is oblivious to what it spreads—in fact, falsehood and fantasy often spread even more easily than the true and the real.

Language has become an integral part of every aspect of human experience, such that we can't even imagine doing some things without being able to talk about them before, during, and after. If thought and language are dependent on each other, then how could thought have been possible in the absence of language?

Thought occurs before language; an infant is clearly thinking and processing the input they are receiving from the world around them as they slowly learn how to affect that world through actions and eventually words. Earlier in our evolutionary history, even before the arrival of anything resembling language as we know it today, we still possessed cognitive abilities similar to those found among the other great apes (our closest relatives). Thought was of course possible before the physiological and cognitive traits necessary for language were fully present in early hominids. But—and this is the crucial part—once the capacity for language *was* part of our intellectual and biological world, it became the organization system for our thoughts. Language alters connections and categories, and it attaches labels to our ever-changing perception of the world.

In the last chapter, we looked at Immanuel Kant's ideas about categories; these ideas have had significant influence on cognitive science as well. The core of Kant's work was about how we know and think about reality: do we experience it as it actually is, or is the experience always mediated by something that can distort or limit our interpretations of it? Newer research in cognitive science suggests strongly that it is the latter; the various sense organs provide the input for experiencing the world outside of ourselves, but that input is then internally processed in ways that are both dependent on past experience and also influenced by the categories and models we cling to. Our sensory input results from the outcomes of processes at work within the world—touch, hearing, sight, and so on are not the objects or processes themselves, but are instead the perceptible results of those objects or processes. Thus, we start out slightly removed from that reality because its perception has already gone through one translation layer (to become the input to which our senses can respond).

There is another source of input that influences our interpretation of all other input, however: past experience. We group experiences and concepts that *seem* similar into categories. These categories organize our experiences into meaningful relationships and provide a basis for understanding—and further categorizing—new input or new thoughts. Sometimes these categories work in our favor: quickly determining whether that loud sound was a gunshot or just a door slamming enables us to make decisions that could be lifesaving. But other times, those categories trick us into making connections that aren't there.

Categories are a product of the semiotic codes used to organize reality and experience, with language being just one kind of semiotic code. The relationship between thought and language, with language providing a means of labeling and revealing connections between our thoughts, is a crucial shaping force on these categories. The categories of experience help us to understand (and file away as further experiences) what *has* happened, and to predict what *will* happen. They also help us to understand (or at least make good guesses at) what is possible.

And whenever we are focusing on what is possible, we have opened the door to magical communication as one means of creating the actual out of the potential.

THE POWER OF METAPHOR

We've already looked briefly at the basic ideas and pursuits behind cognitive science in chapter 1. Linguistics and cognitive science are connected through what has become known as *Cognitive Linguistics*, a branch of linguistics that focuses on the physiological and psychological processing of language. The roots of research into the cognitive aspects of language can be found in the rise of universal grammar as a major concern of modern linguistics starting in the late 1950s.* Linguist George Lakoff (b. 1941) and his collaborators, notably philosopher of language Mark Johnson (b. 1949), chose the name Cognitive Linguistics

---

*Universal grammar is an umbrella term for various theories suggesting that there are innate limitations in human cognition, supported if not created by particular regions in the brain, that determine the possible grammatical structures of human languages. The towering figure in this area of linguistics is linguist and political dissident Noam Chomsky (b. 1928).

in order to differentiate it from universal grammar as another approach to the bridge between cognition and language.

Lakoff and Johnson also coined the name for a crucial idea describing how language transforms our understanding of the world both within and beyond us: conceptual metaphor. First, let's review the general concept of a metaphor.

A *metaphor* is a figure of speech that describes one thing in terms of a different, unrelated thing—we describe something we like as the "bee's knees"; Shakespeare tells us "Juliet is the sun" and "All the world's a stage"; a mobster "smells a rat." *Metaphors form the very foundation of our conceptual system*, enabling us to attach nuance and symbolic meaning to words and other signs. Even magic—especially ritualized magic—is largely an application of metaphor. We may use bells, candles, swords/daggers, robes, and words to represent or call to mind *other* concepts that have symbolic importance within the task at hand. In Masonic lodges, we find hammers, swords, the traditional tools of geometry and bricklaying, and other tools that take on particular significance; the layout and ritualized construction of a Masonic lodge is itself a metaphor for the construction of the cosmos. *Any time we use symbols to add significance to some act, magical or otherwise, we are using metaphor.*

A *conceptual domain* is a set of ideas linked to a specific set of experiences; for example, all the objects, ideas, and processes related to taking a journey are part of a single conceptual domain. A *conceptual metaphor* is a particular type of metaphor that uses a more concrete conceptual domain to describe another more abstract conceptual domain. "More concrete" in this context means something is easier to experience with the senses. For example, when we speak of an argument in terms of being a journey—let's *proceed* in a *step-by-step* fashion to *arrive* at an agreement—we are bringing the abstract idea of argument into terms of something we can more directly describe or recognize in terms of our physical experiences. The actions and ideas associated with a journey then suggest a vocabulary we can use for describing an argument in terms of a more readily accessible experience. *Conceptual metaphors are built into the way we use language in a very deep way*, often to the point we don't even recognize that we are speaking metaphorically because they have become part of the idiom of the language(s) we speak. When we no longer immediately recognize a metaphor *as* a metaphor, we say that it has become conventionalized.

Language is at its core built on metaphor, especially when it expresses things that have no physical analogue in the objective universe: words *themselves* are arbitrary, unrelated collections of sounds that we use to refer to concepts, processes, feelings, and so forth. Words help us to talk about those physical concepts in terms that are more likely to be part of our lived experience since at least the hearing, reading, or speaking of the word is now part of our experience. I can talk about Antarctica even though I've never been there, or talk about boredom even though it's not something I'm experiencing right now. This is perhaps related to the language acquisition process itself: language typically first begins to manifest as part of an infant's development of their sensory-motor representation of the world, and then the developing child becomes capable of expressing more abstract things—but the core conceptual underpinning remains that equates things that can be talked about with things that be touched (or otherwise directly experienced).

Let's look at a few examples of conceptual metaphor. Consider these sentences: He *dove* right into the problem. He'd been *fishing* for the answer for weeks. The answer was *floating around* out there. Finally, the answer *surfaced*.

The conceptual metaphor here is PROBLEMS ARE BODIES OF WATER. (By convention among cognitive linguists, descriptions of conceptual metaphors are written using small capital letters.)

You're *wasting* my time. This gadget will *save* you hours. I don't have the time to *give* you. How do you *spend* your time these days? That flat tire *cost* me an hour.[4]

The conceptual metaphor here is TIME IS MONEY.

And of course, conceptual metaphors abound in magical speech as well, as in this lust spell from the Greek Magical Papyri (spell XXXXIIa. 1–25):

> *As Typhon is the adversary of Helios, so* inflame *the heart and soul of that Amoneios whom Helen bore, even from her own womb, ADONAI ABRASAX PINOUTI and SABAOS;* burn *the soul and heart of that Amoneios whom Helen bore, for [love of] this Serapiakos whom Threpte bore, now, now; quickly, quickly.*[5]

Here, the spell speaks of *inflaming* and *burning* the heart and soul—the conceptual metaphor of LUST IS HEAT. Furthermore, this spell implies that the hatred of an adversary generates a heat that can be redirected (especially when the adversary is the god of the sun, Helios, himself!).

The connection between a conceptual metaphor and what it refers to is based on a *mapping*, which is the way the *source domain* (the conceptual domain drawn from, like *heat*) describes or reveals something about the *target domain* (the conceptual domain that is made more concrete by comparison with the source domain, like *lust*).

Metaphor is a form of analogical thinking that is related to metonymy (the use of some object or visual that is closely associated with something being used to represent that thing). In magical communication, this suggests Frazer's law of sympathy (see chap. 2) and by extension the type of sign called an *icon*. Here the iconic resemblance is not because the metaphor suggests a copy or image of its referent; it is due to the mysterious connection that links both source and target domain, such that the former helps us to better comprehend the latter.

We understand, and can even interact with, gods and goddesses through the same mechanisms in use with processing conceptual metaphors. An image of a divine figure captures some of its essential properties and associations, both making them easier to visualize but at the same time easier to conceptualize. In other words, the appearance and attributes associated with the god help to bring that god closer to our earthbound conceptions. While this can be helpful, especially with trying to communicate something about the god to someone else, it is also necessarily limiting: gods are by their existence and Being more than just what we can describe in human language or visualize in terms of the images available within the mundane world.

Describing the Indescribable

In *Das Heilige* (1917), published in English as *The Idea of the Holy*, the German theologian Rudolf Otto discussed the inadequacy of language for precisely communicating and describing internal states. He employed the word *numinous* (German: *das Numinose*) to describe a feeling or experience not based on sensory experience or reason, the feeling of encountering something "wholly or entirely other."[6] This is the encounter with the divine, the eldritch, the otherworldly, or the mysterious that cannot be convincingly explained away. Because this feeling arises solely from within (even if triggered by something external), *other* concepts or experiences are inadequate to use as points of reference.

> [The experience] may become the hushed, trembling, and speechless humility of the creature in the presence of—whom or what? In the presence of that which is a Mystery inexpressible and above all creatures.[7]

Language finds its most unique uses in the way words are deployed to describe what cannot be seen; this is far beyond simply calling for an object by name rather than pointing at it, or teaching someone how to work with a set of complex instructions for building a canoe only by having them observe the teacher.

INTEGRATIONAL LINGUISTICS

One of the things nonmagicians often get wrong about the magical uses of language—perhaps influenced by watered-down popular depictions of magic in books and movies—is the assumption that just saying the right word or words will *in itself* bring about the hoped-for effect. This reduces magic to just plugging in the right words for the situation. What this misperception overlooks is the fact that the words are just *one* syntagma of signs within the context of the overall sign complex that is being manipulated for operative purposes. In some cases, the words activate or enhance the other signs; in others, the words are merely an outward manifestation of the inner processes of the magician interacting with the other signs found in the context of the situation at hand. The reduction of verbal magic—a *spell*—to the words themselves seems to be related to an often-unexamined assumption in the way languages themselves have typically been studied: this is the assumption that specific parts of a language (its syntax, grammar, vocabulary, etc.) can be studied *without* reference to the real-life communicative situations in which the words are used.

Roy Harris (1931–2015) was a specialist in the history of linguistics, theories of communication, and the works and ideas of Ferdinand de Saussure (he translated the standard English edition of Saussure's *Course in General Linguistics*). Harris was also the founder of what he called *integrational linguistics* (sometimes referred to as *integrationist linguistics* or just *integrationism*), through which he sought to emphasize that linguistic practices are *always* integrated with other behaviors as well. Thus, taking the study of language out of the contexts in which it is used will necessarily rob it of its full contextual meaning. Moreover, the integrational study of language is not just about the context within the immediate situation but recognizes that our entire experience with communication shapes context. In other words, context is not a given but is instead at least partially constructed by the participants in a communication.

In chapter 2 we looked at the work of Stephen Flowers and Scott Shell, who argue that the interpretation of runic inscriptions must take into account the entire context of the inscription and not just the runes themselves. Harris's insistence on accounting for contextual information that transcends just the words being spoken (or written/gestured) fits in precisely with this holistic approach to understanding sign networks in magical contexts.

Context is crucially important for magical communication, and the ways that Harris reminds us that it is an essential part of interpreting mundane communication as well can be easily applied to magical communication. The mutual construction of context by all the participants in a communicative act follows from the way that signs both carry and help to create meaning. Contextualization—determining the applicable context in a given communicative situation—is what leads us to recognize and interpret signs *as* signs; signs can only be interpreted to discover meaning within the context in which they are encountered. *No context, no sign.*

Let's say you are working with a sigil* to attract interesting books to yourself. In theory, you could take any sort of written sign and try to invest it with the meaning behind your magical intent, and that may or may not have the intended result depending on your skill at contextualization and visualization. Context is, however, easier to create and influence when you are working with, and not against, expectations. That is, it is easier to tweak the meaning when you are only looking to make it slightly askew from what most people with a similar linguistic and cultural background would expect. If you struggle to bend context to accommodate the meaning you want the sigil to have, then how is the unmanifest world you are attempting to influence going to have a reasonable chance to understand your communication?

Sigil magic is effective in part because the sigils created through whatever method you prefer are based on systems of communication that *already* predispose their users toward certain contexts. The word method for sigil creation, for example—reducing a statement of intent to

---

*Sigils are pictorial magical symbols. They can be created through a variety of methods, but today are often associated with the "word-distillation" methods pioneered by Austin Osman Spare (see chap. 8).

its bare essentials and creating a sigil from that—leverages all the other parts of the intent that language can help to create through the context in which the original utterance is being used. The sigil is in effect the minimum viable carrier of the entire context of the communication.

The hugely important realization that the *entirety* of an action of communication—and not just the words that may be involved—has to be accounted for when examining *all* types of communicative acts will be a major factor in our discussion of speech acts below as well.

THE PHILOSOPHY OF LANGUAGE

In the early twentieth century, Western philosophy began to reorient itself in what has become known as the *linguistic turn*. This major change in focus was an emphasis on how we come to know and share knowledge about the world through language. The philosophy of language—the use of the tools of philosophical investigation to look at the phenomenon of language itself—is especially interested in questions about how we assign meaning, express intention, and connect the way we speak or write with the ideas and objects that language refers to.

Prior to the linguistic turn, there was an emphasis in philosophy on rationality and the implicit—and sometimes explicit—assumption that humans were rational beings, always relating to the world and its inhabitants in rational ways. As we noted in the prologue to this book, the bet that humans will always act rationally is a poor one to wager. Thus, philosophy shifted toward attempting to understand linguistic behavior revealed through the actual—rather than ideal—actions of people. Through this, more plausible explanations of certain types of thinking, such as magical thinking, became possible.

Because of this focus on language and its relation to the world, the philosophy of language is a useful place for exploring some of our ideas about semiurgy, communication, and magic. As with our discussions of the history of linguistics and semiotics, we will limit our focus to a few essential figures who have something important to say in relation to magical communication: J. L. Austin, Martin Heidegger, and Ludwig Wittgenstein.

Speech Acts and Performative Utterances

John Langshaw Austin (1911–1960) was a British professor of philosophy at Oxford University who was especially interested in *speech acts*—speech that by being spoken produces action in the world. His approach to language was summed up in the title of the collection of lectures published posthumously as *How to Do Things with Words* (1962). Austin was a proponent of the idea that the primary purpose and enduring fascination of the phenomenon of language is not its ability to describe but instead its ability to cause change within and beyond the speaker.

Speech acts convey information, but also perform or cause an action—some concrete response in the phenomenal world. If I ask you to ring a bell to begin a magical ritual, I presume that you are able to understand English, are willing to cooperate, are capable of ringing a bell, and are already familiar with—or can figure out—the process for ringing this particular type of bell. If you then ring the bell, even if you do not accompany that action with any words, you have *still* participated in a communicative act with me, and your response—ringing the bell—was ultimately caused by the words of my request. This idea that not all parts of a communicative act require words to convey meaning should be familiar from our discussion of integrational linguistics as well.

Among anthropologists, linguists, and philosophers who have touched on some aspect of magical communication, Austin and his speech act theory have been common reference points. This is especially true of the class of speech acts called *performative utterances*. Performative utterances are speech acts that *themselves* cause change immediately upon being spoken; they do not depend on a response or some other action being undertaken as a result of the utterance. In contrast to our speech-act example of a request for someone to ring a bell, a performative utterance creates the change *directly*.

The canonical example of a performative utterance is the pronouncement that a marriage has been made official, given by someone who has the authority to do so and who—crucially—performs the correct utterance in the correct context. A justice of the peace officiating at a wedding creates a change in the phenomenal world by saying "I now pronounce you man and wife" at the right moment. There is nothing more that must happen for the change to have taken place; the authority and the context are sufficient for the words to immediately have the intended effect. The same justice saying the same sentence drunkenly at a party does *not* have the same effect because the context does not satisfy what Austin called a *felicity condition*—an aspect of context that must be present for the utterance to perform its desired role. Some of Austin's further examples of performative utterances that are context- and authority-dependent include "I do (take this woman to be my lawful wedded wife)," as uttered in the course of a marriage ceremony, and "I name this ship the *Queen Elizabeth*."[8]

Each of these creates a change of condition *merely by being uttered*. They must be uttered sincerely and correctly. Many forms that performative utterances are required to take are prescribed exactly and any deviation from that renders them ineffective. For example, if you're sitting in the exit row of an airplane, when the flight attendant asks you if you are able and willing to perform the duties necessary in an emergency, you must answer by speaking the English word "Yes." Only this creates the contract required of those sitting in those rows. Anything else—a nod, "Sure," "No"—does not count, because it does not meet all the required felicity conditions.

Stanley Tambiah (see chap. 2) divided performative utterances happening in ritual contexts into two categories: *regulative* and *constitutive*.[9] The former regulate a preexisting activity that is independent of the rules being imposed on it. A mundane example would be the conventions and rules—the semiotic codes—that govern eating, an act that doesn't *require* a fork and knife and good table manners but nonetheless has had those imposed on it in some cultures and contexts. The association between the code and the act has become so strong that most people would not dare to eat around others without following those arbitrary rules of desirable conduct.* A *constitutive* performative act creates (and regulates) something that has no existence outside of the rules; for example, the rules for playing chess or baseball create those specific games even though there are other things that could be done with chess pieces or bats and balls. This is the case for many ritual acts involving performative speech: they have less or even no meaning outside of the ritual context, yet their correct and felicitous performance creates changes that persist even when the ritual has concluded.

Tambiah noted that ritual acts like the installation of a new chief, mortuary rites, a Catholic mass, and "a multitude of cosmic rites and festivals which are self-constituting events" all manifest as constitutive acts.[10] That is, they are based on performative speech that creates and confirms the significance of ritual acts that would otherwise be empty or even mundane gestures. Tambiah also emphasized that magic works according to different models and criteria for success and thus "should also be examined within a performative frame of social action."[11] This opens up a new way to understand magic's internal logic and purpose.

Tambiah primarily studied the magical and religious beliefs and practices of the Sinhalese and Tamil peoples of his native Sri Lanka. His observations apply beyond that culture and place, however. Let's look at one set of examples of using performative utterances from the modern Western magical tradition.

In *The Satanic Rituals* (1971), founder of the Church of Satan Anton Szandor LaVey included one of his most personal and important rituals: *Die Elektrischen Vorspiele* (The Electrical Preludes). There are many features of the "DEV" that showcase LaVey's showmanship, dramatic skill, and experimentation far beyond any more traditional form

---

*Whenever there is an emphasis on the "correct" performance of some common act, we are dealing with a ritual form even if there are no metaphysical or religious implications.

of magic.* Here, however, we'll look at some examples of performative utterances in the ritual (in chap. 8, we will look at other parts of it). In these examples, we will encounter various phrases that nearly always signal the occurrence of performative utterances (whether in semiurgic or mundane contexts).

For a performative utterance to occur in any situation, there must be sufficient authority and context for the speaker's words to carry that weight. In a magical ritual or ceremony, authority comes from sincere, intentional performance of the operation at hand; just reading it in a book, or performing it while joking around with your friends, is not enough. Some rituals or workings, of course, may require that the magician have certain authority, background knowledge, or state of initiation external to the rituals—for example, the magic ceremony for changing wine and bread into the blood and flesh of Jesus.

Now, let's look at a few examples from *Die Elektrischen Vorspiele*. The structure of the ritual has a single celebrant speaking the majority of the words and performing the bulk of the actions.

> *I decree that the glamour be lifted, revealing the face of the Serpent.*[12]

I decree is a phrase that almost always indicates performative speech—it is the statement of a fact or action that becomes a known fact or completed action through the utterance itself.

> *Think not, O men of mildewed minds, that ye can escape the great beasts by entering thy shrines. . . . I know them for I am as one with them.*[13]

This is a more subtle performative utterance; the phrase that trig-

---

*For a thorough history and analysis of *Die Elektrischen Vorspiele*, see chapter 6 of my book *Infernal Geometry and the Left-Hand Path*.

gers it is: *for I am as one with them*. In this instance, the celebrant declares kinship with the "great beasts" and thus claims knowledge of them that will be used as part of the ritual.

> *For know ye well, that the dwellers in the Abyss hunt souls like unto thine to hold in their thrall.*[14]

and

> *Know ye, all who dwell in the light of professed righteousness, that others who know the keys and the angles have opened the gate, and for turning back there is not time.*[15]

Both of these use the same form—the phrase *know ye* [*well*]—to create performative speech, so we can analyze them together. *Know ye* is similar in form and intent to *I decree*; the primary difference is that in this instance the speaker is directing the utterance at specific recipients (or recipients who share some quality or belief). The speaker alters the knowledge and experience of the recipients through the performative utterance.

Performative utterances are a class of communicative acts that produce change in the state of the world or our knowledge of the world. Even for those who are unwilling to accept the usefulness of conceptual models that provide a basis for magical communication, performative speech provides a model for how language can have a quantifiable effect on reality. It does this through no other actions than merely being spoken in the correct context by someone with the correct and context-dependent authority.

The House of Being

Martin Heidegger (1889–1976) was one of the most significant philosophers of the twentieth century.* While his primary preoccupation

---

*He is also one of the most controversial, due to choices and statements he made as an academic in Nazi Germany, but a discussion of that complicated issue is outside the scope of the present book.

was the question of Being—why is there Being instead of nothing and what is the nature of Being?—Heidegger also looked deeply at language and its role in helping us to better understand and discuss Being. A full examination of Heidegger's complex and multifaceted philosophy is far beyond the scope of this book; however, some of his ideas about the intersection of language and Being will help us to understand what it means to transform the magician as part of the pursuit of creating more effective magic.

Restating some of our themes in Heideggerian terms, to know ourselves is to know that we each possess and embody Being, and to transform the magician is to gain greater clarity and expression of ourselves and Being.

Heidegger was especially concerned with the distinction between Being—the mysterious essence of existence itself—and things that *have* Being, which we can call "beings." (In English translations of Heidegger, the standard convention is to capitalize Being when referring to the concept of Being itself; when referring to things that possess or exhibit Being—often called beings in English—the lowercase form is used. Heidegger called this distinction between *Being* and *beings* the "ontological difference.") Being cannot be *a* being, otherwise it would simply be yet another thing that *has* Being. This is similar to how I as an author have "authorness"—whatever particular properties create "authorness," this "authorness" itself cannot *be* an author.

Heidegger referred to us as *Dasein*, never as human beings. *Dasein* is a German word indicating "existence," composed of *da* ("there") and *sein* ("Being"). He considered humans to be unique in that we are creatures who are not always absorbed fully in the moment—we can easily be taken out of the present moment and instead focus on other things that consume our attention.* From a magical point of view, we

---

*Such as any time we find ourselves contemplating the nature of Being, or even with mundane examples like obsessing over whether you remembered to lock the door to your house while you're at work.

can *choose* to see ourselves as other than we are, with the capacity for self-directed, self-willed change. In other words, *Dasein* can perceive and modify its relation to the world by how it manifests Being through language.

For Heidegger, language was one of the essential tools for discovering and understanding Being, as when he observed:

> Language is the house of Being. In its home man dwells. Those who think and those who create with words are the guardians of this home. Their guardianship accomplishes the manifestation of Being insofar as they bring the manifestation to language and maintain it in language through their speech.[16]

To understand why language holds this special place in Heidegger's philosophy, we have to look at his concept of tools and tool use. To him, a tool is far more than just a hammer or the machinery we typically think of today; it is *anything* created by *Dasein* that mediates our experience of the world. A tool is anything that extends—or transcends—our immediate embodied senses to bring us information about the world, or provides us with a way to affect the world and its inhabitants. Thus, tools are something we use to reveal or manifest Being.

This mediation and the tools that work through it, much like a window or even a television, are invisible to us while we use them—we focus on what *effects* they are having rather on the tools and the mediation processes themselves. This transparency is the same whether the tool is concrete like a hammer or abstract like language (or magic). But, *Dasein* that we are, we can *choose* to focus our attention on the tools themselves—recall that in the case of language, this "turning language on itself" is called *reflexivity* (see Hockett's design principles above). By doing this, we become not just passive users of the specific tools but can understand and improve them; as with all things created by humans, humans can change them (some more easily than others, as in the case of large-scale cultural and social institutions).

We've already looked at how we continually recreate meaning through the use of language; that is, meaning is not inherent in words themselves but in the ways that we use them. For Heidegger, language is used for the manifestation of Being, giving it continual expression. Being exists without humans of course, but the understanding and relationship with Being that is unique to *Dasein* is possible through language. In this continual recreation of Being *as understood by and through Dasein*, we use the tools of language to shape our understanding of the world as an expression of Being.

LANGUAGE-GAMES
AND BEETLES IN BOXES

The final philosopher of language we will discuss in this chapter is the Austrian Ludwig Wittgenstein (1889–1951). One of Wittgenstein's central concepts is *language-games*: context-specific uses of language and other aspects of communication that seem to have "rules" that we play somewhat analogously to a game as part of communicating and creating meaning.[17] Language-games also emphasize another core notion in Wittgenstein's philosophy: meaning is use. That is, if we use words in a specific way, and they are then part of a successful communication, then the words carry that meaning. This is one of the core ways that words shift in their expected meaning(s) over time (and through the meaning we bring to the words we use as part of a ritual or other semiurgic act, we adopt this flexibility in meaning for our own magical purposes).

A further wrinkle in finding the "true" meaning of words is the contrast between *descriptive* meaning and *expressive* meaning. Consider these two sentences:

The woman stood in a clearing in the woods and shouted beneath the night sky.
The magician bellowed an incantation to the Seven Stars in a sacred grove within the darkest of forests.

Both could describe the same person doing the same thing, but they likely bring very different pictures to mind. They express different things about the situation being described. These alternate impressions that words call up are called *senses*. As we've already discussed several times, we always must account for context to know which sense of a word is being used. The thing that a sense points to in a given context is called a *referent*—the sense captures some aspect of how you feel about the referent, or what other associations that sense calls up when you hear it or read it. In a profane sense you may just hear the ringing of a bell in a ritual, but you intentionally invest that ringing with meaning that calls forth the significance of the bell; you transform the bell from an indexical sign to a symbolic sign, and by this transformation you add to the sign network (or semiotic web) you are building to carry forth your magic.

Multiple words or phrases can refer to a single referent; for example, "that book" and "my grimoire" can both refer to the same text, but the second expression evokes something quite different from the first in the mind of the reader. This book uses *magic* in a specific sense, which may be different from the sense(s) you had for magic prior to reading it. Senses for words can be closely related to metaphorical or symbolic uses for words; this is one of the reasons the language used as part of the language-game called magic often differs from that used in everyday circumstances. The meaning and associations called up by the different senses of words in this context contribute to the purpose and effectiveness of the ritual; they do this by setting the ritual apart into its own context and meaning space. Learning this language of magic is not just about learning a new definition or sense for these words, but also adjusting your own relationship to the senses you already had for them.

Now let's take a closer look at language-games. These uses of language work with the implied, and often fluid, rules that apply to using language in a particular context or situation. The term "language-game" is *not* meant to imply that language is trivial or "just a game."

Think about the exclamation "Water!" Depending on the language-game (i.e., context-specific use of language), it could be:

- an order or emphatic request
- the response to a question
- a warning that you're about to fall into a river
- a password you're providing so you can enter a speakeasy

As you can see, this is related to the idea of a sense of word, which is also context-specific. And as there is no one sense of a word that is *the* meaning, Wittgenstein argues that the meaning of a word is entirely dependent on how it can be used in a language-game. That is, the meaning of words comes down to how we use them in successful communication.

Linguistic communities (or speech communities) are collections of language users who use language with similar norms and expectations. You are part of multiple speech communities, depending on the different contexts and people you communicate with. Some communities are more or less permanent, like your family; others last just long enough for you to order your morning coffee using that particular language-game.

As an example, let's take a brief look at the linguistic community that is magicians who work with the Renaissance system of angelic magic commonly known as Enochian (see chap. 8 for a more in-depth look at Enochian and the ones who originally received it, John Dee and Edward Kelley). This linguistic community speaks about such strange things as tablets, quadrants, Keys, and Aethyrs in specific ways with particular intent.

Before meeting or interacting with others who work these ideas and techniques, you had most likely read about Enochian in various sources—perhaps a secondary source like Egil Asprem's *Arguing with Angels* or the works of Stephen Skinner, or a primary source like a reprint of Dee's actual diaries. You probably made a good bit of progress based on the way that reading about and working with this system gave you an understanding of what it was about. You likely came to understand it in an even deeper sense when you began to see and talk about how these ideas were used by others. In other words, you experienced some of the different ways that members of the loosely organized Enochian magic linguistic community understand and work with this system, and this taught you new ways to work with and talk about these ideas.

As you communicate with others in this linguistic community, you gain a deeper understanding of the different ways in which they use words which may have other meanings in a different context. Even if, for example, no one defines for you what a key is in this context, you will get a sense of what it means by how the word is used; the more frequently and consistently the word is used, the more quickly you will put together what things these usages have in common. These commonalities reveal what Wittgenstein called "family resemblances" (which we can also call "cluster concepts"): you recognize similarities and repeated patterns to the point where you intuitively see two ideas as being of similar kind.

We come to have working knowledge of what a word means—that is, how to use it in a sentence in a particular situation—through cluster concepts instead of rigid definitions. For example, there may not be any one thing that all games have in common, but they all share at least some things with other members of the group of things understood to be games. These connections enhance the possibilities of what could be considered a game.

Not all things in common in a cluster concept are equal, however. Some are central, and some are on the fringe so that some games would include them, but others would not. Is football a game? Definitely yes. But a sword fight? Seeing how long you can hold your breath underwater? It is not clear whether those count as games, even though they certainly seem to have some game-like characteristics.

What this highlights is that language is a living phenomenon. It changes, and what exactly the words mean to individuals in a given language-game will change. Words take on new shades of meaning and lose others. New ways of expressing thoughts come about as a result and can be leveraged within semiurgy.

Wittgenstein emphasized that meaning is use. As long as a linguistic community uses a word in particular way, *then it has that meaning* (at least within the contexts shared by that linguistic community). This community may or may not span all the speakers of a particular language: think about how many words are strange or unknown to you if listening to a conversation between people a couple of generations younger or older than you. Language use is part of identity; we know others are like us—or compatible with us—in some way because we can communicate effectively with them in the context of the linguistic communities we share. I don't need to be very much like the barista at Starbucks to get the right drink; that short-lived and relatively well-known linguistic game only has one specific purpose and a limited number of expected or possible "moves." I do need to be *enough* like other magicians—or linguists, or semioticians, or writers, or musicians—that they can recognize me as one of their own, so that they recognize me as part of their linguistic community by the ways I use words. *The way we use words is in effect a proxy, an externalization, for part of our identity.*

And so now about that beetle, the subject of a famous thought experiment suggested by Ludwig Wittgenstein.

Let's imagine that every person has a box, and that the box contains *something*. Never mind where the box or its contents came from; what counts is that it is yours and yours alone. Now, suppose we all use the word "beetle" to refer to that thing in our box, but here's the catch: no one can ever look inside someone else's box. You are the only one who can see what your box contains.

Since you can never see inside anyone else's box, and no one else can see inside yours, *we have no way to prove whether the contents of any two boxes are really the same.* The word "beetle" has a difficult time being meaningful in this context: you have no way to verify what others mean by this word, and they have no way to verify what you mean.

This calls to mind what we discussed earlier with our brief look at the German theologian Rudolf Otto. One of Otto's central ideas is that language is inadequate for precisely communicating and describing internal states. He employed the word *numinous* to describe a feeling or experience not based on sensory experience or reason, the feeling of encountering something wholly or entirely other. This feeling, even if triggered by something external, is something only known in all its detail and nuance to yourself; other concepts or experiences are inadequate to use as points of reference.

Minds are like boxes that no one else can see inside: it doesn't matter if we can try to give a rigid, irrefutable definition for "beetle"; "beetle" in this case simply means "what's in the box." As with all words, it's merely a label for a particular concept, or category of concepts, in our minds. This having been established, Wittgenstein argued that we therefore can't refer directly to an internal state. Instead, we must refer to aspects of it that are observable by others. You can't see my stomach pain, but you can see me grab my stomach, hear me moan, and then infer that my stomach hurts (even if I don't say the words "my stomach hurts"). You can do this because you can imagine what internal experiences of your own could lead to the production of signs like this. That is, pain isn't just the internal feeling of physical suffering, it's also those behaviors that can be observed. *Once a concept is externalized in language, the concept is no longer limited to just its internal referent.* This is the same mechanism by which we use magic to carry forth our inner desires and transformations out into the world beyond ourselves.

In the last two chapters, we have presented a broad overview of important thinkers and ideas in semiotics, linguistics, and the philosophy of language. These concepts reveal more nuance in the ways that we can practice semiurgy with precision and depth. Armed with an understanding of cultural semiotic codes, socially created meaning, and the conceptual mechanisms that enable us to use signs and language in both mundane and magical ways, we can now take a detailed look at the history of mythological approaches to magical communication. This will be the final piece that helps us to assemble a comprehensive theory of semiurgy and set the stage for the three "case study" chapters that conclude the main text of the book.

FURTHER READING

Course in General Linguistics by Ferdinand de Saussure (Roy Harris translation)

How to Do Things with Words by J. L. Austin

Key Thinkers in Linguistics and the Philosophy of Language, edited by Siobhan Chapman and Christopher Routledge

Magic, Power, Language, Symbol: A Magician's Exploration of Linguistics by Patrick Dunn

On the Way to Language by Martin Heidegger

Wittgenstein on Mind and Language by David G. Stern

5

LANGUAGE, MYTH, AND MAGIC

I n chapter 2, we took a broad look at the history of ideas in anthropological approaches to magic and religion from the mid-nineteenth century onward. Historically, the precise line between magic and religion has been difficult to draw. As we saw especially with the nineteenth-century anthropologists, many of them took a dismissive view of the beliefs and practices of so-called primitive peoples and this introduced biases that confused matters further. Patricia Cox Miller notes:

> The term "magical" is problematic because of a negative theological bias that the word still carries from antiquity. What was called "magical" was considered by an earlier generation of scholars to be a debased form of religion in which conjuration replaced contemplation and arrogance toward the gods replaced humble submission to them.[1]

Newer attitudes in anthropology, while they have not removed this sort of bias entirely, have shifted in many parts of the discipline toward understanding different cultures on their own terms and respecting their unique expression of what it means to be a human. One of the ways this shift has happened is through coming to view mythology—and the religious and magical beliefs and practices that are illustrated by it—as containing essential truths and cultural blueprints instead of just being inept science.

As we saw with the discussion of Roland Barthes in chapter 3, mythological thinking pervades even modern cultures. He sought to remind us that these codes embedded in modern myths can easily be used *against* us if we forget that they are there. In Barthes's view, myths are a form of communication, but they communicate meaning in layers. The layers hidden beneath the surface are much harder to perceive, but because they are deeper they are more likely to be accepted without being subjected to critical thinking (and thus can "hide" narratives we subscribe to without even being aware of them).

In this chapter, we will look at various mythological figures and narratives to see how a clear reverence for language and especially writing have been revealed through them. Many of these also refer to knowledge of the written and/or spoken word as a powerful tool for affecting the world in mysterious ways—what we have variously called operative communication, semiurgy, or magic.

MYTHOLOGY AND STORYTELLING

The first thing to understand about mythology, especially the mythology of ancient peoples, is that it is *not* primarily a misguided or ill-informed attempt at science. That view of mythology was put forth by nineteenth-century anthropologists, who took a dim view of any culture that did not possess the technology and scientific knowledge they did—especially in the areas subjugated to the empires of Western Europe.

Mythology is a core component of symbolic (ethical) culture, preserving what matters to a given culture about the structure of society and also about the creation of the world and its inhabitants. Myths capture what is important about the makeup of the world and how the gods relate to and interact with people. The stories of mythology serve to give people a way to participate in that mythology. By telling or hearing these stories—and identifying with them through seeing our individual lives as part of the eternal story of myth—we reinforce a particular attitude toward the cosmos and mankind's place within it.

Language makes mythology possible, as it is dependent on the crucial abilities of talking about language itself (i.e., significance revealed through reflexivity), and of talking about those things that are not present in the current space and time (i.e., displacement, or revealing the mythic time outside of time). The stories could have been merely acted out, or portrayed through art, but those would for the most part only capture description, not meaning. However, language adds an otherwise impossible dimension to the narrative as it builds on the way of conceptualizing and describing what is ideal in ways that help to make it real.

Despite our modern use of science and technology for knowing and shaping the world around us, mythology is far from dead even if it may seem that way from a materialist perspective. In the United States we still have—and many still believe in—the "American dream" or the myths about what the Founding Fathers did or didn't intend when they wrote the Constitution. There is also the myth of progress, common throughout the Western world, which is the idea that social concerns will somehow evolve toward their ideal states (which is rather difficult when we have such widely divergent ideas about what those states *should* be). Sometimes ancient myths are recast in modern forms, such as the use of imagery from the myth of Europa and Zeus by the European Union to promote pan-European identity.

Storytelling—whether of cosmic importance like the stories of mythology, or about things on a lesser scale that are nonetheless still worth preserving—connects us with the past to help us see it as relevant to the present. That is, hearing a story and now being able to retell it (perhaps with your own embellishments or interpretations) makes you a *part of* the story. Sometimes it's almost as if we, meme machines that we are, were created so that the kinds of memes we call stories and myths could spread and change over time.

When a story—or myth or meme—changes our outlook, or inspires us to create something new or shape the world to our liking, this is not just storytelling but a form of story-*enacting*. Ultimately, we have used language—via the ideas that can be preserved and spread through it—to modify first ourselves (the inner world) and then impress that change on the outer world. This is the very essence of magic as a process of communication. Not every story is magic, but all magic first began as a story we told ourselves and then it became much more.

DIVINE FIGURES OF LANGUAGE, WRITING, AND MAGIC

Myths providing divine origins for writing and sometimes even language itself are found throughout the world. Most of these are not supported by many surviving records and so there is a limit to what can be said about them with certainty. A few, however, are fairly well documented, such as the ones we will focus on in this chapter.

Thoth

The ancient Egyptian deity Thoth (*Ḏḥwtj*) was strongly associated with writing and language. He was normally depicted with the head of an ibis, but occasionally shown as a seated baboon accompanied by a reed pen and other scribe's tools. He was a mediator in divine disputes, most famously in the conflict between Horus and Set in the Osiris myth cycle. It was also Thoth who recorded the results of the weighing of the heart of the deceased against the feather of Ma'at; this was done to determine whether the soul of the deceased would receive safe passage to the afterlife or be devoured by the monster Ammit.

The influence of Thoth on later ideas about the connection between language and language is profound. He was synthesized with the Greek Hermes to create Hermes Trismegistus ("Thrice-Greatest Hermes") as the legendary author of the texts collectively known as the *Hermetica*, the foundations of Hermetic philosophy and magic. We will look more closely at the Hermetica and related practices in chapter 6.

Thoth was the recorder of all events in the cosmos. Following from his earlier association with the moon, he also oversaw the reckoning of time. This recording role was sometimes extended to bringing events *into being* through the act of writing them down. He also ordered the world by writing down laws—in effect, everything he wrote functioned as a performative utterance (see chap. 4).

Thoth's origins in Egyptian myths are sometimes connected with the advent of language itself; he was the first thought (or utterance) of Ra and arose from thought itself. In other accounts, where he was associated with perception and reason, he thought or spoke *himself* into being—an idea very resonant with J. G. Fichte's "self-positing *Ich*" that we discussed in chapter 3. In addition to connections with writing and language, Thoth is strongly associated with *ḥkꜣ* (*heka*): magic, or what Egyptologist Herman te Velde called *practical theology*.[2] Greek philosophers familiar with Egyptian religion also connected Thoth with *Logos*, the principle of rational discourse and the reasoned understanding of order in the cosmos. In line with the concept of *Logos*, *heka* is not "the word of creation itself, but the mysterious energy which is also expressed in the word of creation."[3] Thus, *heka* is deeply associated with the creation (and maintenance) of the cosmos itself through the power of language to describe or shape the cosmos.

Thoth and Heka

In addition to being a term analogous to what we would call magic (specifically in the way this book is using the term), Heka was also the name of a god that personified this concept of practical theology. Heka was a very ancient figure in Egyptian religion, referred to even in the Coffin Texts (funerary spells written on coffins), which date as far back as 2100 BCE. In spell 261 of the Coffin Texts, he is said to have existed even before duality had yet come into being.[4]

Thoth was called great in *heka*, the lord of *heka*, and learned in *heka*. *Heka* was a dynamistic—energy-based—force associated with the divine itself, and could be obtained by consuming it from the gods. *Heka* was protective magic—especially against scorpions and snakes— but also used as part of postmortem deification in the Duat (the under- world through which the deceased passed, guided by the text popularly known as the *Book of the Dead*). The utility of *heka* in operative com- munication comes through clearly in Thoth's actions concluding the ritual known as the opening of the mouth; this ritual reactivated the senses of the deceased and gave them the power of magical speech so that they could utter the incantations necessary to gain safe passage through the Duat.

Thoth teaches *heka* not only to the other gods but also to humans through his books of wisdom; humans were taught to use it to create incantations and other charms in acts of operative communication. Amulets depicting Thoth were thought to confer and contain *heka* itself—a combination of Frazer's laws of similarity and contagion in practice.

The Egyptian conception of what we would today call the soul was far more complex than the Christian concept of the soul, which was largely inherited from the Greeks. Most Egyptian funeral texts consid- ered that the soul was composed of eight or nine parts that formed an interconnected whole. The *kꜣ* (*ka*) is directly related to the concept and practice of *heka*—the *-ka* in *heka* explicitly references this part of the soul.

The presence of the *ka* determined the difference between life or death—it is a reflection of the combination of all aspects of the body/ soul complex, which can then be projected onto the world and also within the psyche of the individual. The *ka* could remain distinct, coher- ent, and eternal as long as it was nourished properly (this was symbolized by food and drink offerings given to the dead). This coherence, and the effect that the *ka* has on the world, were created and sustained through *heka*, the "consecrator, the initiator, or the strengthener of the *ka*."[5]

The engendering of the *ka* as part of the soul of a person mir- rors the creation of the cosmos itself, both occurring as a result of the descriptive and transformative power of *heka*. Thus, work directed at the *ka*—the coherence of self as the active presence in the world—also leads to becoming a more effective and powerful magician.

Hermes and Mercury

The Greek god Hermes and the Roman god Mercury are very closely related, with Mercury taking on many characteristics resulting from a synthesis first with the Etruscan god Turms and later with Hermes. Both Mercury and Hermes functioned in their respective host cultures as gods of communication: patrons if not inventors of language and writing, acting as messengers between the gods and humanity and mediating between that which is above and that which is below. Additionally, Mercury was the patron of commerce—the exchange of goods instead of the exchange of words. Both gods also functioned as psychopomps (guides for the postmortem travels of souls) and tricksters (gods or other numinous figures who use trickery and secret knowledge to defy social norms).

As gods of communication, they were closely associated with magic. The magical practices of late antiquity in the Mediterranean world bear many communicative features with a focus on written as well as spoken forms. For example, *defixiones* (or "curse tablets") were literally letters to the underworld, typically written on thin sheets of lead and deposited into subterranean locations such as chasms, graves, wells, and caves. The intent was that the numinous beings of the chthonic realm would assist with the fulfillment of the curse (or other spell). Many spells in the Greek Magical Papyri (see chap. 6) contain carefully crafted invocations that intentionally diverge from everyday speech, in addition to having the magician write various magical words on specific materials that the magician would wear (or otherwise use as part of the spell). These same spells and curse tablets often call on regional gods of communication, including Hermes, Mercury, and Thoth—not to ask these deities to perform the work but to invoke and emulate their ability to change the objective universe through the power of speech and writing.

Hermes was often cast in the role of the teacher of magical techniques or revealer of magical items; as such, the magician would call on him to communicate the necessary knowledge for the act at hand. This function of Hermes appears in Homer's *Odyssey*, when Odysseus learns from Hermes about a secret herb for repelling the evil magic that Circe was working on him and his men.

From 305 BCE to 30 BCE, the final dynasty of pharaohs in Egypt was in fact Greek in origin (several of the last dynasties had also been of foreign origin). The founder of this dynasty, Ptolemy I Soter ("the savior"), lent his name to what has since become known as the Ptolemaic kingdom. This period of intense cultural exchange between Greece and Egypt transformed both sides and resulted in two syncretic figures who loomed large in Egyptian magic: Hermes Trismegistus ("Thrice-Great Hermes," sometimes called Hermes-Thoth) and Set-Typhon (the unfathomably ancient Egyptian god Set merged with Typhon, the monstrous serpent who challenged Zeus himself for supremacy among the gods).

As we will examine more closely in the next chapter, Hermes Trismegistus was the patron of what has become broadly known as Hermetic magic. He was credited with writing various books and other works that assimilated practices as varied as astrology (borrowed from Babylonian sources but given a distinctively Greek flavor), the beginnings of alchemy, and other forms of esoteric knowledge and magical practices. A related set of practices, commonly known as Hermetic philosophy, focused on the initiation of the individual into ever more rarefied states of being and perhaps even deification.

Mercury, while intentionally sharing many characteristics with Hermes, still has his own unique stories and characteristics as well. One interesting role showing divine communication of a different sort was his part in the manifestation of dreams. Morpheus was the creator of dreams in the valley of Somnus, but the dreams did not remain there. According to the Roman writer Ovid, one of Mercury's roles was to carry those dreams from the valley to sleeping humans—a gift from the gods delivered by the divine messenger, bridging the realm of the gods and the realm of humans.

Odin

Odin was a prominent god among the pre-Christian Germanic peoples. By the time of the late pre-Christian period in Scandinavia and Iceland he was undeniably the chief god of the Æsir, the gods largely associated with consciousness (the other main tribe being the Vanir, who were generally gods of agriculture and fertility).

Alongside his well-known affinity for war and battle, Odin is also closely associated with poetry, language, and the runes (see chap. 7). Odin is the central figure in the Norse myth of the creation of humanity: the story of Askr (an ash tree) and Embla (an elm, or perhaps a pithy vine).[6] In this myth, Askr and Embla receive from Odin and his brothers various gifts that form parts of their soul, including *önd* ("breath," necessary for life and for speaking poetry) and the same *óðr* ("inspiration") that is the essence of Odin's name (Óðinn).

Odin's name in the Proto-Germanic language has been reconstructed as *Wōðanaz*, which means "master of inspired mental activity." As can be seen in various myths concerning Odin, that inspired mental activity brings about results ranging from poetry and carving runes to inciting war (and many things in between). He does all this in pursuit of the very mysteries of the cosmos itself, exemplified by his knowledge of the runes and the sacrifice of his eye to the Well of Mímir to gain secret knowledge.

Odin is a multifaceted god who is known by many nicknames (Old Norse *heiti*), each revealing some aspect of his often-contradictory character. Odin's true nature is polarian, oscillating between poles of extremes always in the pursuit of knowledge. Some of the nicknames attributed to him reveal these contradictions. He is called both All-father (*Alföðr*) and Eunuch (*Geldnir*); Blind One (*Blindr*) and Flaming Eye (*Báleygr*); Spear-Shaker (*Biflindi*) and Battle-Wolf (*Hildólfr*), but also the less violent-sounding Father of Magical Songs (*Galdrafoðr*);

Sleep-Bringer (*Sváfnir*) and Awakener (*Vakr*); father of the slain (*Valföðr*) yet also protector (*Olgr*).

In a well-known episode from the poem *Hávamál* in the *Poetic Edda*, Odin hung on the world tree for nine nights without food or drink, sacrificing himself to himself with his own spear, until at the moment of death he was suddenly infused with knowledge of the runes—the mysteries of the cosmos. As we will discuss at length in chapter 7, the term *rune* was not originally used to refer to the characters in a system of writing but rather meant a *mystery*—not an everyday mystery like where your keys have got off to, but a mystery of deeper importance—the sort that in many cases we can never fully solve but can nonetheless be transformed through pursuing. Seeking after such profound mysteries opens the door not only to those portions of the mysteries of existence you can unravel, but also leads to that knowledge and experience you must gain as a result of this quest.

Odin and Mediterranean Gods of Communication

In the Roman historian Tacitus's text *Germania*, which is a compilation of secondhand information about the Germanic tribes written in the first century CE, Odin is not mentioned by name; however, the god referred to as Mercurius (Mercury) is clearly Odin (or at least a proto-Odinic figure). It was common in ancient Greece and Rome to interpret the gods of foreign cultures in terms of the nearest Greek or Roman equivalent. The fact that Tacitus identified Mercury and not Jupiter (the supreme god in the Roman pantheon) as the analog to Odin is telling: many of the areas of interest associated with Mercury—such as communication, protection of boundaries, travel, guiding some souls to the afterlife—are easily seen in various myths about Odin.

Writing as a gift or instrument of the gods was a common theme in the ancient world. While the Latin and Greek alphabets (and their predecessors) did not retain divine associations with their origin, writing and communication in general were still strongly associated with

Mercury and Hermes. Odin did not invent the runes; rather, he *discovered* them, after which he began to teach them.

These connections were surely not lost on the first runemaster, the one who through contact with the Roman world (probably as a mercenary) borrowed not only some of the symbols of alphabets from the Italian peninsula, but also the mythological and magical associations with the idea of writing itself. As we will see in chapter 6, the practices recorded in the Greek Magical Papyri—which have origins overlapping with the likely timeframe of the origin of the runes—were systems of operative (magical) communication in their very conception. There are many parallels between these systems and the ideas of operative communication embodied in runes. Whether these are the result of borrowing, or simply independent evolutions of ideas that are similar because of the way that human minds work, is a question that is impossible to answer at this late date. Nonetheless, we can compare these parallels to get a fuller sense of how communication, and especially written forms, could in the right contexts be viewed as divine and potentially magical.

In the beginning was the Word
The Gospel of John opens with this famous line in Koine Greek, intentionally echoing the phrase "In the beginning" which introduces the book of Genesis:

> ἐν ἀρχῇ ἦν ὁ λόγος, καὶ ὁ λόγος ἦν πρὸς τὸν θεόν, καὶ
> θεὸς ἦν ὁ λόγος
> (*En arkhêi ên ho lógos, kaì ho lógos ên pròs tòn theón, kaì
> theòs ên ho lógos*)

In the King James Bible, this line is translated as "In the beginning was the Word, and the Word was with God, and the Word was God."

While "word" can be a valid translation of λόγος (*logos*), depending on context, the Ancient Greek word was used in a variety of senses grouped around the concepts of speech, words, reason, and the results of wielding those concepts. *Logos* became a core idea in Western philosophy as well, beginning with the Greeks; the author of the Gospel of John was no doubt aware of and perhaps even had some training in Greek philosophy. Thus, λόγος did not just refer to a mundane word, but was the *transcendent word* that encapsulated the processes of philosophy (rhetoric, discourse, reason) that are inherent in comprehending the universe and our place within it. In other words, philosophy is in effect a process of learning to communicate more effectively with the world we find ourselves in—not dissimilar to the way we affect the world through language in both magical and mundane senses.

Etymologically, λόγος is also the root of the word *logic*, and it was one of the centerpieces of Charles Sanders Peirce's philosophy of pragmatism. Peirce's meticulous approach to semiotics shows this influence as well, seeking to understand semiosis as a form of rational discourse with the world within and beyond the self. All living things constantly engage in semiosis, but when we—the signifying animal—apply reflexivity to semiosis (i.e., use signs such as words as part of understanding, describing, and adding meaning to semiosis) we are also exercising λόγος.

The deep influence of Logos within the Western philosophical tradition can be seen in the final version of Goethe's *Faust, Part I.* Faust contemplates the meaning of the New Testament and decides to translate the original Greek into his native German. His Bible opens to the first verse of the Gospel of John and he begins with the traditional translation: "In the beginning was the Word." Realizing that "word" was for him inadequate to express the entirety of what he perceived in the original meaning of λόγος, he then tries the alternative translation "In the beginning was the Thought." Closer perhaps, but to Faust this sense of Mind is more reflective than creative (in that it cannot create directly in the world but requires a medium of some sort). He next arrives at "In the beginning was the Power." Satisfying perhaps, especially for those with a certain force of will, but still missing some nuance lost from the original Greek. Finally, he sees that Word, Mind, and Power stop short of actual Deeds; they won't have true effect in the world until made tangible through the Deed. "In the Beginning was the Deed"—the culmination of Word, Mind, and Power made into an active force within the world.

OTHER CONNECTIONS BETWEEN MYTH AND LANGUAGE

The Babylonian Creation Myth in the Enūma Eliš

Our examples so far in this chapter have been from the Mediterranean and European worlds. Egypt was not the only significant philosophical and religious influence on Ancient Greece. The Greeks also notably drew from the Zoroastrian religion of Persia and from the Babylonian culture (including its religion and well-developed practice of astrology).

Mesopotamia—from a Greek word meaning "land between the rivers" (i.e., the Tigris and the Euphrates)—was the ancient name for the region in the Fertile Crescent now known as the country of Iraq. In the millennia before the Common Era, Mesopotamia was dominated at different times by various civilizations within it. The Sumerian civilization was the earliest known one in the region, dating to perhaps as early as ca. 5500 BCE; Sumer is also the source of the earliest known form of writing, a proto-cuneiform system that later developed into classical cuneiform. We will come back to the Sumerian language later in this chapter in the section about the magic of language in modern stories.

Different kingdoms and empires arose, along with a great deal of variation and evolution in religion and mythology. By the time of the Second Babylonian Empire from 626 BCE to 539 BCE, centered around the city of Babylon, the Akkadian language (spread wide during a vast empire of the same name), had come to dominate the region. Unlike the older language Sumerian (which has no known relatives), Akkadian was a Semitic language.* The great Babylonian epic of creation, known

---

*The Semitic branch of the Afro-Asiatic language family includes Hebrew, Arabic, and Aramaic.

as the *Enūma Eliš*, prominently describes the role of language in the Babylonian cosmology and in the main stories within the epic: the creation of the world and the rise of Marduk as king of the gods (and of the universe). The text itself dates to as far back as the Old Babylonian period (ca. 1900–1600 BCE), with this long period of preservation showing how important the epic was to the founding of Babylon and its legitimacy as a regional power. We will not be summarizing the entire text, instead focusing only on parts that reveal something about the Mesopotamian understanding of language's role in myth.

The title *Enūma Eliš* is taken from the beginning of the first line of the epic in Akkadian; in English, this opening runs:

> *When skies above were not yet named*
> *Nor earth below pronounced by name,*
> *Apsu, the first one, their begetter*
> *And maker Tiamat, who bore them all,*
> *Had mixed their waters together.*
> *But had not formed pastures, nor discovered reed-beds;*
> *When yet no gods were manifest,*
> *Nor names pronounced, nor destinies decreed,*
> *Then gods were born within them.*
> *Lahmu (and) Lahamu emerged, their names*
> *pronounced.*[7]

We immediately see the cosmic power of words within the Babylonian religion, equating naming with existence itself. When the epic begins, there is no earth or cosmos, only Tiamat—the salt water of the sea, described as female—and the male Apsu as fresh water. As they mix their waters together, other gods emerge as they have their names assigned and pronounced. This alchemical mixing of waters reflects the region in which the epic was composed and shows its Sumerian roots: the earlier city-state of Sumer was located much closer to the Persian Gulf than the more northern Babylon, and the mythological importance of seawater carried forth as the regional religions evolved over the next several millennia.

Following the birth of Lahmu and Lahamu, more gods follow. Tiamat and Apsu find the noise they create too much to bear and long for peaceful sleep. Apsu and his advisor Mummu advocate killing these other gods so they can have some peace and quiet, although Tiamat the primordial mother of all is firmly opposed to this plan. It is significant that it is Mummu who proposes this plan; his name (a loan word from Sumerian) means variously "life-giving force" or "knowledge," and he is even much later equated with Logos by the Neoplatonists. In essence he is proposing a plan based purely on reason—if the noise bothers you, the logical response is to remove the thing making the noise—without regard to compassion or Tiamat's maternal feelings.

The god Ea—like Mummu, associated with knowledge and creation—discovers their plot and decides to counter it:

> *Ea who knows everything found out their plot.*
> *Made for himself a design of everything, and laid*
> *   it out correctly.*
> *Made it cleverly, his pure spell was superb.*
> *He recited it and stilled the waters.*
> *He poured sleep upon him so that he was sleeping*
> *   soundly,*
> *Put Apsu to sleep, drenched with sleep.*[8]

Here, we see the first of many references to spells—verbal magic. For a culture that regarded speaking something into being as the core act of creation (a type of *performative utterance*), it is not surprising that this idea also extends to further modifications to the results of these initial performative utterances.

Ea kills Mummu and Apsu and creates a dwelling—which he also names Apsu—on top of the fresh water. There, Marduk was born to Ea and his consort Damkina. Ea's father Anu—god of the night sky and its

constellations, and ancestor of many important Mesopotamian gods—
made Marduk "so perfect that his godhead was doubled. Elevated far
above them, he was superior in every way."[9]

Anu is important enough in terms of how the Mesopotamian religions were approached linguistically to be worth a small digression.
In addition to being the god of the night sky and the orderly nature
of the heavens, Anu was—for the Sumerian as well as Babylonian
religion—the source of the legitimacy of power for both gods and
kings.[10] The Sumerian cuneiform character ✳ representing his
name—the sign called *DINGIR*—was also a determinative* used to
indicate that *other* written names referred to gods and goddesses (e.g.,
✳⊣⟨▷⋉ for *ᴰTI.AMAT*). When written by itself, the sign ✳ can,
depending on context, either be a generic reference to a god, to Anu
himself, or to the night sky and its contents. Thus, the character is
both an iconic—resembling a star—and symbolic sign. This certainly
represents a celestial notion of divinity, with likely implications that
the apparent orderliness of the night sky is an archetype for an orderly
and successful rule on earth.

In addition to conferring full godhood on Marduk, Anu also creates four winds—a form of divine breath—for him to wield. These
winds are part of what enables Marduk to speak with the power of Anu
when the time comes.

Tiamat then attempts to promote the god Qingu† to be king of the
gods by speaking the correct spell, in turn granting him certain powers
of magical communication:

> *Then she gave him the Tablet of Destinies and made*
> *him clasp it to his breast*

---

*A determinative is a character which is added to the written form of a word to mark
some attribute of that word, but which does not alter its pronunciation. In the case of
✳, when it is used as a determinative and transcribed into the Latin alphabet it is written as a superscript ᴰ.

†Sometimes written as Kingu.

> *"Your utterance shall never be altered! Your word shall
> be law!"*
> *And Qingu was promoted and had received the*
> *Anu-power*[11]

The *Anu-power* is another reference to the divine kingship that can be conferred only by Anu, the embodiment of the slowly shifting order of the night sky—the *Anu*-power is an indexical sign pointing to Anu whenever it is wielded. Note here that Tiamat is merely asserting it for Qingu, but Anu has *not* in fact granted it (nor does Qingu have the four winds that Anu provided to Marduk to facilitate his divine speech). The meaning of Qingu's name is uncertain, but in Sumerian it may indicate an unskilled laborer[12]—hardly qualification for becoming king of the gods, although Tiamat's ennobling of Qingu was a necessary step in the ultimate ascension of Marduk to that throne.

The Tablet of Destinies is an important artifact as well, even though it is only briefly mentioned in the epic. Nonetheless, its possession for now by Qingu is an attempt by Tiamat to make all utterances of Qingu immediately binding and permanent; in other words, to make all his speech into performative utterances. However, recall from chapter 4 that performative utterances require that all relevant felicity conditions must be met. Qingu may possess the Tablet of Destinies, but his rule is not legitimate because it was not conferred by Anu; that is, he does not possess the divine speech necessary for his words to have the power they purport to have.

Ea witnesses this plot by Tiamat to invest Qingu with divine ruler-ship, and beholds the eleven monsters that she created to fight on her side. He reports back to his grandfather Anshar, who summons all the gods to seek the one who will confront Tiamat. Marduk responds to the call and agrees to be the champion of the gods if they will then recognize him as their ruler. After some doubts and negotiations, they agree, and proclaim through a performative utterance:

> *You are honoured among the great gods.*
> *Your destiny is unequalled, your word (has the power*
>   *of) Anu!*
>
> . . .
>
> *May your utterance be law, your word never be*
>   *falsified.*
> *None of the gods shall transgress your limits.*[13]

"May your utterance be law" creates iconic signs; the utterances manifest an immediate resemblance to law as they are uttered. The words that the other gods wrap Marduk in also become a symbolic sign that all will interpret as the legitimacy of his rule. The way they proclaim this is a deliberate echo of what Tiamat attempted to bestow on Qingu. The difference is this time the right to rule is being conferred legitimately (i.e., by consensus of the other gods, including Anu). But first, they demand of Marduk a test that will prove he truly has the Anu-power (the power of performative speech and dominion over the night sky). They ask that he will speak a word to cause a constellation to vanish, then speak again for it to reappear. Remember that constellations *were* Anu, and the word *Anu* can refer both to any generic god but also to the god of the night sky—conferrer of the right to rule—in particular. Thus, they are asking Marduk for proof that their proclamation worked and that he is able to bring forth Anu's own essence, which he was imbued with after birth. This ability to speak things in and out of being echoes the power of naming through performative utterances that opened the epic. By wielding divine speech to become himself a creator, Marduk fulfills the potential hinted at through the circumstances of the creation of the cosmos itself.

When Marduk leads a host to confront Tiamat, before they engage in battle, they first exchange various spells and counterspells. Marduk taunts Tiamat by telling her that her plot with Qingu was doomed because he did not legitimately possess the Anu-power or the Tablet of Destinies. After more spells and counterspells, Marduk unleashes the four winds that add even more potency to his speech as they create the opening for vanquishing her with weapons as well as words. He then creates the world from parts of her body; what Tiamat—the mother of chaos—had set in motion in the original creation of the cosmos still lives on through everything built on her foundation. Having killed Qingu as well, Marduk takes the Tablet of Destinies from him and entrusts them to Anu—a logical development given the Babylonians' role in the creation of astrology.

The final tablet of the epic describes fifty names for Marduk, showing that as king of the universe he presents a variety of faces, depending on needs and situations. In a connection to the very beginning of the epic (and thus of the universe), one of those names is Mummu—indicating that the life-giving force and supreme knowledge of the universe have now been transferred to Marduk. The epic concludes with a note from its scribe, who "wrote down the secret instruction which older men had recited in his presence, and set it down for future men to read"[14]—making it clear that the epic contains both exoteric and esoteric knowledge that can be read using the correct keys to uncover its meaning.

THE MAGIC OF LANGUAGE IN MODERN CREATIONS

Depictions of magic in fiction are ubiquitous today, especially since the publication of the *Harry Potter* series of books starting in 1997. Most depictions rely more on well-worn tropes than on studies of actual magical practices. However, there are some examples that are useful within the model of magic discussed here, focusing on divine figures of communication and the intersection between magic and language.

Lovecraft, Neomythology, and Magic

Ancient mythology is not the only place where we find references to divine figures of communication and magic. Just as traditional mythology is cosmic in scope—revealing culture-specific ideals about the creation, function, and inhabitants of the universe—neomythology is the creation of *new* stories that offer similar commentary on issues of cosmic importance. Not every work of fiction is neomythology, however. Neomythology can sometimes incorporate material from traditional mythology—like the Marvel comic book universe and Norse gods Loki or Thor, who only bear some resemblance to their older mythological accounts. More often, neomythology is created using mostly or entirely new elements (although because storytelling is built into our memory and cognition in such a deep way, even a new myth with new subjects will likely be reminiscent of other myths in terms of style and structure).

The fiction of H. P. Lovecraft—and others who wrote stories set in his so-called Cthulhu Mythos—features a prominent god who has features modeled on Hermes, Thoth, and perhaps even Odin: the messenger from Outer Gods, Nyarlathotep. Among the Outer Gods, only Nyarlathotep was said to communicate with humans in human languages. As the messenger he interacts with mankind in "forms and communication patterns they are able to comprehend while opening their eyes to wonders beyond the visible world."[15] In the eponymous story (from 1920) in which he is introduced, Lovecraft revealed that Nyarlathotep had "risen up out of the blackness of twenty-seven centuries, and that he had heard messages from places not on this planet."[16]

Nyarlathotep is the embodiment in the Mythos of the importance of communication and secret knowledge selectively shared with a lucky(?) few. Communication of esoteric and cosmically significant knowledge happens through a variety of media in Lovecraft's stories: the stars themselves, dreams, the fabled *Necronomicon* and other obscure books that may or may not exist, folklore, the Shining Trapezohedron, and so on. The *Necronomicon* has in recent years become another example of a hyperstition that has become real (see chap. 1); it has gone from card-catalog entries surreptitiously materializing in Yale University's library in the 1970s to various actual books each claiming to be the "real" *Necronomicon*. Since Lovecraft (and others in his circle who wrote about it) only ever hinted at its contents, who can say with certainty what it did or did not contain?

In his appearances in "Nyarlathotep" and "Dreams in the Witch-House," Nyarlathotep instructs humans in magic—another parallel with Hermes—and induces them to behave in ways often contrary to their own best interests. He is the bridge between the cosmic and the earthbound, appearing with many faces and guises. He does this not only to conceal his true identity but also to reveal different facets of the ways he can reach out to fulfill his mysterious mission—in this way he is much like Odin with his many *heiti* or nicknames (see above).

Sumerian Roots in Modern Creations

In part because of their unfathomable antiquity—and in part because of the region's importance as the birthplace of writing—the language, magic, and religion of Sumer have retained a certain cachet in modern times even as most people know very few details about them. While the true extent of the influence may never be discovered at this point, the location of Mesopotamia and its well-documented connections to the peoples of the Levant likely led to some impression on the Abrahamic religions; this would make Sumerian religion a distant antecedent of the dominant religions in the modern West.

The hyperstition of the *Necronomicon* finally became real in the late 1970s with the publication of the book by that name attributed to the mysterious Simon.* The text of this version of the *Necronomicon* combined various ideas from Lovecraft's works with Sumerian (and Babylonian) mythology. This was done to create something very different from the Book of Shadows–type witchcraft grimoires of the day (even though it still took inspiration from the forms of those books).

---

*Perhaps not so mysterious now; it is widely documented that Simon is Peter Levenda, a member of the New York City scene that was centered around the Magickal Childe bookstore in the 1970s. Levenda has continued to publish both fiction and nonfiction books on various occult subjects.

"Simon" has since published several other books related to this original *Necronomicon*, continuing to expand this syncretism of Mesopotamian and Lovecraftian deities and myths.

In a very different take on the eldritch horror and dim visions of the distant past that Sumerian religion can evoke, Neal Stephenson's pioneering 1992 cyberpunk novel *Snow Crash* centers in part on the implications of Sumerian writing and language in human thought processes. Through the discussions of the Sumerian language, its demise, and the "language virus" supposed to have been spread by the trickster god Enki,* the novel explores many ideas we have discussed (or at least alluded to) in this book: performative speech, universal grammar, and the various ways that words function as a tool for affecting reality.

Stephenson used the name of the Sumerian god Nam-shub (more commonly known as Asaruludu) as the word for a type of "speech with magical force."[17] Nam-shub was strongly associated with magical and medical incantations, though the exact meaning of his name is uncertain. In the novel, a *nam-shub* refers to a self-replicating linguistic or semiotic meme—ideas which once they take hold spread like a virus. These are intended in the novel as a form of *information hazard*: ideas which, even if true or beneficial in certain circumstances, have the potential to be harmful or lead to unexpected results when spreading on a large scale.

In the world of *Snow Crash*, the Sumerian language was once the *only* language and a direct expression of the deep structure of language within the human brain. Sumerian civilization had a foundation of divine decrees called *me*. These were instructions that governed various aspects of Sumerian life, divinely ordered and unalterable as they were encoded and preserved on clay tablets. The *me* tablets were entrusted to the god Enki to safeguard and distribute. Enki had learned how to wield the power of words to rearrange the cosmos:

---

*The older Sumerian form of the Babylonian god Ea, whom we encountered in the discussion of the Babylonian creation myth—the *Enūma Eliš*—earlier in this chapter.

He describes himself as follows: "I am lord. I am the one whose word endures. I am eternal." Others describe him: "a word from you—and heaps and piles stack high with grain." "He pronounces the name of everything created . . ."[18]

According to the novel, the reliance on *me* made the Sumerian people docile and unable to think for themselves, since the language only allowed them to access and express the older structures within the brain. What began as a metavirus—an archetype or pattern for making viruses, both linguistic and physiological—of unknown and possible alien origin had spread so thoroughly that the people could only perform a task or exercise a skill according to the *me* that was decreed for it.

Enki, who had gained the ability to alter and even create new *me*, created a neuro-linguistic virus—a *nam-shub*—to cut off the ability to understand Sumerian. The purpose of this was to spawn the creation of new and increasingly divergent languages as people began to think for themselves and break free from overreliance on divine utterances.

So he created the *nam-shub* of Enki, a counter-virus that spread along the same routes as the *me* and the metavirus. It went into the deep structures of the brain and reprogrammed them. Henceforth, no one could understand the Sumerian language, or any other deep structure-based language. Cut off from our common deep structures, we began to develop new languages that had nothing in common with each other. The *me* no longer worked and it was not possible to write new *me*. Further transmission of the metavirus was blocked.[19]

This event was described in the Bible as the Tower of Babel myth, "a gateway that was opened by the *nam-shub* of Enki that broke us free from the metavirus and gave us the ability to think—moved us from a materialistic world to a dualistic world—a binary world—with both a physical and a spiritual component."[20]

Sumerian then died out as a native language but lived on for at least a couple of millennia as a scholarly and liturgical language; through this the Sumerian myths live on as ideas embedded in other religions even as they are not always recognized as such. Thus, the mechanisms of conformity and control in the major religions of the West were seen as the embedded *me* in the mostly forgotten Sumerian roots of these religions. These survivals of a society run entirely by divine decree are kept from taking over the whole world due to the Babel factor, "the walls of mutual incomprehension that compartmentalize the human race and stop the spread of viruses."[21]

The novel develops as a showdown between a small group of hackers who have learned these forgotten bits of linguistic lore and the L. Bob Rife Bible Institute, led by a media mogul who has financed numerous archeological expeditions in the former Sumer. Rife's goal is to collect as many *me* as possible, and to unleash them along with the metavirus through his vast media network to re-enslave humanity, with him and his followers as its rulers (and as the only ones immune to the metavirus since they know its secrets). The hackers, on the other hand, seek to uncover the words of the *nam-shub* unleashed by Enki as a way to counteract Rife's plans.

From this brief synopsis of *Snow Crash*, especially seen in the context of the present book, we can see a number of ideas about the world-shaping power of semiotics and linguistic signs. Those who can wield them for true transformation, both within and beyond the self, can not only remake the world in the image of their own choosing. As importantly, they can also create a degree of immunity to the attempts by others to embed their own self-serving semiotic codes in our psyches— this is the same goal of the work of Roland Barthes as well, which we discussed in chapter 3.

In this chapter we looked at the deep relationship between mythology and language. In some cases, divine figures were said to have invented (or discovered) language, writing, or poetry (or to be the patron of those engaged in these pursuits). In other myths, ideas about language play a significant role in the narrative. Either way, just as myth often describes and preserves a culture's understanding of the creation and ideal structure of the cosmos and societies, thoughts about the language encoded in myth also form the background for how language—and poetry and writing—are understood in a particular cultural context.

Now we will turn to a brief interlude that describes the approach we will use to look at three case studies—extensive examples of specific techniques, theories, or schools of magic that we will examine in terms of our central thesis of the communicative nature of magic.

FURTHER READING

Language and Myth by Ernst Cassirer
Myth and Philosophy: A Contest of Truths by Lawrence J. Hatab
Myth: A Very Short Introduction by Robert A. Segal
Myths from Mesopotamia by Stephanie Dalley
The Egyptian Hermes: A Historical Approach to the Late Pagan Mind by
    Garth Fowden
The Rise and Fall of the Cthulhu Mythos by S. T. Joshi

INTERLUDE

....

The Methodology for the Case Studies

So far in this book, we've taken a deep dive into important ideas in the history of linguistics and semiotics which help us to understand the essential communicative function of magic. Borrowing a term from French sociologist philosopher Jean Baudrillard, I call this approach to magic *semiurgy*: the creation or manipulation of signs, linguistic or otherwise, to cause specific effects within the psyche of the magician. These effects can then be reflected in changes in the world of the real: the objective universe of matter, physical laws, and other self-aware inhabitants each seeking to understand and affect their surroundings through language and other systems of signs.

Now we will move beyond isolated examples to a collection of chapter-length case studies; these are extensive looks at specific methods, theories, or schools of magic with an eye toward understanding their core communicative features.

The intent behind these case studies is to show how to apply the ideas in this book to *any* magical school, paradigm, or approach to better understand it as a process of communication. My contention throughout is that virtually all forms of magic have communication at their core and that sometimes this core has been obscured by decades if not centuries of obfuscation, confusion, and misunderstanding. By following a methodology very much like that of Roland Barthes, I hope to "peel back" the outer layer of myth we have built up around such practices and provide a more direct look at what really forms the foundations for theory and practice within them.

6

MEDITERRANEAN MAGIC
IN ANTIQUITY

This is the first of the chapters that function as case studies, applying the various ideas we have discussed about linguistics, semiotics, and magic to specific techniques and magical practices. The focus of
this chapter will be the Mediterranean world in classical and late antiquity (roughly the eighth century BCE to the fifth century CE), a period
rife with magical thinking that has been widely studied in the last few
decades. Unlike the issues we will run into with discussing whether runes
were used in magical ways in the Elder Futhark period (see chap. 7),
scholars studying this time period in the Mediterranean world have no
problem acknowledging the widespread use of magic there.

As noted in the previous chapter, the Greek Hermes and Egyptian
Thoth were syncretized into the legendary figure Hermes Trismegistus
("Thrice-Great Hermes"). In the Ptolemaic period of Egypt (305 BCE
to 30 BCE), when the ruling dynasty was of Greek heritage, there was
a significant amount of religious and scientific interchange between
the two cultures. During this time, the striking similarities between
Hermes and Thoth led to a blurring of the lines between the two and
the attribution of writings on magic and philosophy to the combined

Hermes Trismegistus. This syncretism continued as Egypt became part of the Roman Empire following the death of Cleopatra VII—yes, *that* Cleopatra—in 30 BCE.

In this chapter we will look primarily at selections from the Greek Magical Papyri (*Papyri Graecae Magicae*, commonly abbreviated to *PGM*) and two texts from the Nag Hammadi library known as *The Thunder, Perfect Mind* and *The Discourse on the Eighth and Ninth*. These will not be line-by-line analyses, but instead will highlight specific lines or sections that illustrate some notable use of linguistic or semiotic concepts that form the basis these texts' magical communication. We will also examine the phenomenon of *defixiones* or curse tablets, actual letters inscribed on lead sheets and deposited into the chthonic realm in order to manifest their intent.

THE GREEK MAGICAL PAPYRI

History and Collection

Unlike the Nag Hammadi library, which we will look at later in this chapter, the Greek Magical Papyri (*PGM*) are not a single set of texts. While the texts classified as magical papyri span from the second century BCE to the fifth century CE, they have been assembled roughly in the same order as they have come to light through the antiquities trade beginning in the early nineteenth century. The *PGM* are a significant primary source about the magical practices of Greco-Roman Egypt; they are considered part of the broader body of texts known as the *Hermetica* (due to the frequency with which Hermes is addressed or appealed to by the spells).

Before we look at some of the individual spells, we must note a couple features of Mediterranean magic—both oral and written—that occur throughout the *PGM*. The first is the use of unpronounceable, or nonsense, words—variously called *voces magicae* ("magical names"), *ephesia grammata* ("Ephesian words"), or barbarous names. The second recurring feature is a form of magical signs incorporated into the text, called *charaktêres*, often found in Greek magical texts of the period.

Ephesia Grammata, Voces Magicae, and Barbarous Names

The Ἐφέσια Γράμματα (*ephésia grámmata*) were originally an inscription of six words—written in the Greek alphabet—of unknown origin and meaning on the temple of Artemis in her cult center of Ephesus.

ασκιον κατασκιον λιξ τετραξ δαμναμενευς αισιον

askion kataskion lix tetrax damnameneus aision[1]

The original group of words came to be regarded as an extraordinarily powerful magical formula to be used for a variety of purposes (e.g., ending possession by evil spirits, averting evil in general, bringing luck).[2] Speaking them aloud was the key: their power lay not in their meaning (which was unknown) but in their sound itself. These words were so famous that they occur in many magical writings in the ancient world, even in some early Christian texts. The term *ephesia grammata* was later extended to *any* unknown or unpronounceable words used a magical context, although the Latin phrase *voces magicae* is often used in scholarly works as a more generic name for all types of unpronounceable magic words.

Nonsense words are embedded in popular ideas of magic even today, ranging from "mumbo jumbo" as a description of words—magical or otherwise—that sound impressive but don't make sense, to the common "Abracadabra!" in stage magic. On *voces magicae* as a core feature of Mediterranean magic in antiquity, H. S. Versnel comments:

> The powerful sounds acquired an additional function as they were understood to be the secret names of mysterious deities invoked in the spells. In other words, we perceive a new *theogonia*, a process of explosive creativity in which divine powers emerge from powerful words. The names of these new gods and demons easily

amalgamated with other existing names that were also characteristic of magical formulas but which, from the beginning, were imagined as names of real gods or demons.[3]

Even more to the point, the Greek grammarian Diogenianus observed that "those who intoned them conquered in everything."[4] Who wouldn't want to use such words in their magical spells?

Recall the importance of naming things to call them into existence. We have seen this as far back as the early Mesopotamian religions all the way through to today. It is not certain whether the magicians of this period saw themselves as appealing to an otherwise unknown god for assistance or *creating*—at least for the duration of the magical act—an unknown god by naming it into existence. However, in either case the magician is externalizing something within themselves, calling it forth so that it can be communicated with; the resulting meaning from their conversation then creates the desired change by having spoken it into being.

As the signifying animal, we are always seeking to create patterns and significance out of the signs—linguistic or otherwise—that we encounter. Some combinations of nonsense syllables may remind us of other actual words, setting off the meaning-seeking mechanisms within our minds. Others help us to focus on the emotional instead of the intellectual content of what is being said.

Another related usage of words whose meaning is unknown to the magician using them is the concept of *barbarous names*, from the Greek βάρβαροι (*bárbaroi*) referring to those who did not speak Greek. These were generally transcriptions of foreign words into Greek; it's quite possible that many *voces magicae* are foreign words (or corruptions of foreign words) whose source and original form are simply unknown (or forgotten). These words automatically had some magical power by virtue of transgressing against the host culture of the magician; many Mediterranean cultures had a notion that the mysterious and the foreign were inherently magical.

The capacity for language is an integral part of the way that humans interact with and affect the world around them. This ability to create change through language is not always dependent on the meaning behind what is said; we can also reach beyond the rational parts of our minds through these various forms of phatic speech—speech that bypasses the normal ways of forming and recognizing meaning. In doing so, we integrate the rational with the nonrational, tapping into parts of ourselves that cannot be fully expressed in words.

Charaktêres

Charaktêres were a "non-semantic hieroglyphic system for ritual purposes."[5] They appear in a variety of magical texts and especially on amulets that also included images of gods (often Hermes). These look like random doodles but in fact were a systematic group of signs used as part of the written forms of otherwise spoken spells and rituals. They were a written parallel to the spoken *ephesia grammata* or *voces magicae*.[6]

The purpose of the *charaktêres* is perhaps best described from within the Greek Magical Papyri themselves, with this explanation from *PGM* I. 272–76* following a list of such glyphs:

> But be careful not to lose a leaf [and] do harm to yourself. For this is the body's greatest protective charm, by which all are made subject, and seas and rocks tremble, and daimons [avoid] the characters' magical powers which you are about to have. For it is the greatest protective charm for the rite so that you fear nothing.[7]

Their origin is not entirely understood, but it is likely that they were either imitations of petroglyphs or of letters (or hieroglyphs) seen in foreign writing systems. In the search for ever more potent sources for foreign words and writing to incorporate into the increasingly syncretic

---

*In scholarly works, spells from the *PGM* have a numbering scheme based on the collections published by philologist Karl Preisendanz in 1928 and 1931. Individual spells are generally referred to by document number (in Roman numerals) and line numbers within that document. For example, the spell commonly called the "Headless Ritual" is *PGM* V. 96–172: document 5, lines 96 to 172.

Greek (and later Roman) magic, "the mysterious symbolic qualities with which Greek ignorance of their true character endowed the hieroglyphs, became, therefore, their main charm and attraction."[8] The net effect was not unlike the use of barbarous names in magical operations described in the previous section, and worked in a very similar way.

Spells from the PGM

Now, we will turn to an analysis of the communicative features of a selection of spells from the Greek Magical Papyri. Various features will occur again and again; while there wasn't a single template that the spells were derived from, the underlying theory of magic in that time and place resulted in certain repeated patterns to aid in the spells' efficacy. This reflects commonly held attitudes about magic and language—and highlights the pragmatic attitude toward magic as being focused on results through the repetition of patterns that *work*.

Nearly every spell in the *PGM* involves invoking or otherwise interacting with one or more gods. Sometimes it is a well-recognized god—Hermes, Thoth, Set-Typhon. In other instances—the majority, in fact—it as a god identified by one or more barbarous names (although sometimes identifiable roots in these names suggest connections to a known god). Rarely is this done to ask the god to work on the magician's behalf. The far more common approach is to ask the god for some piece of knowledge or ability, or to raise the state of being of the magician up to the level of that god to claim access to the god's knowledge and ability. This is Frazer's law of sympathy in action; the magician is externalizing some part of himself to interact with it in terms of the god invoked, creating context and authority for the performative speech within the spells.

All renderings of the English text, as well as the titles, of the *PGM* spells below are taken from the translations compiled and edited by Hans Dieter Betz in *The Greek Magical Papyri in Translation, Including the Demotic Spells*; words within brackets are emendations that have been commonly accepted by scholars.

PGM I. 1–42 For Acquiring an Assistant Daimon

In the very first entry in the *PGM* we find some features that will manifest in various ways throughout the rest of the spells. The stated purpose of this spell is:

> A [daimon comes] as an assistant who will reveal everything
> to you clearly and will be your [companion and]
> will eat and sleep with you.[9]

The magician is instructed to write down strings of vowels based on a visual pattern:

> and take [a piece of choice papyrus], and inscribe in
> myrrh the following, and set it in the same manner
> [along with the] hairs and fingernails, and plaster it with [uncut]
> frankincense [and] old wine. So, the writing on [the strip] is:
> "A EE ÊÊÊ IIII OOOOO YYYYY ÔÔÔÔÔÔÔ."*
> [But write this, making] two figures:[10]

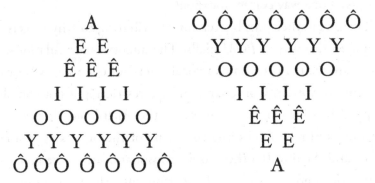

The vowel dialogue

---

*Modern renderings of the rituals in the Greek Magical Papyri nearly always transliterate the Ancient Greek letters in barbarous names into the equivalent Latin characters. Letters written with a circumflex (Ê, Ô) indicate the long vowels instead of their short counterparts (*eta* vs. *epsilon*, *omega* vs. *omicron*).

Here, we can see the obvious pattern: the seven vowels in the Greek alphabet are shown in order, with each one repeated the same number of times as its position in the list of vowels. This functions loosely as a type of *voces magicae*, but the vowels were also associated with a variety of collections of seven things, most notably the designation of planets as inherited through Babylonian sources. Some spells, because they refer specifically to intoning the vowels at night, were likely referring either the Seven Stars (known as the Big Dipper in American English) or the Seven Sisters (commonly known as the Pleiades).[11] Regardless of the specific association, it is clear the magician is making a connection with phenomena of cosmic importance by writing (and later intoning) the vowels in this way, and is also claiming mastery over the cosmos by knowing the sound which creates each part of it. This is also shown by the directions of the triangular arrangement of the letters. In the first, the sounds are shown originating from above and spreading out upon the earth: the heavens above speaking to the magician. In the second, however, the magician speaks them to the heavens, impressing their desire on the cosmos. This functions as the creation of a dialog with the unmanifest, rather than just a one-way communication.

There's another possible reason contributing to why vowels were often used this way in *PGM* spells. The quality of articulation—how sounds are made in the human vocal tract—of consonants is distinct from that of vowels. Consonants involve restricting if not completely stopping the flow of breath; vowels, on the other hand, do not restrict that flow and rely on altering the shape of the oral cavity using the tongue and the lips. In other words, consonants are discrete, but vowels are continuous—one vowel can flow into the next, unimpeded. Intoning vowels allows us to resonate with the vastness of the cosmos, choosing places where we can be in harmony with it or go against its flow. In this sense, magical uses of vowels would function as iconic signs due to their conceptual resonance with the vast universe.

Following the use of the syntagma created from all the vowels that connect the will of the magician with the impressionable cosmos, the daimon that has been invoked appears in the form of a falcon; the magician then communicates with this daimon using barbarous names and metaphorical associations:

> *A EE ÊÊÊ IIII OOOOO YYYYY ÔÔÔÔÔÔÔ, come to me, Good Husbandman, Good Daimon, HARPON KNOUPHI BRINTANTÊN SIPHRI BRISKYLMA AROUAZAR [BAMESEN] KRIPHI NIPOUMICHMOUMAÔPH. Come to me, O holy Orion, [you who lie] in the north, who cause [the] currents of [the] Nile to roll down and mingle with the sea . . .*[12]

Note the use of conceptual metaphors, with the results of the invocation expressed in terms of motion ("come to me") but also in terms of orientation to the cardinal directions. Conceptual metaphor is an important feature of language in general as we seek to better understand the abstract in terms of the concrete. Used in magical acts, the desired results of the magic are anchored to the world of the real and take on a concrete reality of their own.

After describing the invoked daimon in terms of the Egyptian myth of the sun's daily travel across the sky and then through the underworld, the magician reveals their knowledge of the true name of the daimon:

> *[This] is your authoritative name: AKBATH ABAÔTH BAKCHABRÊ*[13]

This passage calls to mind the importance of names in both Mesopotamian and Mediterranean magic: to give a name to something is to bring it into being, and to know or guess the true name of a god (or other inhabitant of the numinous realm) is to have some measure of control over it (or least to be able to seek its favor).

PGM I. 232–47 Memory Spell

This spell not only contains several direct symbolic references to Hermes, but also introduces an interesting sympathetic magic technique—one that functions as magical communication. The spell is intended to enhance memory, an important skill for a magician.

The spell specifically calls for—and gives a recipe for—a myrrh-based ink that was sacred to Hermes. A long string of *ephesia grammata* are to be written on papyrus using the ink then washed off into water from seven springs.

KAMBRÊ CHAMBRE SIXIÔPHI HARPON CHNOUPHI
BRINTATÊNÔPHRIBRISKYLMA ARAOUAZAR
BAMESEN KRIPHI NIPTOUMI CHMOUMAÔPH
AKTIÔPHI ARTÔSE BIBIOU

BIBIOU SPHÊ SPHÊ NOUSI NOUSI SIEGÔ SIEGÔ
NOUCHA NOUCHA LINOUCHA LINOUCHA CHYCHBA
CHYCHBA KAXIÔ CHYCHBA DÊTOPHÔTH II AA OO
YY ÊÊ EE ÔÔ.[14]

In addition to the by now expected stream of untranslatable magical words, there are other features worth noting in this example. First, there is the repetition of many words in the second line (the first word of that line in fact echoes the last word of the first line, tying the two lines together as a narrative device). One theory about the intended use of *ephesia grammata* is that by bypassing the logic, interpretative parts of the intellect they facilitate an altered state of consciousness unrestrained by rational thought:

One doesn't so much listen for sense or reason as experience efficacy—to get caught up in the rhythms, the repetitions, the descriptive words that build on each other.[15]

Further to the use of repetition, these words function as a mantra and deepen the trancelike effect of the magical speech.

The vowels—all seven are given at the end and repeated, but not in alphabetical order as we have seen in other instances—were likely sung as they were written on the papyrus, and they anchor the unknown barbarous names back to the known world. This forms a bridge from the prerational world of communication with unknown intelligences through unknown words connecting to the cosmos which resonates with the very vowels themselves.

The magician then drinks the water over seven days while the moon is in the east. The recipe for the ink not only includes seven parts of various ingredients but also includes seven wings of the ibis—a bird sacred to both Thoth and Hermes, thus emphasizing the spell's association with gods of magical communication. In addition to the associations with seven (seven vowels, seven planets, seven notes of a musical scale, etc.) which add a mystical familiarity to the spell, the repetition of sevens within it functions as a narrative technique. This makes it more memorable (useful for a memory spell!) and implies other connections to occurrences of seven in magical contexts, something found throughout the Greek Magical Papyri.

The drinking of the ink used to write out the spell enacts Frazer's law of contagion; the ink in the water was in contact with the numinous words and after externalizing the words by speaking and writing them, the words are now internalized and made a part of the magician's body. The mind has communicated with the phenomenal world and given its words physical presence through an indexical sign, and now the results of the spell have been reabsorbed into the body so that they can take effect to bring about the ultimate goal of the spell: to enhance the magician's memory.

PGM V. 96–172 The Stele of Jeu the Hieroglyphist in His Letter

The spell colloquially known as the "Headless Ritual" is probably the most well-known one in the Greek Magical Papyri. The Headless

Ritual was one of the first spells in the *PGM* to be available in English translation, first appearing in Charles Wycliffe Goodwin's *Fragment of a Græco-Egyptian Work Upon Magic* in 1852 (although with the barbarous names replaced with ". . ."). The more widely available (and more complete) version was published in E. A. Wallis Budge's influential *Egyptian Magic* (1899), which became a central text in the Egyptomania of the day and its intersection with the occult. The ritual was adopted by the Hermetic Order of the Golden Dawn in London at the end of the nineteenth century. Following his departure from the Golden Dawn, British occultist Aleister Crowley later adapted and heavily modified it into one of the central rituals—now known as *Liber Samekh*—of his magical philosophy, Thelema.

In this section, we will be looking at the original spell from the *PGM*; in the section on Aleister Crowley and Thelema in chapter 8 we will look at the history of *Liber Samekh* and the markedly different version of the spell found there.

The spell calls itself a *stele*: a stone or wood slab, taller than it is wide, that served as a common type of monument or marker in the ancient world. While steles were an obvious antecedent of modern gravestones, they served a much wider variety of purposes. Egyptian graves often featured wooden steles inscribed with spells, such as those from the *Book of the Coming Forth by Day* (more commonly known as the *Book of the Dead*). Referring to the spell as a stele has semiotic implications; the author wanted to call up references to the types of writing that would feature on these markers or their permanence. This could have been due to the spell's perceived importance or even because the spell could have some postmortem significance that is encoded in the text itself.

The rite invokes Ἀκέφαλος (*Aképhalos*), which means the "Headless One"—a deity about which we have little concrete information despite its multiple appearances in the Greek Magical Papyri and other magical writings from antiquity. Since it has no head—where the eyes would normally be—it is almost invariably described as having sight in its feet; this inversion of norms is no doubt part of its power within magical operations.

Many of the spells in the *PGM* contain preparation instructions appended to the end of the rite. More rarely, as in the case of the Headless Ritual, those instructions also include text to be spoken as part of the preparation for the rite; as a result, adaptions of the rite often move these instructions to the beginning for convenience (as I will do here).

> *Write the formula on a new sheet of papyrus, and after extending it from one of your temples to the other, read the six names [AÔTH ABRAÔTH BASYM ISAK SABAÔTH IAÔ], while you face north saying, "Subject to me all daimons, so that every daimon, whether heavenly or aerial or earthly or subterranean or terrestrial or aquatic, might be obedient to me and every enchantment and scourge which is from God." And all daimons will be obedient to you.*[16]

Note that the letters forming the sequence of names begin with *alpha* and end with *omega*—the beginning and ending of the Greek alphabet that is used to give speech a physical presence in the phenomenal world. Invoking both the beginning and the end expands the consciousness and scope of power of the magician; his awareness must become vast if not infinite if he is to be able to become enough like the Headless One to be able to communicate with it as equals.

The summoning of the Headless One ascribes to it various pairs of opposing attributes:

> *I summon you, Headless One, who created earth and heaven, who created night and day, you who created light and darkness; you are Osoronnophris whom none has ever seen; you are Iabas; you are Iapos; you have distinguished the just and the unjust; you have made female and male; you have revealed seed and fruits; you have made men love each other and hate each other.*[17]

Attributing a catalog of paired opposites to a god as part of an invocation is a common linguistic feature of magic spells in the Greco-Roman world (we will see this again the discussion of *The Thunder, Perfect Mind* later in this chapter). These opposites are extremes, showing the awesome breadth of the god's power and influence. They also defy easy categorization, transcending rational explanations of what the god is capable of affecting. In essence, they are paradoxical semiotic codes that we must decode to arrive at an understanding of the true nature of the god. Using linguistic signs in this way expands the sign network—or semiotic web—that the magician intends to affect.

The magician identifies himself with Moses—the lawgiver and writer of stone tablets. This spell combines Hebrew references with the usual syncretism of Greek and Egyptian ideas. Some of the barbarous names used in the ritual are genuinely of unknown origin, however some are well known in the Greco-Roman world (IAÔ, SABAÔTH, ABRASAX) or are transparently borrowed from Hebrew (ISAK, ADÔNAI).

The magician further identifies himself as a messenger of the legendary Pharaoh Osoronnophris, who will now summon the Headless One by his *true* name, as part of what now seems to have shifted to a sort of exorcism instead of invocation:

> *. . . this is your true name which has been transmitted to the prophets of Israel. Hear me, ARBATHIAÔ REIBET ATHELEBERSÊTH [ARA] BLATHA ALBEU EBENPHCHI CHITASGOÊ IBAÔTH IAÔ; listen to me and turn away this daimon.*[18]

Knowing the true name of this god earns the magician the right to communicate with it. As the prelude and preparation notes, the daimon to be turned away is subject to the command of the magician as well as the Headless One. The magician raises himself up in power and understanding to be able to communicate with the Headless One, and then, having entered into communication with him, exercises his powers to command that daimon that prevents the fulfillment of his desires.

> *I call upon you, awesome and invisible god*
> *with an empty spirit*[19]

The "awesome and invisible god with an empty spirit" is then named through a string of *voces magicae* punctuated with a sequence of the vowels. The phrase "empty spirit/air" appears often in *PGM* spells that reference Set-Typhon (always with the "awesome/terrible and invisible" epithet). This, then, seems to connect the Headless One with Set-Typhon or at least indicate they are often invoked together due to their similar areas of power and significance.

> *He is the lord of the gods; he is the lord of the inhabited world;*
> *he is the one whom the winds fear; he is the one who*
> *made all things by the command of his voice.*[20]

This is a powerful sequence of epithets that employ conceptual metaphors and reveal the scope of power of this terrible and invisible god. He is lord of both the gods and the *inhabited* world; this is no nature god but rather one who guides civilizations. He has the power of performative speech, able to create through the "command of his voice" (see the discussion of the *Enūma Eliš* in chap. 5). The winds fear him because his voice—borne on divine breath that powers his speech—is stronger than them.

> *I am the headless daimon with my sight in my feet; [I am] the*
> *mighty one [who possesses] the immortal fire; I am the truth who*
> *hates the fact that unjust deeds are done in the world; I am the*
> *one who makes the lightning flash and the thunder roll; I am the*

> *one whose sweat is the heavy rain which falls upon the earth that it*
> *might be inseminated; I am the one whose mouth burns completely;*
> *I am the one who begets and destroys;*
> *I am the Favor of the Aion; my name is a heart encircled*
> *by a serpent; come forth and follow.*[21]

The invocation has been successful: the magician has now gone from invoking the Headless One to manifesting him. The act of *ph-ntr*—the Egyptian term for raising oneself up to reach or become a god—is complete.

This sequence of conceptual metaphors illustrates not only the awesome power of the god but also focuses on the cosmic maintenance for which the Headless One is ultimately responsible. He wields fire and embodies truth—both attributes of Ahura Mazda ("Wise Lord"), the supreme god in Zoroastrianism* (a significant and influential religion in the Mediterranean world). The connections with thunder and lightning (and creation and destruction) also serve to equate the Headless One with other supreme gods in the various cultures of the region.

Don Webb notes that "the 'Holy Headless One' is identified in other texts as being behind the constellation Draco. He is Set in his form of the Bata serpent."[22] This suggests part of the significance behind the heart being "encircled" with a serpent: it may be intended to evoke the Ouroboros—the serpent swallowing its own tail, a symbol of eternal cycles in both Hermeticism and Gnosticism—but also reveals that the heart so enchanted has become divine.[23]

---

*Zoroastrianism originated in ancient Persia, now known as Iran, as early as the second millennium before the Common Era. The Persian language and its ancient ancestors (including Avestan, the language of Zoroastrianism's founder, Zarathustra) are Indo-European languages.

SELECTIONS FROM
THE NAG HAMMADI LIBRARY

The collection of Coptic texts known as the Nag Hammadi library was discovered near the Egyptian town of the same name in 1945. The fifty-two separate treatises are generally classified as Gnostic literature, although some early Christian and Hermetic texts are found among them as well; the manuscripts themselves date from the third or fourth century of the Common Era, but some of the material recorded may be earlier.

In this chapter we will examine two texts within the Nag Hammadi library: *The Thunder, Perfect Mind* and *The Discourse on the Eighth and Ninth*. These selections show other ways that the mysteries of language had become a general feature of the religious and magical approaches throughout this time and place.

Unlike the spells of the Greek Magical Papyri, many of the works in the Nag Hammadi library focus on imparting a particular understanding of divinity and the soul. Rather than being instruction manuals, they are for the most part works of theory although specific techniques can be gleaned from some of them (as we will see in part of *The Discourse*). Their general purpose was to communicate something about the divine and to show the initiate how to attain that same understanding for himself.

The Thunder, Perfect Mind

This text as a revelation from an unknown goddess does not neatly fit into a particular Mediterranean tradition, although there are obvious parallels with female wisdom figures such as Sophia in Gnostic literature. The connection with thunder is presumably meant—following Hebrew and Greek sources—to associate this female manifestation of divinity with the *highest* gods (Yahweh, Zeus) who also had thunder and lightning under their command.[24]

> *I was sent forth from [the] power,*
> *and I have come to those who reflect upon me,*
> *and I have been found among those who seek after me.*
> *Look upon me, you (pl.) who reflect upon me,*
> *and you hearers, hear me.*
> *You who are waiting for me, take me to yourselves.*[25]

These opening lines establish the transcendent source of the divine speaker through conceptual metaphors, such as REVELATION IS MOTION, KNOWLEDGE IS A MIRROR, and DIVINITY IS KNOWN THROUGH SEARCHING (see chap. 4). These figures of speech also emphasize that knowledge of her is only available to those who seek her through engaging in these same metaphorical actions; her revelations are only meant for certain ears.

> *For I am the first and the last.*
> *I am the silence that is incomprehensible*
> *and the idea whose remembrance is frequent.*
> *I am the voice whose sound is manifold*
> *and the word whose appearance is multiple.*

This is the beginning of the paradoxical pairs of contrasting opposites, not unlike the opening passage of the Headless Ritual; through these the middle way of understanding is sought. These opposites strain the limits of rationality—the objects of rational thought cannot be both extremes at once—and so open the gate to a more intuitive, nonrational means of understanding. These attempts to express the ineffable in words only offer a glimpse of what her existence and power really entail; the gaps can only be filled in through direct experience of her.

> *I am the utterance of my name.*[26]

Self-creation through the manifestation of a word or name is a feature we have seen in multiple contexts, including German philosopher J. G. Fichte's "self-positing *Ich*" (see chap. 3).

> *Why have you hated me in your counsels?*
> *For I shall be silent among those who are silent,*
> *and I shall appear and speak.*
> *Why then have you hated me, you Greeks?*
> *Because I am a barbarian among [the] barbarians?*
> *For I am the wisdom [of the] Greeks*
> *and the knowledge of [the] barbarians.*
> *I am the judgment of [the] Greeks and of the*
> *barbarians.*
> *[I] am the one whose image is great in Egypt*
> *and the one who has no image among the barbarians.*[27]

The inherent magic of foreign things was a recurring theme in Mediterranean magic and the religions of antiquity. Use of these foreign ideas and deities in magical practice did not necessarily indicate *approval* of them, only that they had power which could be leveraged for certain magical acts. This rather pointed criticism of the Greeks seems to imply that she is far more greatly respected by the Egyptians and so-called barbarians than by the Greeks, even as only the Egyptians had given her a name (i.e., image). Yet, she *is* known to the Greeks even if they only associate her awesome wisdom and power with non-Greek things. In other words, they have accepted foreign names for her even if they have not given her a name themselves.

> *I am the knowledge of my inquiry,*
> *and the finding of those who seek after me,*
> *and the command of those who ask of me,*
> *and the power of the powers in my knowledge*
> *of the angels, who have been sent at my word.*[28]

These are not exactly performative utterances but are related in that they describe the process that leads to their realization. Each of these is the inevitable outcome—*telos*, in Aristotle's philosophy—of the given process, with the outcome pulling the process forward toward that end. We inquire *so that* we gain knowledge, we seek *so that* we find, and so forth. The goddess makes it clear that doing these actions for their own sake will lead to the desired outcomes, outlining in classic Gnostic concepts a process of knowing divinity through the correct actions and frame of mind.

> I am the knowledge of my name.
> I am the one who cries out,
> and I listen.[29]

Naming is knowing. This text was written around the time that Neoplatonism was becoming a prominent movement in Greek culture, and it is another reflection of Platonic ideas about names and words cast into a worldview that assimilated Hebrew and Egyptian ideas as well.

This also shows how the goddess is to be known through externalizing aspects of the self of the initiate. To know something is to have internalized the impression and understanding of that thing. This process implies that the thing known was either originally external to the magician or *has been treated as external* in order to have a dialogue with it to deepen the understanding of it. This type of dispassionate examination requires interacting with the object of the examination as if it were outside the self—literally to objectify it to see it in ways not possible when it is only seen as part of the psyche. In other words, she is teaching a way to deeper knowledge through *de*-identification followed by *re*-identification.

The same applies to hearing her own cry; one of Charles Hockett's design principles of language (see chap. 3) is *interchangeability*: the speaker can both speak and hear the same sounds. In this text she is also both speaker and hearer. This anthropomorphizes her to an extent, but also reveals a path toward knowing her since her initiate can cry out and she will hear it just as she cries out so that those who know her can hear.

> *Hear me, you hearers,*
> *and learn of my words, you who know me.*
> *I am the hearing that is attainable to everything;*
> *I am the speech that cannot be grasped.*
> *I am the name of the sound and the sound of the name.*
> *I am the sign of the letter*
> *and the designation of the division.*[30]

She is to be known through the magic of language—naming things into existence and describing that which already exists so that it can be taught and shared. She is not only identified with spoken language, but written language as well: the "designation of the division" gives her *individual* existence, setting her apart from a formless jumble of letters to create coherence and individual words. The meaning of these words can be evaluated both separately and as part of a more complex text. She is *the* syntagma: the combination and ordering of the individual sounds and letters into more complex signs of ever-expanding meaning.

> *For many are the pleasant forms which exist in*
> *   numerous sins,*
> *and incontinencies,*
> *and disgraceful passions,*
> *and fleeting pleasures,*
> *which (men) embrace until they become sober*
> *and go up to their resting-place. And they will find me*
> *   there,*
> *and they will live,*
> *and they will not die again.*[31]

These are the concluding lines of *The Thunder, Perfect Mind*, revealing the ultimate purpose of the text: a path toward knowing and enacting the eternal soul free from the tyranny of matter. The path for accomplishing this is, as we have seen, fraught with paradox and the inability to describe in words the entirety of the experience. However, knowing her Name—and through that knowing her—is a critical part of the path and she is to be found in the interactions between these extremes.

The Discourse on the Eighth and Ninth

The other text we will look at in the Nag Hammadi library is, in contrast to most of the others in the collection, primarily Hermetic with its emphasis on Hermes Trismegistus as initiator. Nonetheless, it still contains elements typically associated with Gnosticism, such as an emphasis on attaining purity and its cosmological outlook (which is the source of the commonly used title for the text).

The entire discourse is couched in a conceptual metaphor: the connection of a cosmic rebirth in nine spheres surrounding the earth to nine months of human gestation. In the first seven of these spheres, the known planets of the day "wander" about the sky (see the discussion of *PGM* I. 1–42 earlier in this chapter). The eighth and ninth spheres are the beginning of the divine realm and thus the avenue for perfection:

> At death the soul would journey through the seven spheres, and after successful passage it would reach the eighth and the ninth, the levels at which the soul could experience true bliss. Furthermore, the eighth and the ninth spheres can also indicate advanced stages of spiritual development.[32]

Thus, the initiation into this knowledge described in the text is the formal beginning of the journey as well as the induction into a brotherhood dedicated to this pursuit. However, there is a prior journey which must have been taken for the initiate to arrive at this point, which is alluded to but not described in the text: the attainment of a particular level of purity of life and mastery of the wisdom contained in certain books.

Historian Christian Bull notes that, in common with similar texts in the Greek Magical Papyri, *The Discourse* shows distinctive signs of "ritual realism." That is, it is likely reflective of actual Hermetic rituals and initiations, with the experiences it is designed to facilitate intended to be experienced as real.[33]

> *[My father], yesterday you promised [me that you would bring] my mind into [the] eighth and afterwards you would bring me into the ninth. You said that this is the order of the tradition.*[34]

The opening of the discourse makes it plain that this is an initiatory dialogue, and that the student is seeking to be initiated into a specific tradition that holds certain ideas about the nature and possibilities of the individual soul. In semiurgic terms, the initiate wants to gain knowledge of a semiotic code about the nature of reality that is different than those codes he currently knows about. Similarly, the tradition is bound to a specific speech community, and the initiate wants to learn to speak its language. Note also that this transmission of knowledge is the fulfillment of a performative utterance: the promise of the Father to lead the initiate into this knowledge.

The Father in the ritual dialogue is Hermes Trismegistus, consistent with the core Hermetic idea that the secret transmission ultimately has divine origins. Hermes Trismegistus himself, although largely a syncretic blend of the gods Hermes (Greek) and Thoth (Egyptian), has been euhemerized (i.e., reimagined as a human, albeit an exceptionally knowledgeable and powerful one).

> *Indeed the understanding dwells in you; in me (it is) as though the power were pregnant. For when I conceived from the fountain that flowed to me, I gave birth.*[35]

After the Father—in an inverse of the expectations of the natural world—states he has given birth to this "power" just as children are born, the initiate makes the further connection with this SHARED TRADITION IS FAMILY conceptual metaphor, noting:

> (Initiate): Then, my father, I have many brothers, if I am to be
> numbered among the offspring.[36]
> (Father): Therefore, my son, it is necessary for you to recognize your
> brothers and to honor them rightly and properly,
> because they come from the same father. For each generation
> I have called. I have named it, because they were
> offspring like these sons.[37]

The representative of the power—the initiator, the Father—has named his offspring into being. He speaks, and they are born.

> (Hermes): My son, they are spiritual ones. For they exist as forces
> that grow other souls. Therefore I say that they are immortal."
> (Initiate): "Your word is true; it has no refutation from now on.
> My father, begin the discourse on the eighth and the ninth,
> and include me also with my brothers.[38]

The Father can speak *only* truth, and what he desires will come to pass when he speaks it into being through his performative utterances. The response from the initiate—"Your word is true"—is reminiscent of the absolute power of divine speech in the *Enūma Eliš*, possessed by the god of the constellations and source of the divine right to rule, Anu (see chap. 5).

> And it is right [for you] to remember the progress that came to you as
> wisdom in the books. My son, compare yourself to the
> early years of life. As children (do), you have
> posed senseless, unintelligent questions.[39]

Knowledge of the wisdom contained in certain books is one of the two prerequisites for the initiate to receive this wisdom from the Father (the other is to have attained a level of ritual purity guided by certain rules that are not included in this text). What has been written down of the truths of this tradition is both eternal and true; the permanence of the writing reflects the permanence of the wisdom itself.

There is another subtle (yet common in initiatory traditions) conceptual metaphor here as well: IGNORANCE IS CHILDHOOD. The maturity attained through the wisdom being communicated is a rarefied and more profound version of the wisdom attained through age alone.

> *He created everything. He who is self-contained cares for everything. He is perfect, the invisible God to whom one speaks in silence—his image is moved when it is directed, and it governs—the one mighty power, who is exalted above majesty, who is better than the honored (ones), Zoxathazo a ôô ee ôôô êêê ôôôô êê ôôôôôô ooooo ôôôôô uuuuuu ôôôôôôôôôôôô ôôô Zozazoth.*[40]

The names Zoxathazo and Zozazoth—bookending the vowels—are extremely similar to names found throughout the *PGM*,[41] and we have already seen many examples in this chapter of this characteristically Hermetic usage of vowels.

From his previous studies, the initiate would already understand the purpose of the vowels: the ascent of the soul through the seven planetary spheres to where the eighth sphere begins. As we discussed earlier in this chapter, the seven vowels are closely associated with the seven planets, sonically evoking their essence and functioning as symbolic signs through their culturally conditioned associations with the planets. When everyday speech is spoken, the vowels provided language with a foundation within the physical cosmos; words bridged the gulf between the physical world and the divine world. In magical and religious contexts, speaking or singing the pure vowels connected the singer directly with the divine realm.

> *Let us pray, my father: I call upon you, who rules over the kingdom of power, whose word comes as (a) birth of light. And his words are immortal. They are eternal and unchanging.*
>
> . . .
>
> *Lord, grant us a wisdom from your power that reaches us, so that we may describe to ourselves the vision of the eighth and the ninth. We have already advanced to the seventh, since we are pious and walk in your law.*[42]

The difficulty of describing the ineffable rears its head as we have already seen in *The Thunder, Perfect Mind*. This is part of the prayer being taught to the initiate, wherein the godhead being invoked calls to mind the "Let there be light!" opening of the book of Genesis in the Bible. Light may be the medium, but the *linguistic sign*—the word—is the critical thing being transmitted. The words, once spoken, are eternal and unchanging, and provide a pathway toward divinity for any who can not only hear and understand them, but also speak them in further creative acts.

> *For we have walked in [your way, and we have] renounced . . . , so that your [vision] may come. Lord, grant us the truth in the image. Allow us through the spirit to see the form of the image that has no deficiency, and receive the reflection of the* pleroma *from us through our praise.*[43]

Pleroma is a concept in Gnosticism—a feature of their loosely organized linguistic community—that describes the spiritual universe as the abode of God and the totality of the divine powers and emanations. There is an interesting parallel being drawn here between truth and images, both directly seen and reflected. The conceptual metaphor

TRUTH IS A MIRROR guides the imagery, emphasizing this connection of truth with the special kind of sight only available to the few who have learned how to gain access to it.

We see further evidence of divine communication as well; apprehension of the *pleroma* is the product of this dialogue with the divine and the desired response to the right questions.

> *I will offer up the praise in my heart, as I pray to the end of the universe and the beginning of the beginning, to the object of man's quest, the immortal discovery, the begetter of light and truth, the sower of reason, the love of immortal life. No hidden word will be able to speak about you, Lord. Therefore my mind wants to sing a hymn to you daily. I am the instrument of your spirit; Mind is your plectrum.*[44]

This stanza, in the form of a prayer to be said by the new initiate, is an excellent example of the type of speech used in magical and religious contexts that intentionally differs from profane speech. It is rich and poetic, showing new ways to connect with the divine as it uses this imagery to attempt to describe the ineffable. It is trying to bring the divine closer, to make it more understandable and attainable—and ultimately easier to engage in dialogue with.

Various conceptual metaphors permeate the passage, including INITIATION IS A JOURNEY, KNOWLEDGE IS DISCOVERY, TRUTH IS LIGHT, TEACHING IS SOWING SEEDS, and SPIRIT AND MIND ARE MUSICAL INSTRUMENTS.

In this stanza we also find the use of paradox—"the end of the universe and the beginning of the beginning"—emphasizing that this type of knowledge of the divine is not solely rational. Perfection is to be found partially through contemplation of this truth that cannot be completely plainly stated in words.

The Father—Hermes Trismegistus—now praises the successful initiate and gives him further instructions:

> *For I have received life from you, when you made me*
> *wise. I praise you. I call your name that is hidden within*
> *me: a ô ee ô êêê ôôô iii ôôôô ooooo ôôôôô uuuuuu*
> *ôôôôôôôôôôôôôôôôôôôôôôô. You are the one who exists with the spirit.*
> *I sing a hymn to you reverently. My son, write this book for the temple*
> *at Diospolis in hieroglyphic characters, entitling it*
> *"The Eighth Reveals the Ninth."*[45]

The sequence of vowels here, sung out loud during the ritual but silently afterward, is identical to the first time they were sung, *however* this time the barbarous names are not present. The initiate is now able to access the Eighth and the Ninth and no longer has a need to invoke the divine because he has taken his place in their abode.

The use of reflexivity stands out here as well: the ritual is the source of the book that it is written in. Thoth writes things into creation—something has come into being because it has been written down. The ritual is completed through the newly initiated magician recording it; they *become* Thoth through replicating one of his central actions. It should be noted that knowledge of hieroglyphics was quickly fading during the time the texts in the Nag Hammadi library were being written down. That the book should be written in hieroglyphs—even though the original version of this text is known to have been in *Greek*—shows the roots of some of the text in Egyptian ideas and ties it to more archaic traditions. Reverence for esoteric knowledge found in old texts is built into the seeming permanence of writing itself.

> *And write an oath in the book, lest those who read*
> *the book bring the language into abuse,*
> *and not (use it) to oppose*
> *the acts of fate.*[46]

The purpose of the oath is more interesting for our purposes than the oath itself. While certain prior knowledge is required for the one undergoing the ritual, the admonition of the oath reveals that much of the power in the ritual lies *in the words themselves and the signs they call to mind*. Reciting certain parts of the book without the requisite knowledge and ritual purity could be disastrous spiritually. Protecting the text—so that it only falls into the hands of those who have proven worthy to possess it—is one of the functions of the brotherhood using this text as an induction ritual. The idea that some books are *dangerous* in the wrong hands underlies everything from mass book burning/banning to the eldritch tomes (the *Necronomicon*, the *Pnakotic Manuscripts*, etc.) found in Lovecraft's mythos. This is a sinister fear hidden within Frazer's law of contagion—once you've been touched by a dangerous idea, you can never completely clean it out of your mind. Therefore, the text of this *Discourse*, like countless others before and after it, must be guarded from misuse; it should only be available to those who are capable of responsibly using the power within.

CURSE TABLETS
AND EXECRATION TEXTS

Curse tablets (Latin: *defixiones*, Greek: κατάδεσμοι [*katádesmoi*]) were a common magical technology in the Greco-Roman world, appearing as early as the fourth century BCE. They did not seem to be associated with any particular school of magical or religious thought, but they would employ certain common forms and phrases that give them some cohesion as a specific type of semiurgy. They did not always take the form of curses, but that was a common enough use that it has become the general name for the technology (spells for lust directed at specific targets were the second-most-common category among surviving examples).

Curse tablets are interesting to our thesis of magic-as-communication because they are literally letters to the chthonic realm, typically carved on thin lead sheets. They were then deposited into caves, chasms, graves, or the like—anywhere there is an opening into the earth, ideally one where the tablet could not then be easily retrieved. The intent behind depositing the tablets in such places was to petition their inhabitants—gods and other numinous beings, or the deceased—to carry out the curse. The use of curse tablets became so common that an entire cottage industry sprang up dedicated to creating tablets with the curses pre-written for a variety of situations; the customer had only to scratch in the name of the intended victim and deposit the tablet in an appropriate place.

Lead was readily available as a side product of both the silver-mining and pewter-making processes, and indeed was relatively common as a durable yet soft writing material that could be easily reused as well. Certain physical features—its weight and coldness to the touch—took on semiotic associations for the task of sending curses and spells to the chthonic realm (returning the lead to its source). Through the law of similarity, the heaviness of lead would make one's enemies heavy and less able to act.[47]

Defixiones show many of the hallmarks of magical communication we have identified with other forms of Greco-Roman magic: *charaktêres*, palindromes, series of carefully crafted vowels, barbarous names, and other seeming nonsense.[48] These features were found alongside others we have seen in the *PGM*, such as the use of names of gods adapted from Hebrew and other sources, and repeated ritual formulas.

The scholar of religion John Gager describes an example from a well in the Agora (the central public gathering place in Athens), which was intended to break up a love triangle.[49] This tablet was likely produced as part of a set that could be adapted to a specific target, with other surviving examples showing similarities in the opening language and the inscription style. The tablet begins by invoking a long barbarous name composed of many repeated sounds:

BÔRPHÔRBABARPHORBARBARPHORBABARPHORBABAIÊ.⁵⁰

As with other uses of such names in the *PGM* and elsewhere, the meaning was intended for the *numinous* realm to interpret and was not necessarily meant to be intelligible by the person issuing the curse. There are multiple references in the tablet to "chill[ing] them" (the members of the love triangle), and the "gloomy air" and "darkened air of forgetfulness" brought about by the denizen of the underworld who will enact the curse—conceptual metaphors that signify LUST IS HEAT and THE UNDERWORLD IS DARKNESS.

The tablet also invokes the dreaded Set-Typhon among the gods capable of bringing about this chilling: "Typhon KOLCHLO PONTONON Seth SACHAÔCH EA, Lord APOMX PHRIOURIGX who are in charge of disappearing and chilling."⁵¹ This continues the idea of syncretism of Greek and Egyptian sources and methods, but also shows a way of communicating with these known and unknown gods to call upon their help that—as we'll see with execration texts below—has roots that go back several millennia. Curse tablets connect then-current Greek magic with forms and techniques—based on communication between the mundane world and the numinous world—that had been used for millennia in Ancient Egypt.

Execration Texts

There is a related technology from Ancient Egypt that was likely an influence on the techniques used in curse tablets. *Execration texts* (sometimes called proscription lists) were curses written on clay images representing their target or on specially prepared bowls. In either form, they were then ritually destroyed, and the pieces often buried. Execration texts—which are found as early as the Sixth Dynasty (2345 BCE to 2181 BCE)—were typically directed at enemies of the pharaoh or of the state. At various points in its long history, Egypt was in conflict with neighboring states and tribes (especially ones in the Near East) and during these times execration texts would become common; the texts formed a magical compliment to whatever military, economic, or diplomatic struggles were also in play.

Beyond their use of language, execration texts have a rich semiotic foundation. Egyptologist Robert Ritner noted that the text itself on these items often simply listed the name of the target and perhaps their offense; thus, the magic derived not from the text but from other factors of the object and process.[52] In other words, as we discussed in the context of Scott Shell's work with the sign networks of rune inscriptions in chapter 2, we must take into account the semiotic whole—not just one aspect of the text—in order to determine that these are indeed examples of magical semiosis. Figures used as execration texts were typically bound before destruction, a common technique in Egyptian magic signifying (in this context) "hostile restraint."[53] All these factors—the image and the binding, the inscription of the name—are also examples of Frazer's law of similarity in action: what is done to the image magically transfers to the person(s) identified through the image. In terms of the overall sign network—the semiotic web—in use, the image has an *iconic* relationship with its target, and through this semiotic relationship the target is also magically the recipient of the actions done to the image.

In the Ptolemaic period (305–30 BCE), the targets of these execration texts began to shift more toward *personal* enemies of the person creating and desecrating them. Of course, as we've discussed throughout this chapter, this is the same time period when the syncretization of Hermes and Thoth is taking place and magical practices based on the mysterious power of language are proliferating throughout the Mediterranean region. It seems that the idea behind execration texts began to blend with other magical forms already being practiced to create an even more prevalent form of magical communication.

Magic was widely used in the Mediterranean world prior to the dominance of Christianity, and the common methods and theories employed invariably show a strong connection to the linguistic and semiotic magical forms we have discussed in this book. The prevalence of written and verbal magic demonstrates this, and it is further enhanced through the use of iconic, indexical, and symbolic relationships as part of the semiotics of effective semiurgy. In the next chapter, we will follow some of these ideas about the magical power of writing and words further north as we see their echoes in the runes— echoes that may well have been inspired by cultural transmission as the Germanic tribes had more commercial and military contact with the remnants of the Roman Empire.

FURTHER READING

The Greek Magical Papyri
    Hermetic Magic: The Postmodern Magical Papyrus of Abaris by
        Stephen E. Flowers
    Seven Faces of Darkness: Practical Typhonian Magic by
        Don Webb
    The Greek Magical Papyri in Translation, edited by
        Hans Dieter Betz
    The Tradition of Hermes Trismegistus by Christian Bull

The Nag Hammadi Library
    "In Praise of Nonsense: A Piety of the Alphabet in Ancient
        Magic" in *The Poetry of Thought in Late Antiquity* by
        Patricia Cox Miller
    The Nag Hammadi Library, edited by James M. Robinson
    The Thunder, Perfect Mind: A New Translation and Introduction
        by Hal Taussig, Jared Calaway, Maia Kotrosits, Celene Lillie,
        and Justin Lasser

Magic in the Greco-Roman World

Magic and Ritual in the Ancient World, edited by Paul Allan
Mirecki and Marvin W. Meyer

*Materia Magica: The Archaeology of Magic in Roman Egypt, Cyprus,
and Spain* by Andrew Wilburn

Curse Tablets and Binding Spells from the Ancient World by John
G. Gager

7

RUNES AND SEMIURGY

WHAT ARE RUNES?

From the mid-twentieth century onward—especially in English-speaking lands—many people first became aware of runes through the works of J. R. R. Tolkien. In *The Hobbit* (1937) and *The Lord of the Rings* (1954), runes were a system of writing used by the inhabitants of Middle-earth called dwarves. There was little magical about runes in Tolkien's stories, other than the kind of runes called "moon-letters"—these were written with a silver pen and usually could only be seen by the light of a moon in the same phase and season as that when they were written.

Tolkien was a professor of English at the University of Oxford, with a special interest in Old English and Old Norse language and literature. As such, he was well-versed in the history of runes, although he was beholden to the British academic dogma of the day that saw runes as just another form of alphabetic writing and overlooked—or at least downplayed—their apparent magical uses.

What, then, are runes historically, and how do they fit into our discussion of communication as a fundamental aspect of magic?

In the most mundane sense, runes are characters that were used for writing short inscriptions in the early Germanic languages prior to the adoption of the Latin alphabet for writing those languages. In the Proto-Germanic language—the reconstructed language that is the common ancestor of all the modern Germanic languages—the word *rūnō* means "mystery." *Rune* is simply the modern English derivative of that word.

The use of *rune* to refer to the characters is a later association than the meaning of "mystery." Historically, ancestors of the modern English word *stave* (or *runestave*) were sometimes used for the characters. In fact, the uses of runes have always been closely associated with written or carved forms of the languages written in the different varieties of runes. The technical vocabulary associated with writing in the modern Germanic languages still shows this heritage. For example, the English word *write* comes from the Proto-Germanic *wrītaną*, meaning "to carve" or "to write" and was originally associated with carving runic characters. In another example, the element *stab* in the modern German noun *Buchstab* ("letter") is cognate with English *stave* and *staff* (that is, they share the same etymology).

Drawing on the etymological data, as well as the historical mentions of runes in the various lore, however, it is clear that the concept of a rune is first and foremost that of those archetypal Mysteries that underly all things, actions, and occurrences. The characters, especially in acts of magic—operative communication—are both representation of and gateway to the Mysteries that always lie hidden behind them.

Runes and Magic

While there is still some controversy over the extent to which runes were used for magical operations, there is nonetheless significant evidence that suggests they were often used in magical contexts at different points in history. Indeed, in the almost completely illiterate cultures that originally created and used runes for writing, the very act of writing itself—carving or writing ideas into physical existence—was magical and mysterious (not to mention reserved for the exclusive use of those few who had received specific and secret teachings). This attitude toward writing, in cultures where it was rare and rarely taught, was hardly exclusive to the rune-using early Germanic cultures.

In his 1984 doctoral dissertation *Runes and Magic: Magical Formulaic Elements in the Older Runic Tradition*, Stephen E. Flowers extensively documents the use of runic formulas (repeated patterns with some apparent magical intent). He precedes this by developing a semiotic theory of magic based on using symbols to communicate effectively with the phenomenal world to bring about the change the magician desires. He then evaluates these uses of runes in terms of that theory to support the assertion that they are at least *in part* magical and not exclusively mundane usages.

There are four main types of formulas documented in *Runes and Magic*:

1. runemaster formulas (or *ek* ["I"] formulas)
2. symbolic word formulas (such as the words *alu* or *laukaz*)
3. graphic formulas (ordered collections of runes)
4. operative formulas with a magical intent suggested by their construction and phrasing[1]

All of these are *syntagmatic* uses—they are combinations of signs that convey meaning beyond just the meaning of the individual characters and the words created from them. Recall from chapter 3 that a syntagma (pl. syntagmata) is a building block of meaning within a sign system such as language. As syntagmata are built on top of each other, more and more meaning accumulates that transcends the meaning carried by the building blocks in isolation.

The association of rune formulas with singing and poetic forms was no doubt partially done to aid in their memorization. It also reinforces the connections between Odin and runes: he was the conduit of inspiration for poetry, and also the one who discovered (not invented!) runes in the mysterious fabric of the cosmos itself.

As should be clear even with this brief introduction to runes, their historical associations and uses are quite compatible with the central thesis of this book regarding magic as a communication process.

RUNES AS A SYSTEM OF OPERATIVE COMMUNICATION

Literacy and the technology of writing in the ancient Germanic world were reserved to an elite few. Writing was only done when the intent behind a particular act of operative communication needed to be impressed directly onto the observable world. This approach to literacy and writing changed as the various Germanic tribes became Christianized.

We do not have a great deal of specific information on how runes were historically used as an operative tool. However, among our reconstructions and best guesses based on the available historical information, certain patterns emerge again and again. This situation contrasts with much of Mediterranean and later medieval magic, which took place in cultures that were comparatively widely literate and whose magical forms were based on the written word as merely one use among many for the technology of writing.

HISTORICAL AND LINGUISTIC ROOTS OF THE RUNES

The oldest universally accepted runic inscription is the Vimose comb, found in Denmark and dated to approximately 160 CE. A writing system will have generally been in use for some time—as much as a century or two in the case of ancient scripts—before the earliest examples that we can recover today. Based on this rule of thumb, we can place the origin of runic writing possibly as early as the late first century BCE. If some other possible—but not conclusive—runic finds are taken into account, this time of origin might be pushed another century or so earlier.

The different types of runes, depending on time period and location, are each referred to as a *Futhark** or *Futhorc* due to the sound values of their first six characters.[†] There are three primary historically attested varieties of runes, each showing only minor variations in the forms of the individual characters over their history (more on these below).

The Runes in Relation to Other Alphabetic Systems

In contrast to the well-known sources of the Greek, Latin, and Hebrew alphabets—all ultimately derived from the Phoenician alphabet—the runic Futharks have no clear predecessor from which they were borrowed in their entirety. There are a number of elements in the Futhark that seem to come variously from Greek, Latin, and/or North Etruscan alphabets, sometimes but not always maintaining the same pairing between symbol and sound. Other runestaves, often corresponding to sounds unique to (or at least more common in) Proto-Germanic, seem to have been created anew *or* were perhaps adapted from existing signs like those that can be seen on prehistoric Scandinavian petroglyphs.

The *idea* of writing was certainly borrowed—likely in military or trading contexts—from Germanic encounters with Romans or other literate cultures near the northern parts of the Italian peninsula. At the probable time of borrowing, the Germanic tribes were well known for serving as mercenaries in the Roman army; this would have provided ample opportunity for becoming acquainted with state-of-the-art systems of writing as well as an introduction to the power of literacy for its use in magical contexts (see chap. 6).

---

*Futhark is also often used as a generic name for any of the different varieties of runes, as in "the different Futharks show some variations depending on the times and places when they were written."

[†]The [th] sound was written as a single rune (Þ) in all of the different Futharks.

Three curious things happened in this process of partial borrowing, however. First, as mentioned before, some of the characters were borrowed along with their associated sounds, but the *order* of the symbols was not.

The second unexpected thing is that the adaptation and creation of the runes did not lead to relatively widespread literacy in the Germanic tribes, as it had in the Greco-Roman world.* The Elder Futhark—the oldest form of the runes—was in use from around the beginning of the Common Era to approximately 750 CE. Over this substantial time period, the Elder Futhark largely retained its order and its orthography (i.e., the appearance of the written/carved individual characters). This consistency strongly suggests that there was some sort of organized effort to maintain the standards of runic learning and use.† This in turn suggests that the ordering of the runestaves was not arbitrary but instead encoded some sort of symbolic metacommentary on the names and meaning of the runes themselves, which made the order important to preserve.

The third and perhaps most curious thing about the partial borrowing of the characters that correspond to individual runes is that the names of the characters were *not* borrowed. In fact, the individual runestaves have names that alliterate with the sounds that the staves reference in writing, and those names are *themselves* words that have meaning. The meaning, shape, and the place of the rune in the overall order are gateways to the mystery signified by the rune. The meanings of the names for letters in the Greek alphabet—*alpha*, *beta*, *gamma*, *delta*, et cetera—have no significance in and of themselves although they do also alliterate with the sound the letter represents.

The names of the individual runes, along with the metaphysical

---

*Even in the Greco-Roman cultures, the overall literacy rate probably did not exceed 15 percent—a very respectable number in the context of the ancient world.
†The modern Rune-Gild considers itself to be the spiritual successor of this surmised archaic runic guild. See Edred Thorsson, *History of the Rune-Gild: The Reawakening of the Gild 1980–2018* (Gilded Books, 2019).

significance of the names and the cosmology they reflect, are used in a metonymic* way in certain types of rune formulas. That is, in a formula that repeats the rune *fehu* (ᚠ) eight times, the *concept* of *fehu* (accumulated movable wealth) is what is being invoked. This type of repetition is a common type of word formula in magic in the ancient world and may have been borrowed by the first runemaster through his exposure to Mediterranean forms of magic and their respective alphabets.

SEMIOTICS AND METAPHOR IN THE DIFFERENT FUTHARKS

As noted previously, the names of the runes are themselves words with meaning. For example, the first four runes of the Elder Futhark, with their reconstructed Proto-Germanic names, are:

1. *fehu*—cattle, signifying movable wealth
2. *ūruz*—the aurochs, a large and now-extinct European bovine known for its fierce nature and large horns
3. *thurisaz*—the original meaning is uncertain, but the word later evolves into *thurs* in Old Norse, signifying a type of primitive and malevolent being not possessing full consciousness
4. *ansuz*—a god of consciousness; later becomes *áss* in Old Norse (pl. *æsir*), referring to gods such as Óðinn, Týr, and so forth

This occurrence of single characters signifying both *sound* and *words with specific meaning* is not found in ancient alphabets used to write other Indo-European languages. That is, there is no meaning for the name of the letters in the Latin alphabet, or its ancestor the Greek alphabet. The letters in the predecessor of the Greek alphabet—the Phoenician alphabet—*did* have names that were also normal words in the Phoenician

---

*Adjectival form of metonymy, a figure of speech where something concrete that is closely associated with a particular thing is used to represent that idea.

language. For example, the first Phoenician letter, *'ālep*, meant "ox, head of cattle"; the second letter, *bēt* meant "house"; and so forth.

The association of the words with the individual runestaves is literal but also highly symbolic. For example, *fehu* carries with it associations not just of the exoteric meaning of "movable wealth" (in the form of livestock) but also the implications, benefits, and drawbacks of wealth. Further into the symbolic realm, it also suggests the ability to acquire not just external wealth but also the internal acquisition of self-knowledge, which can be transformed into visible, external manifestations through actions.

In chapter 4 we looked at *conceptual metaphor* in the context of the work of George Lakoff and Mark Johnson. Conceptual metaphor is a critical feature of expression through language, serving to aid in the understanding of abstract concepts (source domains) in terms of more concrete ones (target domains). This is done naturally, often without the speakers and listeners even aware they are employing metaphor.

In terms of runes, there are a variety of source domains that are drawn upon (see the table in the section on the Elder Futhark below). The individual runes—opening the door to the mysteries encoded by the runes—are the target domain. We might explain "movable wealth" in terms of livestock (a common symbol and vehicle of status and influence in the precapitalist world). The same concept in turn explains more abstract notions of wealth: personal power and charisma, influence, social status. Cattle are the gateway to more and more abstract versions of the comparatively concrete things that the possession of cattle can represent. This is easily seen from the encoding of this metaphorical significance in the various rune poems. For example, in the Old Icelandic Rune Poem stanza for *fé* (Old Norse and Younger Futhark equivalent to *fehu* in the Elder Futhark), we see the rune used in a more general sense signifying wealth:

> *Fé (wealth) is the quarrel of kinsmen*
> *And a flare 'neath the floodtide,*
> *And the serpent's path* [2]

The first line is fairly straightforward: acquiring and distributing wealth can certainly cause familial discord. What of the second and third lines? While they can be interpreted literally, their relation to the concept of wealth is less obvious, which implies they are intended metaphorically (perhaps in relation to a semiotic code no longer known).

Metaphors embedded in the names (and related images) of the different runestaves open new avenues of understanding. The more vivid the imagery used in a magical act, the more the intent—what is desired as the outcome—can be effectively visualized and thus more likely to come to be.

The Elder Futhark

The Elder Futhark, consisting of twenty-four staves, was in use until around the year 750 CE (Table 7.1). The Elder Futhark has a rough one-to-one correspondence with the sounds of the Proto-Germanic language that it represented in the early inscriptions. Later Elder Futhark inscriptions in certain geographical areas are sometimes referred to as representing "Proto-Norse," a stage of the language that would further evolve and differentiate into Old Norse.

TABLE 7.I
THE ELDER FUTHARK 24-RUNE SYSTEM

No.	Sound	Shape	Name
1	f	ᚠ	*fehu*
2	u	ᚢ	*ūruz*
3	th	ᚦ	*þurisaz*
4	a	ᚨ	*ansuz*
5	r	ᚱ	*raiðō*
6	k	ᚲ	*kēnaz*
7	g	ᚷ	*gebō*
8	w	ᚹ	*wunjō*
9	h	ᚺ	*hagalaz*
10	n	ᛏ	*nauðiz*

No.	Sound	Shape	Name
11	i	ı	*īsa*
12	j	↷	*jēra*
13	ei	ʃ	*eihwaz*
14	p	ᚲ	*perðrō*
15	-z	Y	*elhaz*
16	s	ᚻ	*sōwilō*
17	t	↑	*tīwaz*
18	b	ᛒ	*berkanō*
19	e	ᛗ	*ehwaz*
20	m	ᛗ	*mannaz*
21	l	⌐	*laguz*
22	ng	◇	*ingwaz*
23	d	ᛞ	*dagaz*
24	o	ᛟ	*ōðila*

The Younger Futhark

The Younger Futhark—which underwent a reduction in number of characters from twenty-four to sixteen, despite a simultaneous *expansion* in the sound system of the Old Norse language—was in use from around 750 CE until it was largely supplanted by the Roman alphabet in the late Middle Ages (Table 7.2). It is not known for certain why the number of characters contracted; this is somewhat unusual in the history of alphabetic writing systems, as usually the number of symbols will expand to accommodate evolving sounds in the language that the alphabet is normally used to write.

The Younger Futhark could be used to write Old Norse quite effectively,* but doing so required more specialized knowledge about how certain runes were now used to write multiple sounds in ways

---

*It should be pointed out that all the long-form texts written in Old Norse and Old Icelandic, such as the Eddas and the numerous sagas, were not written with runes of any kind but rather in a regional variation of the Latin alphabet.

not always discernible by context alone. That is, it was perhaps made more complicated in order to preserve the limited number of people who were able to read and write using the system. Some of the specific orthographical changes as compared to the Elder Futhark, like ensuring that every rune had a vertical line, were perhaps due to the increasing number of carved runestones (where consistent vertical lines help with the aligning of runes into lines with consistent height).

TABLE 7.2. THE YOUNGER FUTHARK 16-RUNE SYSTEM

No.	Sound	Shape	Name	Exoteric Meaning	Esoteric Meaning
1	f	ᚠ	*fé*	Cattle, money, gold	Dynamic power
2	u/o/v	ᚢ	*úr*	Drizzling rain, aurochs	Fertilizing essence
3	th/dh	ᚦ	*thurs*	Thurs (giant)	Breaker of resistance
4	a	ᚬ	*áss*	*The* god (= Odin)	Word-power, sovereign force
5	r	ᚱ	*reið*	A ride, thunderclap	Spiritual path or journey
6	k/g/ng	ᚴ	*kaun*	A sore	Internal fire or protection
7	h	ᚼ	*hagall*	Hail	Ice seed form
8	n	ᚾ	*nauð*	Need, bondage, fetters	Need-fire, slavery/ freedom
9	i/e/)	ᛁ	*íss*	Ice	Contraction, *prima materia*
10	a	ᛅ	*ár*	Good year, harvest	Blooming into manifestation
11	s	ᛋ	*sól*	Sun	Sun wheel/ crystalized light
12	t/d/ nt/nd	ᛏ	*týr*	The god Tyr	Sovereign heavenly order
13	b/p/ mb	ᛒ	*bjarkan*	Birch (-goddess)	Gestation/birth
14	m	ᛘ	*maðr*	Man, human	Ancestral divine order

No.	Sound	Shape	Name	Exoteric Meaning	Esoteric Meaning
15	l	↑	*lögr*	Sea, waterfall	Life energy/ organic growth
16	-R	⅄	*yr*	Yew, bow of yew wood	Telluric power

The picture of whether runes were sometimes used in magical ways is clearer in the Younger Futhark period, even as the number of purely mundane uses of runes greatly increased.

Two of the most-cited references to rune magic in the Younger Futhark period are in *Egils saga Skallagrímssonar.*[*] The central character of the saga, Egill, explicitly uses runes for magical purposes in a pair of episodes. In the first, he suspects that the contents of his drinking horn have been poisoned. He carves a rune on the horn and reddens it with his own blood, with the intent that it will confirm or deny the presence of poison; the horn dramatically bursts asunder, confirming the poison. Here, it is not enough merely to utter the word or name associated with the rune, but it must be given physical presence on the very object it is to affect. Egill communicates directly with the object, using the carved and stained rune to convey his intent and receives a response in the form of the destruction of the horn.

Also in *Egill's Saga*, the daughter of the farmer Thorfinn has fallen ill and her condition worsens after another farmer's son attempts to cure her by carving runes on a piece of whalebone. Egill notices that the runic formula on the whalebone was carved incorrectly, thus further sickening the girl; he resolves this by scraping off the runes and casting both the scrapings and the rest of the bone into the fire. He then replaces them with a properly executed runic healing formula, after which the girl arises, cured of her illness although still weak.

Here we again see the importance of giving runes physical existence, carving the runic formula with all its layers of meaning directly onto an

---

[*]*The Saga of Egill Skallagrímsson*, usually just referred to as *Egill's Saga*.

object. In contrast to the episode with the horn, the whalebone is not the final recipient of the magic but rather a tool for carrying the operative communication to its recipient (the farm girl). This passage also illustrates the vital importance of carving runes *correctly*: ill-carved runes cause more harm than good. It was not enough for Egill merely to scrape the runes off the whalebone; the object and the runestaves themselves had to be transmuted and destroyed to remove their adverse influence—another instance of the law of contagion in action (see chap. 2).

Both episodes speak to the numinous, magical associations that runes could take on in the right circumstances. Not every runic inscription in the Younger Futhark is inherently magical, but some inscriptions can be understood as magical when other parts of the context—the semiotic whole—in which they are carved is *also* magical.

The Anglo-Saxon (Anglo-Frisian) Futhorc

A separate evolution of the Elder Futhark is the Anglo-Saxon (sometimes called Anglo-Frisian) Futhorc, which consists of twenty-nine to thirty-three runes, depending on timeframe and location. These runes are first attested around 500 CE—branching off not long before advent of the Younger Futhark—and are primarily associated with the Old English period of Great Britain.

As the Old English language developed from Proto-Germanic, there was an expansion of the number of vowel sounds (not unlike parallel developments in Old Norse). In contrast to the Younger Futhark, however, the Anglo-Saxon Futhorc retained (with some minor variations) all the runes of the Elder Futhark and over time added new ones to accommodate sounds in Old English that were not present in Proto-Germanic. Some of the sounds presented by the Elder Futhark did undergo changes. Notably, the sound of the fourth rune *ansuz* changed from an [a] to [o] while the name (which ultimately become *ōs*) and appearance of the rune also shift slightly as well (from ᚠ to ᚩ). These particular changes will be discussed in more detail below in the section about the rune poems.

There is very little extant Old English material that directly alludes to magical uses of runes, although much evidence of a general magical outlook remains as part of numerous folk magic charms and spells. The most famous of these is a text known as "The Nine Herbs Charm," in which Woden (Odin) slays a serpent using nine *wuldortānas* ("glory twigs"); the nine glory twigs are widely surmised to be runic in nature. Another instance of residual belief in runes as magical can be seen in Bede's account of the capture of the nobleman Imma. After Imma's bonds fell away, which Bede attributed to the prayers being said for him by his kinsman among the clergy, Imma's captors accused him of knowing and concealing certain runic spells for the loosening of bonds.

These episodes do suggest that there was clearly a vestige of a folk belief among the Anglo-Saxons that runes can be used for magical purposes, but we must be careful about assuming too much about earlier pre-Christian beliefs based on folklore alone.

MYTHIC ORIGINS

It is not possible to separate the study of the runes from knowledge of their divine patron, Odin (Old Norse Óðinn). Stanzas 138–39 of the *Hávamál*, a poem in the *Poetic Edda*, describe how he gained knowledge of the runes:

> *I know that I hung on a windy tree*
> *nights all nine*
> *Wounded by the gar (spear) given to Óðinn,*
> *myself to myself,*
> *on that tree, of which no man knoweth*
> *from what roots it rises.*
> *They dealt me no bread nor drinking horn,*
> *I looked down,*
> *I took up the runes, roaring I took them*
> *And fell back again.*[3]

It is important to note that Óðinn does not *invent* the runes, he *discovers* them in his moment of deepest despair on the edge of the spear point that separates life from death. The discovery of the runes revitalizes his nearly dead form, and he immediately knows that this knowledge is worthless if he merely hoards it for himself. As he falls back to the ground of Midgard, thus ending his ordeal, he begins to work to reshape the cosmos in an image of his choosing. He does this not according to whim but based on his newfound understanding and makes these tools available for use by those who aspire to the same knowledge and potency.

The Etymology of Óðinn

The very name of Óðinn reveals some of his connections with poetry, spells, and other forms of verbal and written magic. The original Proto-Germanic form of the name—*Wōðanaz*—can be translated as "master of inspiration." The root of the name, *wōð-*, in turn derives from either a Proto-Indo-European root meaning "to be excited" or one meaning "to blow." Both possible roots are revealed in the context of the myth of the creation of humanity from the trees Askr and Embla. In the version of this myth in stanzas 17 and 18 of the poem *Völuspá* in the *Poetic Edda*, the divine trio of Óðinn, Hœnir, and Lóðurr* travel along the coast and find two trees to whom they give certain gifts so that they become the first humans. Among these gifts are *önd*, given by Óðinn, and *óðr*, given by Hœnir.

Óðr is an Old Norse word derived from—and meaning the same as—Proto-Germanic *wōðaz*. *Önd* is an Old Norse word meaning "breath." Both gifts are of vital importance in the composition and performance of poetry, and in related activities such as singing incantations and magical songs. Inspiration—*óðr*—is required to be able to conceive of a new way to configure the self or the phenomenal world; breath—*önd*—is needed to speak those desires into existence.

---

*The latter two are very likely hypostases of Óðinn: different "faces" of the same god, emphasizing different attributes.

THE RUNE POEMS

No written records of the names of the runes of the Elder Futhark survive from the archaic period, assuming they were ever written down or standardized to begin with. The likely names have been reconstructed as Proto-Germanic words based on sound changes established through historical linguistics. The prime source of evidence for the names is the rune poems, of which there are three primary ones. These consist of brief poetic statements about the hidden lore of individual runes, which also serve as aids to memorizing their names, order, and lore.

The three most well-known rune poems are the Old English Rune Poem, likely dating to the early ninth century and referring to the Anglo-Frisian runes, and the two poems referring to the Younger Futhark: the Old Icelandic Rune Poem, and the Old Norwegian Rune Rhyme.* Linguistic features of the latter two poems confirm that the text contained in them dates to approximately the twelfth century at the latest.

Note, however, that none of these poems correspond to the Elder Futhark. If there was ever an "*Ur*-poem"—a more ancient common source poem (or poems) that inspired the later rune poems that have survived—it was either never written down or no copies survive. We cannot rule out the possibility that a long oral tradition preserved the ancient lore in poetic form. Other Indo-European cultures of course did this, and to suggest that the Germanic peoples could not have done that if they wished would only play into stereotypes about the Germanic tribes as "noble savages" (like those portrayed in Tacitus's infamous *Germania*).

Hints of Magical Communication in the Rune Poems

Let's look at a stanza from one of the rune poems that connects runes with magical communication.

---

*Two lesser-known poems are the Early Modern Swedish Rune Poem and the Abecedarium Nordmannicum. See *The Rune Poems: A Reawakened Tradition*, edited by P. D. Brown and Michael Moynihan (Arcana Europa, 2022), for more information on all the rune poems including new translations and commentary.

Old English Rune Poem, stanza 4:

> *(Mouth) is the source of all speech,*
> *wisdom's upholder, and a comfort for counselors;*
> *for every earl, happiness and hope.*[4]

The reconstructed name of the fourth rune of the Elder Futhark, *ansuz*, is a Proto-Germanic word for a god. This name later became *áss* (pl. *æsir*) in Old Norse. Óðinn, as the first independent and self-aware being in the Norse mythology, is the exemplary "sovereign god" (*áss*).

However, the name of the rune in this poem has shifted to a homophone (soundalike word): Latin *ōs* (mouth).* Whether this was done under Christian influence or as part of concealing the true name with a pun is uncertain—however, because of the very close associations between Óðinn and speech and poetry the latter explanation is perhaps the more likely one.[†]

The associations between Óðinn and speech run deep in Northern Germanic lore. He is the patron of poets, who draw on the inspiration he has mastered and teaches. He is also connected with the breath; in the account of Askr and Embla mentioned earlier in this chapter, he provides these protohumans with breath (Old Norse *önd*), which is even considered to be a part of the body/soul complex of humans. Breath, of course, is a vital component of speech, especially the speech of poets—skalds—who must master the breath in order to maintain the necessary rhythms of their speech (just as they must remain open to inspiration so they can speak words of mythic and eternal truth).

---

*A similar homophonic shift happens in the Old Norwegian Rune Rhyme, where the rune name refers to an inlet—the mouth of a river opening to a larger body of water.
†The Old English word *ōs*, meaning "a god," is retained in various names like Oswald ("god power") and Osgood ("god [is] good"); these names date from an early period and did not originally refer to the Christian god.

RUNIC FORMULAS

One of the better-attested approaches in the runic corpus is the use of formulas to convey magical intent. Among other things, these can be used to sanctify an object, to use an object as part of a curse, or to enlist the object in causing or preventing the occurrence of some phenomenon. In a culture where literacy was rare and carried with it a perception of being something magical or at least extraordinary, writing or carving the formula into physical existence added a potent dimension to the operation by imprinting the intent onto the very fabric of the material universe.

Four common types of formulas found in inscriptions are:

1. runemaster formulas (also known as *ek* ["I"] formulas, where the carver of the runes asserts his qualifications and right to carve them)
2. reused symbolic words and phrases, such as *alu* ("sacred intoxicating drink"), *laukaR* ("leek"), and the *ek erilaR* ("I, the Eril [runemaster]"), or *þórr vigi* ("May Thor bless [this object]")
3. individual runestaves repeated for symbolic numbers of iterations—usually groups of three or eight runestaves—used to emphasize and compound the meaning behind the name of the stave so repeated
4. seeming gibberish; random runestaves repeated, likely to evoke an effect similar to glossolalia ("speaking in tongues")

The formulas themselves then become runes—syntagmata, or collections of signs that take on meaning beyond merely their component parts, which in turn serve as building blocks for operative acts.

These types of formulaic speech use well-known and repeated phrases that serve a ritual purpose by connecting this act with others that have come before; these may be references to mythic operations (such as "May Thor bless [this object]") or part of a formula horde that can be invoked when needed (such as the aforementioned runemaster formulas and symbolic word formulas). Formulaic speech is not at all limited to runic contexts; a well-known example is the "imperishable fame" formula that appears in a variety of contexts throughout the ancient Indo-European world.*

All of these types of formulas can be interpreted as syntagmatic uses of runes: both the ideographic meanings (from the component runes themselves) and the meaning of the words combine to convey meaning beyond just their component parts.

Let's look at the *ek erilaR* formula first. For example, on the famous Lindholm bone amulet, the inscription begins: *ek erilaR sā wīlagaR ha(i)teka* ("I, the Eril, am called the crafty one"). The title Eril became synonymous with "runemaster."[5] The name is found in inscriptions, usually as part of a statement about the carver's worthiness and qualification.

The runemaster identifies himself with the transcendental archetype of "runemastery," with the proof being in part his ability to inscribe runes at all. By doing so, he declares his kinship with the source of this magical stream, and by extension, declares himself for the duration of the operation to be acting *as* Óðinn.

The *ek* formulas also work with the law of similarity, one of the aspects of James Frazer's anthropological theories on magic that have retained usefulness among more modern views (see chap. 2). This is the equivalent of the Egyptian process *pḥ-nṯr*—the magician raising himself to the same level as the god whose powers he wishes to employ. Because of its dependence on context, communication is most effective among communicants who are similar in some way: they speak the same language, have some commonalities in their backgrounds, or are participating in a situation where context conditions how their

---

*Found, among many examples, in Homer's *Iliad* as κλέος ἄφθιτον (*kléos áphthiton*), and अक्षितम् श्रवस् (*śrávas ákṣitam*) in the *Rig Veda*; both phrases can be translated as "imperishable (or undying) fame."

attempts to communicate with each other are interpreted. In magical communication this similarity can be created through identification with the god who has the skills and expertise to bring about the desired change.

By identifying with these attributes, the magician is claiming them as part of himself (at least for the duration of the rite). He can now do the very things that gods with those abilities can do. In the same way that myth relates what those gods can create or modify within the world, the magician now has the ability to do likewise.

Another type of formula uses the repetition of certain runestaves some significant number of times in an inscription, most often three or eight. This approach is commonly used in formulas of desire and in curses. For desire, the formula is used for calling a specific concept to the runemaster. *Fehu* (ᚠ), signifying movable wealth, is a common one of course. The rune *nauðiz* (ᚾ), "need," is found repeated eight times in curse formulas, calling forth unfulfillable need upon one's enemies. Alternately, the runes *ansuz* (ᚨ) and *teiwaz* (ᛏ) are repeated to invoke the favor—or attributes—of the gods Óðinn and Týr, respectively.

The formula *alu* (ᚨᛚᚢ) is common as well, appearing in over twenty Elder Futhark inscriptions. The Proto-Germanic word *alu* is the root of our modern English word "ale," and in its original form refers to any intoxicating drink. *Alu* typically occurs at the end of runic formulas and is used to sanctify the preceding words, sealing their magical intent and making sacred both the inscription and the object it is inscribed on.

Bind Runes

A fifth type of pattern found in Elder Futhark inscriptions could in some circumstances also be classed as a type of formula: a *bind rune* is a combination of two or more runes into a single symbol, with the meanings of those runes combined to form a new syntagma as well. We should treat bind runes carefully, however, based on context. In many cases, especially

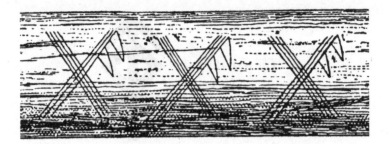

Bind runes on the Kragehul spear shaft

on earlier inscriptions, they seem to have been done merely to save space and don't necessarily carry any additional meaning. However, they did later begin to appear to have significance of their own, especially in contexts where there is no apparent space-saving motive.

Let's look at a historic example of a bind rune first, then at a modern one. The Kragehul spear shaft, dated to approximately the fifth century, contains an Elder Futhark bind rune that appears to have been deliberately encoded as such for its meaning (rather than as a way to conserve space in the inscription). The three identical bind runes in the inscription are generally accepted as being composed of the runes *gebo* (X, the [g] sound) and *ansuz* (ᚠ, the [a] sound). Recall that gebo means "gift" and ansuz is a word for "a god" (often specifically Óðinn), and the idea of a gift from or to a god closely associated with war seems fitting for a spear shaft. We should note that there is no reason to presume that there must have been one and only one meaning for the bind rune that could have been understood by the runemaster who carved this (or those reading or hearing the inscription).

For a modern example of the technique of creating a bind rune, we can look at the one created and popularized by Stephen Flowers that encodes the Old Icelandic phrase *reyn til rúna* ("seek the mysteries"). This bind rune, written using the Younger Futhark since that was the rune row appropriate to the times and places where Old Norse and Old Icelandic were spoken as primary languages, combines the *týr* rune (ᛏ, the [t] sound) with two *reið* runes (ᚱ, the [r] sound).

The reyn til rúna
bind rune

From an operative communicational—or semiurgic—perspective, bind runes are another syntagmatic use of runes. That is, the individual runes have a meaning and sound of their own, but the combined figure encodes meaning and intent that transcend that of the runes in isolation. Bind runes are a purely written, not spoken, form of magical communication; since there are often multiple ways to read the individual runes that may comprise a bind rune, it is possible and even likely for the reader of the bind rune to find different runes (and thus different meanings) from those intended by the one who carved (or wrote) it.

THE ARMANEN RUNES

Guido von List (born Guido Karl Anton List, 1848–1919) was an Austrian mystic, novelist, and journalist who was prominent in the *völkisch* and pan-Germanic movements in German-speaking lands in the late nineteenth century. Inspired from a very young age to learn about and revive the religious beliefs of the ancient Germanic peoples, List later became the central figure in the reawakening of esoteric interest in runes in the first couple of decades of the twentieth century.

Although many of List's teachings about the history and meaning of the runes contradict accepted historical and linguistic narratives, it must be understood that his ultimate aim seems to have been much more about creating a new syncretic form of rune work than recreating strictly historical forms. In this he was heavily influenced by his earlier association with Theosophy, especially its emphasis on combining the beliefs and practices of various cultures based on similarities and com-

patibility of the ideas—whether those similarities were due to borrowing, having a common ancestry, or mere coincidence.

In 1902, while his eyes were bandaged for eleven months following
surgery for cataracts, List had the visions and insights that led him to
formulate the idea of what he called the Armanen runes (Table 7.3).* This
set of eighteen runes was based on the sixteen-rune Younger Futhark,
with specific changes and expansions derived from his reading of the final
section of the *Hávamál*, known as *Rúnatáls þáttr Óðins* ("Odin's Rune
Song"). That section begins with the stanzas quoted before about Odin's
winning of the runes after hanging on the World Tree Yggdrasil for nine
nights; it ends with a collection of eighteen magic spells or incantations.

These spells are not explicitly referred to as rune songs although
their context suggests that they certainly could be. Several of these spells
clearly reference runes and so the idea that they are describing runes has
been an enduring one; it seems reasonable to accept that these pivotal
eighteen stanzas are indeed likely referring to runes or at least incantations featuring runes. One thing to note about them is they describe the
result, purpose, or usage of the "rune songs," *not* the actual text of the
spells that accomplish these things. For example, one reads:

> *A twelfth (spell) I know: when I see aloft upon a tree*
> *A corpse swinging from a rope,*
> *Then I cut and paint runes*
> *So that the man walks*
> *And speaks with me.*[6]

Nonetheless, List read these eighteen spells as descriptions of runes
and largely followed the Younger Futhark order in hypothesizing the
Armanen runes, which he claimed were in fact the *original* form and

---

*List postulated an ancient Germanic society of priest-kings called the *Armanen* (the
tribal name of the "Herminones" cited by Tacitus in Germania supposedly represented
a Latinized version of the name of this society). This body of priest-kings were, to List,
the original runemasters.

arrangement of the runes. This assertion is usually one of the specific things cited for rejecting List's ideas by those who take a more historical and/or academic approach to runes. But again, List's goal was not so much to foster historical interest in runes as much as it was to rekindle *mythical* and *esoteric* interest in them recast in a modern form.

List's Armanen runes are sometimes erroneously identified with the Nazis' use of runes. The Nazis' rune imagery was not part of any systematic philosophy or practice but was rather an appeal to the mythic past intended to function primarily on an emotional level.* The source of much of the usage of runes by the Nazis was in fact due to the influence of Karl Maria Wiligut[†] on *Reichsführer*-SS Heinrich Himmler as his personal spiritual advisor. Wiligut had been originally inspired by List, but largely developed his own theory of runes in a very idiosyncratic and ahistorical way supposedly derived from a family religion passed down to him from father to son.

TABLE 7.3. THE ARMANEN 18-RUNE SYSTEM

No.	Shape	Name	Meaning
1	ᚠ	FA	Primal fire, change, re-shaping, banishing of distress, projecting-generative principle, primal spirit
2	ᚢ	UR	Eternity, consistency, physician's rune, luck, telluric magnetism, primal soul
3	ᚦ	THORN	Action, will to action, evolutionary power, goal-setting, rune of Od-magnetic transference
4	ᚨ	OS[‡]	Breath, spiritual well-being, word, radiating Od-magnetic power

*For a thorough examination of the truth, fiction, and occasional wishful thinking behind the topic of Nazi occultism, see Stephen E. Flowers's *The Occult in National Socialism: The Symbolic, Scientific, and Magical Influences on the Third Reich* (Inner Traditions, 2022).

[†]See Flowers's and Moynihan's *The Secret King: The Myth and Reality of Nazi Occultism* (Feral House, 2007). This volume collects, translates, and analyzes virtually all of Wiligut's extant writings (such as they are; Wiligut's preferred mode of teaching was mouth-to-ear to individual students so there is limited written material from him).

[‡]An alternate name for this Armanen rune is OTHIL, with the meaning(s): "Arising, the power of the word, receptive power."

No.	Shape	Name	Meaning
5	ᛈ	RIT	Primal law, rightness, advice, rescue, rhythm
6	ᚴ	KA	Generation, power, art, ability, propagation
7	✳	HAGAL	All-enclosure, spiritual leadership, protectiveness, harmony, cosmic order, the midpoint of order
8	✝	NOT	The unavoidable, karma, compulsion of fate
9	I	IS	Ego, will, activity, personal power, banishing, consciousness of spiritual power, control of self and others
10	ᛉ	AR	Sun, wisdom, beauty, virtue, fame, well-being, protection from specters, leadership
11	ᚼ	SIG	Solar power, victory, success, knowledge, realization, power to actualize
12	↑	TYR	Power, success, wisdom, generation, awakening, rebirth in the spirit, spiraling development
13	ᛒ	BAR	Becoming, birth, the third birth in the spirit, concealment, song
14	ᚱ	LAF	Primal law, life, experience of life, love, primal water, water and ocean rune
15	ᛉ	MAN	Man-rune, increase, fullness, health, magic, spirit, god-man, the masculine principle in the cosmos, day-consciousness
16	ᛦ	YR	Woman-rune, instinct, greed, passion, matter, delusion, confusion, death, destruction, the negative feminine principle in the cosmos, night-consciousness
17	✝	EH	Marriage, lasting love, law, justice, hope, duration, rune of trust and of the dual (twin) souls
18	ᛡ	GIBOR	God-rune, god-all, cosmic consciousness, wedding together of powers, the generative and receptive, sacred marriage, giver and the gift, fulfillment

List's writings on runes were for the most part more theoretical than practical; he insinuated in various places that there *were* specific practices associated with his theories, but they needed to be learned directly from him or his students. Several German rune magicians influenced by List did, however, produce much more written material on the practical points of working with the Armanen runes. Among these were Rudolf John Gorsleben with his *Hoch-Zeit der Menschheit* (Zenith of Mankind), although like List he focused on theory instead of practice in his written works. Siegfried Adolf Kummer, on the other hand, focused on practical work in his short *Runen-Magie* (Rune-Magic) and *Heilige Runenmacht* (Holy Rune Might). Friedrich Bernhard Marby had name recognition and influence surpassed only by List and Gorsleben. Karl Spiesberger arrived on the scene later than the others just mentioned, and he was also a high-ranking member of the Fraternitas Saturni.* His small 1954 volume *Runen-Magie* (Rune Magic) focuses on practical uses of the runes and shows the eclectic influence of Spiesberger's work in the Fraternitas Saturni. For an overview of these and other twentieth-century German rune magicians, see *Rune Might: The Secret Practices of the German Rune Magicians* by Edred Thorsson (Inner Traditions, 2018).

Because of the inherently eclectic approach that List encouraged, these other German rune magicians innovated in various ways with the practices that are now included under the banner of the Armanen runes.

Communicative Features of Armanen Runes

As the Armanen runes are part of an esoteric and flexible system, it is difficult to say with certainty what is and isn't a part of it. However, we can identify some core practices and approaches with roots in List's works.

---

*The Fraternitas Saturni is an eclectic magical order founded by Gregor Gregorius (Eugen Grosche) in 1926. For an account of its early history and practices, see Stephen Flowers's *The Fraternitas Saturni* (Inner Traditions, 2017).

There is an emphasis on spoken runes and rune formulas, combined with using the hands for *mudras* (hand gestures signifying specific runes) and tracing runes in the air. There is less emphasis on inscriptions (written or carved), and little mention of using runes for divination. We must be cautious about contrasting this balance of techniques against what we know of likely uses for runes in the Elder Futhark and Younger Futhark periods; since only inscriptions on durable materials would still be available to us, there may be a significant bias due to the specific media of the remaining evidence so we simply can't know how widespread oral- or gesture-based runic practices may have been in antiquity.

The Armanen practices have also tended to focus on runic mantras. The latter possibly were imported by List due to his influence from Theosophy (which drew heavily on Hindu practices, at least as they were understood in Europe in the nineteenth century). List created an entire "mystery language" based on the rune names as "seed" words for building complex verbal formulas that also convey the meanings of the component runes. Since this technique is so critical to his theory of semiurgy using runes, we will devote a section to it below.

Among the Armanen runic pioneers, Guido von List was especially fascinated by language and the ways it could be manipulated for magical practices. Drawing on the discussion of language-games in chapter 4, we can definitely see List's work with seed words as an innovative language-game with its own rules and assumptions. List was also prone to use folk etymologies* to tie ideas together. Even if these connections do not have validity in terms of the actual verifiable etymology of words, they *do* have validity in the context of List's idiosyncratic language-game, which results from the way he attached consistent meaning to these particular manipulations of phonemes (the component sounds of a language).

---

*A folk etymology is a mistaken assumption about the origin of a word based on other words with which it happens to share sounds.

List associated eighteen runes—the Younger Futhark plus two runes he claimed had been lost or suppressed—with the eighteen spells in the *"Rúnatáls þáttr Óðins"* section that closes the *Hávamál*. List emphasized that one does not need to know the words of the spell itself if the associated rune is known; through metonymy, the runestave and sound open the door to create the same effect.

This type of verbal magic facilitated by symbols embodies many of the principles of semiurgy that underly this book. The runestaves—as with any other magical symbol—are anchors in the objective universe for the subjective (i.e., individual, self-directed) practices of the magician. The gestures, words, and symbols utilized are part of a complex sign-network that the operator creates to encode their intent—they then use this encoded intent in communication with the unmanifest to bring about their desire.

List's Formula

List saw history and cosmology in terms of cycles: what happens has an antecedent in what has happened before, and what perishes will be renewed when conditions are once again favorable. This fits in with the myth of Ragnarök—a renewal of the world following its destruction by strife among the gods—as found in the Eddas. Interest in the mythic principle of Ragnarök had also then recently been popularized by the last of the operas in Richard Wagner's Ring Cycle, *Götterdämmerung* ("Twilight of the Gods," 1876).

List encoded this view of cycles in his magical formula *Entstehen—Sein—Vergehen zum neuen Entstehen*: "arising, being, passing away to a new arising." For List, this formula was also embodied in the myth of Wuotan's (Óðinn's) winning of knowledge of the runes through his nine-night ordeal hanging from Yggdrasil. Wuotan realizes that his knowledge of himself and the world is limited, willingly undertakes the ordeal, and at the moment of death he is suddenly infused (and renewed) with a new understanding via the runes.

The runes are used to write new realities in being, and they do so in part subject to the conditions that are common to all kinds of communication. They are dependent for meaning on context, so that even the same words (or same runes and runic formulas) can take on different meaning in different situations and times. When a runic formula is spoken or carved, everything about the time, place, intent, and the person engaged in the runic operation affects the significance and effectiveness of the operation. Thus, even operations that appear the same on the surface as previous ones are in fact partaking of List's formula; they arise, exist on their own terms yet tied to time and place, and then cease to exist where they (and their results) will then be created anew through future operations. This takes List's formula from being not only about macrocosmic and mythic concerns to affecting the microcosm of an individual magician as well, with each cycle building on the previous ones.

Seed Words: The Kala

List was very interested in the hidden meanings of the sounds that combine to build words (in linguistic terms, these are the phonemes [sounds] that are used in morphology [the formation of words from individual sounds]). List called his system of sonic analysis *Kala* and while he only wrote of it in a passive sense (for analyzing the meaning in existing words/formulas), it can also be adapted for creating *new* words/formulas as a tool in magical operations and mantras.

Crucial to his theories are what he called *seed* or *kernel* words. Using the sounds signified by the Armanen runes, there are ten distinct consonant sounds and five distinct vowel sounds;* these combine as pairs of consonants and vowels (in either order) to form the seed words. All of the names of the runes (many of which correspond to these combinations of vowels and consonants) are also considered seed or kernel words.

---

*He treats the sounds [th] and [d] as equivalent, as well as the pairs [p] / [b] and [k] / [g]. In linguistics, sounds that are considered as the same for phonetic purposes even though they can be heard as distinct are called allophones.

TABLE 7.4. KEY TO THE LISTIAN MYSTERY LANGUAGE

		I — primal fire, cause or power	II — primal air, desire or will	III — primal earth, ability, art, magic	IV — primal æther, the act	V — primal water, law, law of nature	VI — heavenly fire order	VII — heavenly fire order in spiritual interior	VIII — midgard fire order in material exterior	IX — all-light forming traits	X — moon completion
1. cause or power / 2. desire or will / 3. ability, art, magic / 4. the act	A	FA	RA	KA ga	ThA da	NA	SA	TA	BA pa	LA	MA
5. law, law of nature / 6. order	E	FE	RE	KE ge	ThE de	NE	SE	TE	BE pe	LE	ME
7. spiritual order	I	FI	RI	KI gi	ThI di	NI	SI	TI	BI pi	LI	MI
8. material order / 9. forming traits	O	FO	RO	KO go	ThO do	NO	SO	TO	BO po	LO	MO
10. completion	U	FU	RU	KU gu	ThU du	NU	SU	TU	BU pu	LU	MU
1. cause or power / 2. desire or will / 3. ability, art, magic / 4. the act	A	AF	AR	AK ag	ATh ad	AN	AS	AT	AB up	AL	AM
5. law, law of nature / 6. order	E	EF	ER	EK eg	ETh ed	EN	ES	ET	EB ep	EL	EM
7. spiritual order	I	IF	IR	IK ig	ITh id	IN	IS	IT	IB ep	IL	IM
8. material order / 9. forming traits	O	OF	OR	OK og	OTh od	ON	OS	OT	OB op	OL	OM
10. completion	U	UF	UR	UK ug	UTh ud	UN	US	UT	UB up	UL	UM

This chart from Edred Thorsson's *Rune Might* (Table 7.4) shows the sounds and some of their associated significance:

As an example, using this chart to determine the true meaning of the rune name *FA*, List would say that the following combination of meaning emerges: *F* = "primal fire" + *A* = "cause or power, the will to express it, realization of the necessity of deeds."

Similarly, the name Wuotan (rendered as U-O-T-A-N to fit the sounds in the *Kala*) would be explained through this type of investigation as: "in the completion of the plan" + "in the physical order of the forming of the necessary traits of the world" + "cause or power, the will to express it, realization of the necessity of deeds" + "primal water."

This type of analysis is possible because historically the runes have been *ideographic*—having names that themselves bear meaning—in addition to being an alphabetic script where the letters indicate specific sounds. These dual layers of meaning provide for possibilities for deriving significance from their meaningful combinations (syntagmata) that are not possible with a purely alphabetic script. This is why, for example, *isopsephy* (adding the values of the Greek letters in a word to form a number) must rely on number/order alone; the extra layer of meaning in the names of the individual runestaves creates a much richer matrix of possibilities.

This type of thinking shows the extent to which List focused on seeing new possibilities for how runes could be understood and used. The fact that he then claimed that his insights revealed the *original* shapes, names, and practices behind the runes is a function of his mythological approach: seeing myths as both concealing and revealing what is eternally True. This aspect of List's work is often missed, or is poorly understood, by those who dismiss List's work purely on historical grounds.

CONCLUSION

Runes have been the subject of intense study from historical, linguistic, semiotic, and esoteric perspectives, especially in the last 120 years or so. That they continue to hold such fascination (even from those who see nothing at all magical about them) only confirms the inherent Mystery behind them that is encoded in their very name.

Since the use of runes in writing—not to mention association with song and poetry—is a fundamental part of their history and mythology, they are a communicative system at their core. This holds true for both their use in mundane communication and in operative (magical) communication. As this chapter has shown, the runes are fertile ground for applying the ideas of magic-as-communication that are the basis of this book.

FURTHER READING

Historical Information about Runes and Rune Magicians
Runes: Literacy in the Germanic Iron Age by Stephen Pollington
Runes: A Handbook by Michael Barnes
The Rune Poems: A Reawakened Tradition, edited by P. D. Brown and Michael Moynihan
The Secret of the Runes by Guido von List (translated with commentary by Stephen E. Flowers)

Academic Studies Looking at Magical Uses of Runes
Runes and Magic by Stephen E. Flowers
The Application of Peircean Semiotics to the Elder Futhark Tradition by Scott Shell

Practical Magical Uses of Runes
Helrunar: A Manual of Rune Magick by Jan Fries
Runa: The Wisdom of the Runes by A. D. Mercer

Rune Might: The Secret Practices of the German Rune Magicians by Edred Thorsson

The Big Book of Runes and Magic by Edred Thorsson (combines and consolidates information from his books *Futhark*, *Runelore*, and *The Runecaster's Handbook*)

8

MODERN APPROACHES
TO SEMIURGY

In the first two case studies, we looked at the communicative features of both late antique Mediterranean magic and runes. Now we will examine several modern schools of thought on magic that show different ways to approach what we have called *semiurgy*, or operative communication. Two types of magic will connect several of these approaches: sigils and Enochian (or angelic) magic.

Modern sigil magic has some roots in the Renaissance. However, sigil magic as most magicians know it today bears a heavy influence from the theories and practices of twentieth-century British artist and occultist Austin Osman Spare (whose magical work was popularized by the Chaos Magic current that began in the 1970s in the UK).

The other connector, Enochian magic, took shape with the scrying experiments of John Dee and Edward Kelley beginning in the late sixteenth century. New approaches to Dee's work by the Hermetic Order of the Golden Dawn at the end of the 1880s set the stage for many of the practices of Enochian magic since that time.

In this chapter, we will trace some of these semiurgic connectors as well as look at other ways that different modern schools of magic—both formally organized and not—have utilized many of the concepts we have covered thus far. First, let's take a brief look at what sigils and Enochian are in historical terms.

THE EVOLUTION OF SIGILS

Sigils as understood in the late medieval and early Renaissance period were pictorial representations of various demons, spirits, and even angels. In some cases, they were created by tracing patterns in magic squares of letters or numbers; in other cases, the source of their attribution is unknown. The word *sigil* comes from Latin *sigillum*, meaning a "seal": just as the impression in a wax seal stands for the signature of the person who stamped it, a sigil in this older sense stands for the particular numinous entity associated with it. Semiotically, they are symbolic (or unmotivated) signs, with the association between the sign and its referent being an arbitrary one (i.e., fixed by convention).

Two of the most famous collections of such sigils are Heinrich Cornelius Agrippa's planetary signs in his *De Occulta Philosophia* and the seals of the seventy-two demons in the anonymous *Ars Goetia* from the *Lemegeton Clavicula Salomoni* (commonly known as the "Lesser Key of Solomon"). These sigils have been repeated in numerous grimoires since their publication, presented as equivalents of the "true names" of the entities and intelligences signified by them.

These types of sigils function as a sort of bridge between linguistic and nonlinguistic symbolism. All the same ideas about what it means to know the name of something—to control it, to describe it, to give it existence—apply whether the sigil is based on words, pictures, or both. *Sigils are another way of creating something more concrete for the mind to focus on in order to bring the abstract, the numinous, and the mysterious closer.*

Ancient Roots

The technology behind these Renaissance and Early Modern sigils has roots going back into the dim past even before writing was invented.

Petroglyphs (images engraved in rock) and pictographs (images painted on rock) up to 20,000 years old have been discovered on every continent except Antarctica.* While we can't be sure at this late date, the general consensus is that these images—some of which are clearly symbolic and not representative—held cultural and even cultic significance that made it important to leave them in a permanent medium. In some cases, they may have even been a form of proto-writing, communicating limited information (as opposed to true writing, which can be used to express an unlimited range of types of linguistic communication). In other instances, they may have provided a visual focus for magical or religious practices as something shared among people with a common semiotic code for understanding and affecting the world around them.

The letterlike images called *charaktêres* in ancient magical texts (see chap. 6) can resemble medieval and modern sigils as well, especially in the commonly found form with straight lines capped in small circles.

As we have seen with the type of sign called a *symbol* by Peircean semioticians, the arbitrary (i.e., determined by convention) meaning of these prelinguistic signs can be every bit as real and profound as that of more well-known arbitrary signs. Such signs carry meaning and significance in the context where they are used, much in the same way that a particular gesture or ritual tool has meaning that is tied specifically to their use in a ritual context. They retain this meaning even if they have no significance outside of this context that is part of the language-game of ritual magic.

Austin Osman Spare and Sigils

A more recent and enduringly popular type of sigil magic can be traced to the work of British magician and artist Austin Osman Spare (1886–1956). A renowned painter and sketch artist in his youth,

---

*And hopefully will never be found there, given the warnings of H. P. Lovecraft in *At the Mountains of Madness*!

Spare never attained the station in the art world to which he at one point seemed destined. He spent his later years destitute, frequenting a handful of pubs in London and making art that he sold cheaply just to survive. Nonetheless, his influence on late twentieth-century magic is profound, especially in the world of Chaos Magic.

Spare invented a new method for creating sigils, based on formulating a written statement of desire and then reducing the component letters to a visual form that captures the "essence" of those letters. Thus, his sigils were symbolic reductions of the original statement, which could then be "charged" and implanted into the subconscious mind of the magician. I talk about a few Spare-inspired methods of sigil construction in *Infernal Geometry and the Left-Hand Path,* and give the following example based on striking duplicate letters from a statement of desire then further reducing it to a visual form. This form evokes—but does not completely replicate—the letters in the original sentence:

MY WILL IS TO SEEK MYSTERY IN THE MUNDANE
MY WILL IS TO SEEK MYSTERY IN THE MUNDANE
M Y W I L S T O E K R N H U D A

Sigil example

Spare wrote about various methods of charging sigils and then intentionally forgetting their meaning in order for them to be effective. On the techniques of charging and forgetting, he suggests:

Vacuity is obtained by exhausting the mind and body by some means or another. A personal or traditional means serves equally well, depending on temperament; choose the most pleasant; these should be held in favour, Mantras and Posture, Women and Wine, Tennis, and the playing of Patience, or by walking and concentration on the Sigil, etc., etc.[1]

We will look more closely at this and other aspects of Spare's unique—and fundamentally communicative—magical techniques later in this chapter.

ORIGINS OF ANGELIC/ENOCHIAN MAGIC

John Dee was one of the most fascinating people of the Elizabethan era, a true Renaissance man who had success in a variety of fields during his lifetime and an enduring legacy in the history of Great Britain on the world stage. He also had—much to the chagrin of his biographers, who would rather focus on his considerable mathematical and political accomplishments—a profound effect on the history of Western occultism.

Starting around 1580, Dee began to devote more and more of his time and attention to magic. One of Dee's primary goals with this pursuit was to learn how to more effectively read the Book of Nature, an enduring idea in Christian theology. Galileo coined the phrase, but the foundation was much older: natural philosophers would seek to know God through the wonders and mysteries of creation, to be "read" alongside the books of scripture. One of the ways to read this "book" was through mathematics, a subject upon which Dee had built his early fame. Another approach, which was quite popular at the time, was to seek to discover the original language used by Adam.

The book of Genesis attributes the first language to Adam, as he was charged by God—*prior* to the expulsion from Eden—to speak and assign names to everything in nature. If the language of Adam could be recovered somehow, it would provide the most primordial and unsullied key to knowing nature through the true names of all its components. When Dee began to work with a succession of scryers, one of his primary goals was to make contact with angels who could perhaps be persuaded to reveal this language to him. His diaries, especially once he began to work with a seer with a rather shady background, Edward Kelley, show quite a bit of success with gaining access to what he called the Angelic or Adamic Language (but which is now usually referred to as Enochian).

The history of "Enochiana" is intricate, and many of the practices associated with it today are more influenced by later adaptions of the material (such as by the Hermetic Order of the Golden Dawn) than the practices described in Dee's diaries.

Uncovering the Language

The transmission of the language to Dee through Kelley was painstaking, received one letter at a time as the angels pointed out the relevant letters (through some method not fully understood even though we have Dee's diaries attempting to describe it). Eventually, this process resulted in, among other transmissions, eighteen "Keys" in the Angelic Language and one call to thirty "Aethyrs." After the transmissions, the angels would translate them, with Dee attempting to match the English with the Angelic words. This fits into typical Renaissance ideas about magic: the core techniques often revolved around learning the names and other identifying information about both angels and demons then seeking (if not compelling) their help.

One of the enduring questions around Enochian is whether it is an actual language, with consistent vocabulary, grammar, and syntax. While there is some identifiable vocabulary, and the words are used relatively consistently, linguist Patrick Dunn observes that a true grammar and syntax are lacking.[2] This has not stopped major figures in occultism from the time of the Golden Dawn onward from asserting that they were "fluent" in the language.

After Dee's death in 1608 (or 1609), many of his documents and diaries ended up in the hands of the noted antiquarian Sir Robert Cotton. They were later made available to classical scholar Meric Casaubon, who published records of the angelic conversations in 1659 as *A True & Faithful Relation of What Passed for Many Yeers between Dr. John Dee and Some Spirits*. His purpose in publishing the material was to discredit Dee and warn against such attempts to interact with angels, since in Casaubon's opinion Dee was really talking with evil spirits. On top of that, there were many errors in the Enochian text in *A True & Faithful Relation* (possibly intentional, but also quite likely just mistakes in the typesetting of an unknown language).

Rather than acting as the intended warning, the Casaubon text helped to reintroduce Dee to occultists of the day. Over two centuries later, after various isolated attempts by other occultists both to use the Casaubon text and to revisit the original texts of Dee's diaries, the Hermetic Order of the Golden Dawn would incorporate a new approach to Enochian magic into the very foundation of their practices. Now, we will take a closer look at this crucial bridge from the origins of Dee's angel magic to the ways it is usually practiced today.

THE GOLDEN DAWN AND ENOCHIAN

Founded in 1887, the Golden Dawn (GD) sought to refocus Western occultism away from an emphasis on Eastern philosophy, as had become the norm with the influential Theosophical Society (founded just a couple of years earlier). To that end, the founders of the GD emphasized Hermetic magic, a preoccupation with Egypt, and the work of John Dee, while attempting to tie to it all together with their own idiosyncratic understanding of the Kabbalah.

One of the Order's founders, W. W. Westcott, came into the possession of what has become known as the Cipher Manuscript. This manuscript, encoded in a simple substitution cipher, contained outlines of the first five initiation rituals for a secret initiatory organization. Another of the founders, Samuel Liddell Mathers, fleshed these out to create initiations that could be used to make this secret society into something real. In an attempt to give this this new organization a plausible yet fanciful backstory connecting it to Rosicrucianism—one of the recurring metaphysical hyperstitions that had gripped seekers in Europe for centuries—Westcott then forged letters from a "Fräulein Sprengel" who supposedly represented a secret Rosicrucian order in Germany. This gave Westcott, Mathers, and the third founder, William Woodman, the provenance they felt they needed.

This entire episode is full of types of magical communication. It begins with an obsession with the magical power of foreign things, an attitude also found throughout the Greek Magical Papyri. The founders emphasized the importance of a *written* backstory to give their claims more weight. The Cipher Manuscript was encrypted in a rather amateur and easy to crack manner, based on a technique in an early Renaissance work on cryptography by Johannes Trithemius called *Polygraphia*. Trithemius even gave his practice of cryptography an element of magical communication, calling it a "secular consequent of the ability of a soul specially empowered by God to reach, by magical means, from earth to Heaven."[3]

The Cipher Manuscript included references to Enochian magic, and the incorporation of Enochian into the initiation rituals took it into a significantly different direction than Dee's original work. As part of the integration of the Enochian material into their magical and initiatory system, the founders of the Golden Dawn began with some reimagining of those tables based on the Cipher Manuscript. The four-quadrant division of Dee's Great Table (of angelic names) associated with the first grades of the GD was mapped onto the four classical elements—earth, air, fire, and water. This became the key for mapping the Enochian tables onto the Kabbalistic tree of life.[4] In light of what we have discussed so far in this book, it should be clear that the founders were adding their own signs into the semiotic web of the original Enochian material—a web that, until then, had only been loosely defined. They were attempting to connect this web with others to form a totalizing—all-encompassing—system that unified various strains of Western occultism. Whether the connections were already there—as they claimed as justification for elaborating on the connections—or not is irrelevant, at least in terms of their effectiveness. What matters is that they created some measure of cohesion and coherence out of these amalgamations, and then used them in fairly consistent ways alongside the new connections they had made. They used signs to lie—à la Umberto Eco's definition of semiotics—but in doing so created new truths that forever changed the way Enochian was approached.

There are various signs and conceptual metaphors at play in the incorporation of Enochian into the Golden Dawn's initiation rituals, products of Mathers's attempt to permanently alter the sign network of Enochian practice. The initiation candidate's expectations, the various symbols and signs used as part of creating the ritual environment, and the solemn profundity of the ritual and its language would have all made them more open to incorporating these new ideas into their own personal network of signs (or *phaneron*; see chap. 4). Their frequent characterization of the language as "secret" incorporates another sign: *things that are secret carry an implication that they are more important* (otherwise why bother to try to keep it secret?).

The Order took the practice of Enochian magic into new areas, and added new symbolism to it that was not explicitly in Dee's original diaries. Most of the uses of Enochian since the time of the Golden Dawn—the Kabbalistic associations, the use of the Nineteenth Key and the Aethyrs*—have been more influenced by the GD itself than based on Dee's practices. Such is the nature of ideas that spread memetically: they are not always copied perfectly, the source is rarely remembered,

---

*In Enochian magic, the thirty Aethyrs are numinous realms accessible through the use of the last of the nineteen invocations (or Keys) provided to Dee and Kelley by the angels.

and they are always interpreted and modified in the context of the interpreter's own background, biases, and intentions.

ALEISTER CROWLEY AND THELEMA

Aleister Crowley (1875–1947) was one of the most infamous and influential magicians of the twentieth century. He joined the Golden Dawn in 1898 and was forced out in 1900 (along with co-founder Samuel Liddell Mathers) as part of a schism that was in large part caused by him due to his lifestyle and personality.

Crowley had an uncanny ability for quickly absorbing new occult knowledge and drawing connections within it; despite his short tenure in the Order, he learned and applied various magical techniques and adapted them to his own preferences and understanding. Rituals that have been mainstays of the Golden Dawn—such as the lesser banishing ritual of the pentagram and their idiosyncratic work with Enochian magic—took on new forms in the light of Crowley's development of a new magical philosophy that he called Thelema.

There have been immense amounts of ink spilled on the history and legacy of Aleister Crowley and his magickal* writings. Here we will focus on a few features of his philosophies and practices that have particular implications for our exploration of magic as a process of communication.

The Vision and the Voice

While references to it pop up again and again in Crowley's writings, the most prominent usage and development of Enochian magick in his vast body of work is in *The Vision and the Voice*. This is the record of a lengthy series of visions he had while scrying the thirty Enochian Aethyrs primarily in 1909, undertaken with his protégé and scribe,

---

*Crowley preferred to spell "magick" with an additional "k" for stylistic, philosophical, and numerological reasons.

Victor B. Neuburg. One of the most prominent of these encounters, gained through scrying the thirteenth Aethyr, named ZIM, is the one that led Crowley to proclaim he had attained the grade of Magister Templi in the magical organization he created called the A∴A∴.

The Golden Dawn incorporated Enochian into its initiations and made it a topic of scholarly study for its members; Crowley, years after his break with that organization, was interested in exploring the implications of Enochian as a full-fledged magical system (especially with regard to the potential of magically exploring the numinous realms known as the Aethyrs).

In his work with Neuburg in the Tunisian desert in 1909, Crowley undertook the scrying himself (using a large topaz as a "shew stone"), with Neuburg as his scribe; Crowley also considered Neuburg to be a gifted clairvoyant and his presence there was intended to enhance Crowley's work accessing the Aethyrs. Here we see several hallmarks of magical communication. Crowley was working with the Enochian, or angelic, language, which was the product of John Dee's search for the oldest and purest language for connecting with the divine. He used the topaz in part for its semiotic significance but also as a medium for the communication: he encountered the visions while looking into this both literal and figurative lens, enacting a conceptual metaphor for pulling the objects of his desire for knowledge closer. Instead of trying to recall his experiences later, where they would be more colored by the imperfection of memory and perhaps even unintentionally embellished, Crowley dictated them to Neuburg as they were appearing.

Despite their vivid and often otherworldly flavor, Crowley knew that the visions were the result of exploring new signs and connections within the semiotic web of his own mind:

> By making the relevant Call and concentrating on the topaz, Crowley could enter the Aethyr. He was clear about what this meant: "When I say I was in any Aethyr, I simply mean in the state characteristic of, and peculiar to, its nature." In other words, Crowley recognized that

this was a similar experience to that of astral travel; it was conducted within his own mind.[5]

Crowley's experience of scrying was something like a waking dream induced from the imagery set in motion by his receptive exploration of the Aethyrs. In contrast to his earlier experience of the reception of *The Book of the Law*,* in the desert with Victor Neuburg he was primarily working with visuals (although there were also some experiences with voices). The language of these dreamlike visions was "often peculiar and haunting to the rational self-conscious mind and has symbols for its 'words.' Symbols are the units of the distinctive language of subconsciousness."[6]

The visions Crowley derived from these explorations added to the language and signs of his developing magickal philosophy of Thelema, especially in the symbolism behind the abyss and Choronzon—the being who dwells in the abyss waiting to block the adept's quest toward enlightenment. To Crowley, the abyss and Choronzon had a real, external existence, but at the same time they were highly symbolic with Choronzon being "a manifestation of the dark, repressed components of the psyche."[7] As with all symbols, there is shared meaning with all those who include the symbol as part of their speech community, but also personal experience and context that make each manifestation of that symbol partially shared and partially unique. A symbol such as Choronzon—whether or not it has a referent in the phenomenal world or only brings out something in the magician's own psyche—becomes like a vessel that can be filled with whatever is needed to be confronted by the magician. The experience and its results are conditioned by accounts of those uniquely personal shadows lurking beneath the conscious awareness; this is what Choronzon helps the magician to bring into the light.

---

*This book, dictated to Crowley on April 8–10, 1904, by what he understood to be a disembodied intelligence named Aiwass, is the foundational text of Thelema.

Liber Samekh

Following the example of the Golden Dawn, Crowley took various explicit and implicit influences from the Greek Magical Papyri. He well understood the power of barbarous names in magical rituals, observing that:

> It may be conceded in any case that the long strings of formidable words which roar and moan through so many conjurations have a real effect in exalting the consciousness of the magician to the proper pitch—that they should do so is no more extraordinary than music of any kind should do so.[8]

The central Thelemic ritual *Liber Samekh* was originally based on the Headless Ritual from the Greek Magical Papyri (*PGM* V. 96–172; see chap. 6). It was probably Crowley who introduced the ritual to the ceremonial inventory of the Golden Dawn, and he immediately began to update and adjust it to make it fit more cleanly into the Order's system that synthesized Egyptian ideas, Enochian, Kabbalah, and other aspects of Western occultism. Crowley's initial version was included as a preliminary invocation in Samuel Liddell Mathers's edition of the *Lesser Key of Solomon*.

The most immediately obvious change Crowley made was to adjust "Headless" to "Bornless." He did this by taking the root *képhalos* ("head") in the ritual's deity Akephalos (the "Headless One") and drawing a connection to the Hebrew word for "head," ראש (*rosh*). *Rosh* can also mean "beginning" (as in Rosh Hashanah, the Jewish New Year). Thus, putting it back in the negative would yield "not (or without) beginning" or, viewed in a more metaphorical sense, "bornless." This is somewhat like the idea of a folk etymology that we briefly discussed in the context of Guido von List's playful approach to stretching real and imagined word origins to create additional meanings and connections. As with all language-games, they are "true" to the extent they create something that is understood by a particular linguistic community; this technique also adds connections that individuals can further embellish as part of their own meaning-making.

Crowley did similar machinations with the barbarous names in the original ritual. However, it was not until the completed version of *Liber Samekh* in 1921 that a full revision of those names was ready along with a highly detailed Qabalistic key to offer Crowley's interpretations of their meaning.* Keep in mind that while some of those names—for example, "Isak"—were just transliterated Hebrew, there are many others whose original meaning is not known (assuming they were intended to have a specific meaning at all). But again, what Crowley does is valid *in the context of creating a new ritual from the original*; not only does he change the title and the name of the primary deity being invoked, but he also significantly alters and extends the structure of the ritual itself.

The purpose of Crowley's *Liber Samekh* is to facilitate the "Attainment of the Knowledge and Conversation of [the] Holy Guardian Angel."[9] Conversation in this context is not merely mundane conversation in the sense we use the word today; it also suggests the original sense of the Latin roots, which mean "to keep company with."

As in the original, the Headless (now Bornless) One creates earth and the heavens, night and day, darkness and light, and so on. The Bornless One is identified with the Holy Guardian Angel (HGA) of the magician; thus, invoking this creative aspect of the HGA emphasizes the individual's ability to create their own understanding of reality through altering their perception of it through the signs they choose to focus on. In other words, as we noted in chapter 3, the realization that you are in control of how you create meaning and significance underpins all effective magic (and opens even more potent doors for the magician who understands the semiotics implicit in all magic).

Crowley moved the setting of the ritual from Israel and its prophet Moses to Egypt, where he has made Ankh-f-n-Khonsu—the owner of

---

*Crowley preferred the spellings Qabala (sometimes Qabalah) and Qabalistic.

the Stele of Revealing* and one of the magical names that Crowley took for himself—the prophet instead. This was done to realign the symbolic setting of the ritual to set it explicitly within the symbolism derived from his work with the ideas in *The Book of the Law*. That is, he swapped symbolic signs that were not part of the interpretation he preferred for the sign network encoded in the ritual and replaced them with new signs that suggest the desired interpretation.

Let's look at an example of this etymological device.

In the original Headless Ritual, the first three of the *voces magicae* for the true name of the Headless One are given as ARBATHIAÔ REIBET ATHELEBERSÊTH.[10] Crowley broke some of them into additional words while making certain changes in spelling to facilitate interpretation through his understanding of the Hermetic Qabalah:

> AR: "O breathing, flowing Sun!"
>
> ThIAF: "O Sun IAF! O Lion-Serpent Sun, The Beast that whirlest forth, a thunderbolt, begetter of Life!"
>
> RhEIBET: "Thou that flowest! Thou that goest!"
>
> A-ThELE-BER-SET: "Thou Satan-Sun Hadith that goest without Will!"[11]

Another significant structural change that Crowley made was to use the preparation statement given at the end of the original ritual as a refrain throughout *Liber Samekh*. Crowley also modified this refrain to include references to all four of the classical Greek elements: earth, air, fire, and water:

> Hear Me, and make all Spirits subject unto Me, so that every Spirit

---

*An ancient Egyptian stele (see chap. 6) that Crowley encountered at the Cairo Museum just prior to his experience with *The Book of the Law*. Crowley considered this stele as a key to the reception of the book as his discovery of the stele opened his eyes to his true destiny as the founder of a new philosophy and religion.

> *of the Firmament and of the Ether: upon the Earth and under the*
> *Earth: on dry Land and in the Water: of whirling Air, and of rushing*
> *Fire: and every Spell and Scourge of God may be obedient unto me.*[12]

The repeated use of this refrain, and its elemental associations, reinforces that the magician is constructing their entire perspective on the universe through these fundamental building blocks and signs, adding to the cosmos-creating abilities of the Bornless One.

Aleister Crowley was one of the most prolific writers on esoteric topics in the twentieth century. An entire book could be devoted to analyzing the semiotic and communicative features of his hugely influential approach to magick, and so here we can only give a short overview of his unique and fascinating way of approaching these topics.

AUSTIN OSMAN SPARE
AND THE LIMITS OF LANGUAGE

We have already looked at Spare's profound influence on modern techniques of sigil magic as filtered through the Chaos Magic current. This was a significant element in his magical work, but there are other aspects of his theories and techniques that will also interest us from a semiurgic perspective.

Kia and Neither-Neither

The core of Spare's concept of self and magic is *Kia*, "the primal, cosmic life force which can be channelled into the human organism, Zos."[13] Spare often wrote of it in paradoxical terms, always focusing on the difficulty of understanding what it actually is and suggesting different ways of transcending the tendency of the rational mind to get in the way of truly knowing Kia. The Kia, as a numinous concept, shares in the same problem of "describing the indescribable" that Rudolf Otto grappled with (see chap. 4). As words were inadequate, Spare emphasized crafting ways of directly experiencing Kia—this included his experiments with automatic writing, whereby he entered into a receptive state and wrote what came to mind without consciously attempting to interpret or filter it.

Closely related to Kia is one of Spare's techniques for communicating with it (or at least, learning to listen to it): reaching the state he called *neither-neither*. In this state, the mind has stopped trying to reconcile pairs of opposite concepts and accepted that both extremes are true and false at the same time. Peter Carroll described the mechanism as a progressive process of specialized meditation:

> The mystic (you) meditates for a time on a particular idea, then meditates on its polar opposite. Existence and non-existence are often chosen. Thirdly, you meditate on the simultaneous presence of both qualities. Illumination arrives if you can complete the fourth stage of meditating on the simultaneous absence of both qualities, which forces the process of conception beyond its normal limits.[14]

Implicit in *neither-neither* is that the magician does not fully believe either member of such pairs: contradictory truths are held in the mind simultaneously. This malleability of belief is a core concept within Chaos Magic, which owes a massive debt to Spare's ideas and techniques. The emphasis shifts from faith—whether faith in a god, or faith in science, or anywhere in-between—to working with conceptual models that are true and effective within the context they are being used. Within that context, signs take on meaning and significance they do not otherwise possess and become one of the partners in communication that the magician converses with to bring about their desire.

The Alphabet of Desire

Another of Spare's idiosyncratic creations is the *alphabet of desire* (also called the *atavistic alphabet*), which he used for creating sigils in addition to his language-based word method. These glyphs corresponded to various manifestations of sexual expression, which he believed was the root of effective magic. Rather than being just another set of characters for writing ordinary language, the atavistic alphabet was supposed to have a direct—rather than symbolic—connection to the self and to channel the magician's desires unfiltered. This is a perennial idea, as we've already seen in the context of the similar goals of John Dee's work with angelic or Enochian language. Indeed, Dee's angels shared a unique writing system with him and Edward Kelley and—coincidentally or not—it bears more than a passing resemblance to the glyphs from Spare's alphabet of desire.

Unlike the angelic alphabet, however, Spare did not intend that his alphabet would be applicable to anyone but him (and in the last few years of his life it was perhaps no longer even useful to him).

> Spare's Sacred Alphabet will never be deciphered completely, because it doesn't fully add up; he claimed in the Fifties to have forgotten the key, and it is likely that many of the characters were invented simply out of graphic pleasure. It would, in any case, be personal to Spare himself, as he always stressed: he wrote in a later book that each of us has our own arcana—our own symbol system, memories, reference points. As one of his best commentators puts it, there is for every individual "the sacred alphabet of the mysteries that each one of us contains."[15]

The alphabet of desire was an expression of Kia; the individual nature of this sacred alphabet arose out of the individual connection to Kia, with the state of *neither-neither* as the bridge. This alphabet is a sign network—both in the semiotic sense and in the conventional sense of a collection of related glyphs used for creating especially powerful sigils. Just as the sigil is *not* the desire, merely a symbolic expression of it which is necessarily incomplete, the alphabet of desire is *not* Kia but merely a personal representation of some small part of it that can be expressed in graphical, symbolic form.

We will revisit some of Spare's ideas and techniques later in this chapter in the context of their adoption (and modification) by the Chaos Magic current beginning some two decades after Spare's death.

THE EARLY YEARS OF THE CHURCH OF SATAN

Anton Szandor LaVey (born Howard Stanton Levey; 1930–1997) founded the Church of Satan on April 30, 1966. The history of the Church of Satan, with varying degrees of objectivity, has been covered elsewhere but here we will look at some specific aspects of the Church's practices that illustrate various concepts in magical communication.

As we will see throughout this section on LaVey and his ritual style, he was a master of using language for dramatic effect and employed many of the techniques we have examined such as performative utterances.

Satanic Angel Magic

Unlike with the Golden Dawn and the practices associated with Aleister Crowley's Thelema, Anton LaVey did not use the original translations of the Enochian Keys from John Dee's diaries. Instead, he created what he called "an archaic but Satanically correct unvarnishing of the translation employed by the Order of the Golden Dawn in the late Nineteenth Century."[16] This largely involved replacing references to God with Satan, but it also went deeper in subtle ways often overlooked by those who reacted to his changes with indignity.

LaVey noted the "barbarous tonal qualities"[17] of the sounds of the Keys in the original Enochian and understood the ritual effectiveness that arose from this. This was representative of his flair for dramatic ritual, but also reveals that he understood the power inherent in bringing language into the ritual chamber in ways that break normal patterns of sounds.

LaVey did not use the Enochian Keys as part of scrying or conversation with demons, but rather incorporated them into his rituals as additional invocations to reinforce the underlying purpose of those rituals and enhance the atmosphere of the ritual chamber. The associations he brought to the meaning and intent of the Keys function as additional signs in the semiotic web of the ritual; they are part of ensuring that as many signs as possible within the context of the ritual carry meaning that enhances the chances for success.

The Law of the Trapezoid and Enochian

One of LaVey's other original contributions to the Church's use of Enochian was a brief commentary preceding each of the Keys. These commentaries tied his modifications to the translations together with his preferences for which Keys should accompany specific types of rituals. For example, he described the Sixth Key thus:

> The Sixth Enochian Key establishes the structure and form of that which has become the Order of the Trapezoid and Church of Satan.[18]

The opening of the Sixth Key in Dee's original translation is:

> *The spirits of the 4th Angle are Nine, Mighty in the firmament of waters: whome the first hath planted a torment to the wicked and a garland to the righteous*[19]

Contrast this with LaVey's rendering:

> *The spirits of the fourth angle are Nine, mighty in the trapezoid, whom the first hath formed, a torment to the wretched and a garland to the wicked*[20]

The "firmament of waters" became the trapezoid: the symbol for LaVey's Law of the Trapezoid, which was the foundation and totem of his magical practices and theories, inspired by William Mortensen's theories of photograph composition called the *command to look* and the "strange angles" often mentioned in H. P. Lovecraft's works. LaVey never gave a succinct definition of the Law, but Michael Aquino summed it up as:

> All obtuse angles are magically harmful to those unaware of this property. The same angles are beneficial, stimulating, and energizing to those who are magically sensitive to them.[21]

A "torment to the wretched" certainly represents the effect that such strange angles have on those not attuned to them, while a "garland to the wicked"—not to the *righteous* as in the original translation of the Key—describes the beneficial effect those same angles have on those who know and work with the Law.

Ritual Style

Anton LaVey had a very distinctive ritual style, and some key components of that were his use of magical communication, fiction, and neomythology. All of his rituals in *The Satanic Rituals* reflect these three elements to some extent. These rituals included commentary LaVey wrote to introduce each of them and give an embellished backstory. The "tall tale" backgrounds are an essential part of the semiotic codes of these rituals, creating new connections for the participants to work within as part of capturing the right attitude and atmosphere for their effectiveness.

These backstories portray the rituals as previously long-secret rites now being revealed, yet another sign in the semiotic web of each ritual. We have seen in the Greek Magical Papyri and *The Discourse on the Eighth and the Ninth*, for example, similar claims that the magician is receiving a secret teaching or technique and must safeguard it now that they are privy to its secrets.

Several sections of *The Satanic Rituals* have contributed to different neomythologies that have spread throughout the occult world since its publication. LaVey did not create any of them, but his contributions to these neomyths have become part of their lore even if some may not realize their sources. These include the claim that the Yezidis—a non-Muslim religious group living primarily in modern day Iraq—are guardians of an ancient Satanic religion and the assertion that the Nazis were primarily driven by occult interests. Michael Aquino's contributions to *The Satanic Rituals*—the rituals and commentary focused on the world of H. P. Lovecraft—have been significant sources for the occult interest in Lovecraft's works.* The attraction of neomythologies plays on our compulsion to make meaning out of data we encounter, and as LaVey's and Aquino's rituals make clear, neomythology is a powerful source for immersive magical work—the more meaning we can make out of the words, symbols, and atmosphere of a ritual, the more effective it will be.

The Semiurgy of LaVeyan Satanism

At the beginning of *The Satanic Bible*, the Nine Satanic Statements provide a succinct description of the essential attributes of Satan as understood by LaVey. Whether Satan is taken to be literal or symbolic, the *word* Satan is a linguistic sign that carries different meaning for each person who tries to approach it. The Nine Satanic Statements show the specific meaning that LaVey was attempting to invest into this linguistic sign (and which would become part of each Satanist's exploration of what Satan meant *to them*). This is most famously seen in the very first Statement: "Satan represents indulgence instead of abstinence!"[22]

In the later section titled "The Book of Belial," LaVey describes different "categories" that the Satanist can choose to combine and embody. These are not fixed personas but can to an extent be changed as needs and desires change. They are based primarily on visual presentation and associated behaviors, putting them firmly in the realm of using symbolic signs to play into (or against) the expectations of those the Satanist wishes to manipulate. So much of what we perceive about others is based on unanalyzed associations we have with how they look,

---

*These connections are discussed at length in my *Infernal Geometry and the Left-Hand Path*.

speak, and behave. These associations are the products of semiotic codes that come as a "package deal" and can be hard to pull apart and analyze as individual components. As Roland Barthes (see chap. 3) masterfully unraveled, semiotic codes always include unspoken assumptions that are used to embed *other* messages as well. His work on demythologizing these "bundles" of signs to reveal their embedded messages and hierarchies is very compatible with LaVey's suggestions for leveraging the outer signs—dress, mannerisms, speech—as carriers for *new* messages according to the will of the magician.

Performative Utterances to Satan

The Invocation to Satan used as part of Satanic ritual is almost entirely one long performative utterance (see chap. 4). It shows that LaVey well understood the power of performative speech in rituals, which by their design create a context in which the person leading the ritual (the priest/priestess) claims and embodies the authority to speak certain changes into being; these then enhance the effectiveness of the entire ritual. We will now look at a few passages within this invocation.

> In the name of Satan, the Ruler of the earth, the King of the world,
> I command the forces of Darkness to bestow their Infernal power
> upon me![23]

The command is issued to the forces of Darkness and reinforced by the priest's acknowledged allegiance with Satan. This is the *similarity* aspect of Frazer's law of sympathy: by acting in the name of Satan, the priest can share in the authority of Satan to demand that certain things be done solely through the power of utterance.

By identifying Satan as Ruler of earth and King of the world, the priest also anchors the abstract Satan to the concrete world of the here and now. *This has the same semiotic effect whether the priest views Satan as an actual entity or merely as a symbol.*

> *Grant me the indulgences of which I speak!*[24]

This performative utterance is a deliberate connection to the central tenet of LaVey's philosophy: Satan represents indulgence instead of abstinence. As LaVey essentially equates Satan with indulgence, this performative utterance in effect completes the law of similarity equating the celebrant—the priest/priestess—with Satan within the context of the ritual.

> *By all the Gods of the Pit, I command that these things of which I speak shall come to pass! Come forth and answer to your names by manifesting my desires!*[25]

"I command" is yet another phrase that typically introduces a performative utterance. As with all other performative utterances, only those with the proper authority can utter them within the appropriate context—what J. L. Austin called *felicity conditions*. Since we have already established that the person leading the ritual has risen up to embody Satan, the felicity conditions are met that invest their proclamations and utterances with the same power and authority as those of Satan.

Anton Szandor LaVey employed a variety of communication techniques that have also been identified by twentieth-century anthropologists as part of the reason for the efficacy of magic. In addition to his frequent use of performative utterances in his rituals, LaVey well understood the malleability of signs and associations between those signs that the magician could use for affecting the perceptions and even actions of those around them. This type of semiotic hacking is very much in line with the demythologizing work of Roland Barthes that we looked at in chapter 3. Much of LaVey's work utilizing the flexibility of belief, such as the creation of backstories to add to the atmosphere and intent for the rituals in *The Satanic Rituals*, foreshadowed similar work within the Chaos Magic current that took shape later in the 1970s.

THE TEMPLE OF SET

The Temple of Set was founded in 1975 by Michael A. Aquino (1946–2019) and other former members of the Church of Satan. As part of attempting to understand what was unfolding in the wake of a critical policy change by Anton LaVey—one that Aquino and others saw as undermining the integrity of the Church—Aquino sought the advice of the Prince of Darkness (who up to that point he regarded as Satan) in a ritual on June 21, 1975. The response to his question—which was essentially "If this is not the end of the line, then how might we continue our journey along the Left-Hand Path?"—was a text called *The Book of Coming Forth by Night*. Thus, the founding of the Temple of Set is, at its core, an act of magical communication.

The Temple draws on magical techniques and ritual forms from a wide range of traditions (including some that have been developed within the Temple, as discussed in my book *Infernal Geometry and the Left-Hand Path*). The Temple is not a neo-Egyptian religion, and deep interest in Egyptology is not required of its members (known as Setians). The guiding principle and practice of the Temple is *Xeper* (pronounced *KHEF-urr*).* This is a transliteration of the Egyptian word *ḫpr* that, depending on context, means "to become," "to change," "to come into being," and other related concepts. Within the Temple, Xeper is the practice of self-directed evolution of the consciousness of the individual.

Enochian magic and Aquino's new translation of Dee's original text, known as the *Word of Set*, are sometimes overlooked as critical compo-

---

*While we cannot be sure of the exact pronunciation of this (and many other words) in Middle Egyptian, newer linguistic research indicates that the sound at the beginning was likely heavily aspirated with the [k] more of a fricative than a stop (that is, similar to the -ch at the end of words in German). Similarly, the p was probably somewhere halfway between the sounds [p] and [f]. However, the *KHEF-urr* pronunciation is the one commonly used in the context of the Temple, and this specific pronunciation (taken from older Egyptological research that was more current around the time of Temple's founding) is one of the features of that particular linguistic community.

nents in the founding of the Temple, and the *Word of Set* has continued to have an important influence in the philosophy and cosmology of the Temple. We will look at some important semiurgic features of *The Book of Coming Forth by Night* and then will do the same for the *Word of Set*.

First, however, we must briefly take note of the Temple's understanding of Aeons. In the Temple's view, Aeons are not just periods of *time* when certain ideas are dominant; instead, they are worldviews defined and guided by a concept that can be reduced to a single Word (called an Aeonic Word). These worldviews are thus conceptual models that an individual can choose to work with. In the Aeon of Horus—the one created by Crowley through his reception of *The Book of the Law*—the Word of the Aeon is Thelema (θέλημα); the Word of the Aeon of Set is Xeper. This view of Aeons is similar to astronomer Gerald Hawkins's concept of the *mindstep* that he characterized as "a massive change of thinking that alters the relationship of humans to the cosmos."[26] Aeons can be understood without these associated Aeonic Words, but such a Word captures something essential about the meaning and significance of the Aeon. The Word is a sign that facilitates magical communication through the semiotic web of meaning it opens up.

The Book of Coming Forth by Night

For many years, the *The Book of Coming Forth by Night* (or *BoCFbN*) was not available to the public (not intentionally, anyway). This changed with the availability of drafts of Aquino's memoir, *The Temple of Set*, beginning around 2010. The main reason for this change in attitude toward making texts like the *BoCFbN* available was the view that they are nearly meaningless out of context. (Recall our discussion of integrational linguistics in chapter 4, which suggests that *all* communications lose part of their meaning once removed from their original context). By telling the story of not only how and why this text came to be, but also what effect it had on the Temple, Aquino could share the necessary context for a deeper understanding of it.

As Aquino notes, the nature of this communication did not follow what some might assume from popular accounts and stereotypes about this sort of magic:

> The experience was neither one of "dictation" [as with Crowley's *Book of the Law*] or of "automatic writing" after the spiritualist fashion. The thoughts, words, phrases seemed to me indistinct from my own, yet impressed me as both unique and necessary, as though no other sequence would do. Frequently, I paused for a time, waiting for what might occur next.[27]

To examine a few of the semiurgic features of *The Book of Coming Forth by Night*, we must start with its name.

The text popularly known as the *Egyptian Book of the Dead* is more formally titled *The Book of Coming Forth by Day*. This is a collection of spells and other incantations to guide the newly deceased through the underworld. *The Book of Coming Forth by Day* was firmly rooted in an Osirian view of the afterlife, including a temporary rebirth of the deceased before traveling across the sky in the solar barque of Ra in preparation for judgment by Osiris. Thus, in addition to inverting *day* and *night*, *The Book of Coming Forth by Night* explicitly reverses the focus from Osiris to his traditional enemy, Set. By extension, this creates an inversion of the view of the afterlife as well—the Setian afterlife in ancient Egypt was focused on the stars not the sun, as seen in the star maps known as "astronomical ceilings" in the tombs of the Setian pharaohs of the eighteenth and nineteenth dynasties (1550–1189 BCE).

> *Proclaim the nineteen Parts of the Word, and vanquish thus the feeble and corrupt Keys of Enoch, which were but a shadow of my true Word and now are an affront to me.*[28]

Bear in mind throughout this look at the *BoCFbN* that the speaker ("I") is Set. We have seen this type of writing as texts delivered from the perspective of a deity before, for example with *The Thunder, Perfect Mind* (see chap. 6).

This passage refers to the *Word of Set*, which Aquino had only just begun to transcribe at the time of the foundation of the Temple in 1975. Nonetheless, this is the sign network connecting to other attempts from the Golden Dawn to the Church of Satan to find the true importance and practical use of the Enochian material. As we will see in the more detailed discussion of the *Word of Set* below, this has significant implications about the source of the communication with Dee and Kelley and foreshadows its importance to the Temple.

> I am the ageless Intelligence of this Universe. I created HarWer that I might define my Self. All other gods of all other times and nations have been created by men.[29]

"To define" can mean to determine the limits and boundaries of something. It can also mean to communicate the meaning or significance of something, like a word or an experience. Both readings work with the phrase "I created HarWer that I might define my Self." To be distinct, self-aware, and self-evolving, Set must be finite; that is, Set must have limits even if those limits are also capable of expanding. Defining—in the sense of demarcating—where those limits are at a particular moment of comprehension makes it more clear what lies *outside* those limits: the unmanifest and unknown from which Mystery is perceived and pursued. Defining a particular self in the linguistic sense articulates what is essential and unique about that self in relation to other selves.

Set says that only he and HarWer were created without human intervention. This is a core function of what the Temple calls the Gift of Set: the self-awareness and consciousness shared by all humans (and to a varying extent, some if not most animals). Note that such gods are still real in the sense that any god is understood by some to be real, but they are in part shaped by *human* perception of the qualities and attributes the gods are thought to possess. Those qualities and attributes are *not* created, but the god who possesses them and is given a name, appearance, backstory, and so on—this is the part that is created. Whatever our conceptions of gods may be, they are only the perceptions that we are able to express in language; to be worthy of the name, gods must be more than just what humans are able to conceive about them.

Michael Aquino reflected on this nearly three decades after the communication of *The Book of Coming Forth by Night*:

> God-creation is far from a flippancy; indeed it is one of the most, if not indeed *the* most exalted capacities of consciousness. It is the taking of the objective universe, in whole (monotheism) or in part(s) (polytheism), and ennobling its key consistencies and regularities as something inherently glorious beyond their mere existence. Thus they are transformed from the physical to the metaphysical.[30]

The creation of gods is semiurgy in Baudrillard's original sense: the creation of signs (or sign networks) to affect reality or the perception of reality. The signs—linguistic or otherwise—involved in god-making are repurposed if not created, and invested with particular meaning that is reinforced through using these signs in a particular linguistic community. Sometimes the concept of a particular god dies out with the specific linguistic community that had given it a name and identity, but sometimes such a god may spread memetically beyond its original linguistic community. Due to this process the god has now lost some of its original context (and so it may not signify precisely the same things to the new community that copies the divine meme and develops their own idiosyncratic version of it).

> When I first came to this world, I gave to you my great pentagram,
> timeless measure of beauty through proportion.
> And it was shown inverse, that creation and change
> be exalted above rest and preservation.[31]

The Pentagram of Set

This passage describes the essential semiotics of the Temple of Set, using a symbol that is given particular significance within the linguistic community that is the Temple.

The pentagram of Set, as it is known in the Temple, is shown inverse within a circle. The pentagram itself represents the individual psyche—self-aware consciousness—which does not depend on the objective (i.e., material) universe for its existence and subsistence. That is, the psyche in the Setian view is not a product of evolution through natural selection or indeed of the material universe at all. The circle represents that objective universe—the material universe and its laws—and the pentagram does not touch it, so as to signify this essential separation. The psyche does interact with the objective universe of course, mediated through the body and all its processes of semiosis. This connection between the psyche and the objective universe is called the *magical link*.

The last line of The Book of Coming Forth by Night
from the original manuscript

This last line of *The Book of Coming Forth by Night* establishes the Word that creates the Aeon and distills its essence into both a single linguistic and visual sign.

The Word of Set

The *Word of Set* should not be seen as just the "Temple of Set's version of Enochian." It is the result of a magical working in its own right and has deep implications for the cosmology of the Temple.

The Enochian Keys had an often-underappreciated role in the founding of the Temple. In March 1975, Michael Aquino acquired a copy of Meric Casaubon's work on Dee, which we have already noted contained (perhaps deliberately) many errors compared to Dee's original diaries. Aquino undertook some initial experiments with the Nineteenth Key and scrying the Aethyr *ZIM*, which produced results he found "nothing short of astonishing."[32]

Then, in early June, just before the changes that precipitated the departure of Aquino and others from the Church of Satan, he began to write down the first two Keys of what later became known as the *Word of Set*. On June 21, when he sought the advice of the Prince of Darkness, he used the first part of this new translation of the Enochian Keys as part of his invocation. Aquino eventually completed the *Word of Set* in April 1981.

Aquino was clear that his intent was not just to recreate Dee's translation or to make slight aesthetic revisions as had LaVey.

> An "Enochian purist" might question the translation provided by the *Word of Set* in that it is not the English version recorded by John Dee in his diaries. My answer is simply that I approached the Keys not as a historian seeking to reprint what Dee did, but as a magician seeking to operate the same "magical machinery" that Dee did—and to operate it with greater care and precision than he did.[33]

So what is different about the *Word of Set* compared to previous uses of the Enochian material? It was not just a slight tweaking of existing translations but a *new* one that was filtered through the philosophical and cosmological viewpoints of the Aeon of Set.

Let's compare a portion of Dee's original version of the First Key with the *Word of Set*.

Dee:

> *I reign over you, sayeth the God of Justice, in power exalted above the firmaments of wrath: in whose hands the Sun is as a sword and the Moon as a through-thrusting fire which measureth your garments in the midst of my vesture and trussed you together as the palms of my hands: Whose seats I garnished with the fire of gathering and (which) beautified your garments with admiration: to whom I made a law to govern the holy ones and delivered you a rod with the ark of knowledge.*[34]

The *Word of Set*:

> *I am within and beyond you, the Highest of Life, in majesty greater than the forces of the Universe; whose eyes are the Face of the Sun and the Dark Fire of Set; who fashioned your intelligence as his own and reached forth to exalt you; who entrusted to you dignity of consciousness; who opened your eyes that you might know beauty; who brought you the key to knowledge of all lesser things; and who enshrined in you the Will to Come Into Being.*[35]

From the very first phrase we see a profound difference in the nature of the communication. "I reign over you, sayeth the God of Justice" creates a very different relationship between the two parties in communication than does "I am within and beyond you, the Highest of Life." The rendering in the *Word of Set* works with Frazer's law of similarity, creating from the beginning a more equal relationship with the divine, which enables effective communication since the two parties to the conversation are on equal footing. Some of this reflects differing views of the relationship between mankind and the divine, seeding a new semiotic code for understanding this relationship. Aquino was clear he did not wish to supplant Dee's translation; rather, just as with any other interpretation of semiotic codes, translation is *also* context-specific. A translation will emphasize certain aspects of meaning while downplaying others—at the same time it will emphasize different aspects and relationships of the original semiotic code recontextualized into a new one.

Magical Communication within the Temple of Set

The Temple of Set's approach to magic is based on a particular conceptual model. It is focused in part on the interplay between the *objective universe* (the world of matter and its physical laws and inhabitants) and the *subjective universe* (the individual knowledge, experience, and self-awareness of each sentient being within the objective universe).

The Gift of Set—the source of the individual, self-directed *psyche* in all humans—is understood to be nonnatural. That is, it is not the product of evolution or of the perpetual expansion of the universe according to its physical laws. Its source is the god against the gods, Set, and the exercise of this Gift enables the magician to act in some way like Set: to alter the natural order of things according to the will of the magician. We have seen this in other contexts as well, from the *ek erilaR* formula in runic inscriptions (see chap. 7) to various spells in the Greek Magical Papyri (see chap. 6). All of these are instances of what the Egyptians called *ph-ntr*: "to reach a god" or "to employ the magical powers of a god."[36]

There are two main types of magic practiced in the Temple: *Greater Black Magic* (GBM) and *Lesser Black Magic* (LBM).* Greater Black Magic works directly on the *psyche* of the magician and may or may not involve ritual practices. The primary purpose of GBM is to transform *the magician* (i.e., the magician's psyche or subjective universe), and

---

*These are not to be confused with what *The Satanic Bible* called "lesser magic" (manipulating the actions of others) and "greater magic" (used as a synonym for ritual magic).

those resulting changes may or may not have an effect in the objective universe. Lesser Black Magic is applied directly to the objective universe or its inhabitants, impelling—*not* compelling—them to act in accord with the will of the magician.

Let's look at the communication that is built into both types of magic.

Lesser Black Magic is a form of metacommunication. Michael Aquino's definition of it is as follows:

> [LBM] is the influencing of beings, processes, or objects in the objective universe by the application of obscure physical or behavioral laws.[37]

Metacommunication describes those aspects of communication that are nonverbal. This includes physical signs like body language but also many of the things we discussed in chapter 3 concerning the ideas of Roland Barthes: loading the sign networks drawn on by the target of LBM with signs and relationships reinforcing the semiurgist's desires. The attention may be drawn to a particular sign or signs, but the relationships within the entire network carry other information that influences the interpretation of those signs. This is often practiced rather crudely—and nonmagically—by the advertising industry, but in the hands of a magician can be far more subtle and used toward more noble ends than just manipulating someone into buying the right brand of soap.

What contrasts this with simple manipulation is that the magician is not attempting to deceive their target but is instead making certain implications of the sign network easier to find and notice—and these happen to point (as an indexical sign) to the magician's intent. Aquino stresses that the goal is not to manipulate—force someone to act against their will—but instead to encourage the target to harmonize with the intent of the magician so that they *want* to cooperate.

There are no set ritual forms in the Temple, although the outline of a Setian rubric provided by Michael Aquino in the Temple's basic texts (many republished in his *The Temple of Set*) does provide a form that is used by many Setians since it functions as a sort of shared magical language. Space limitations prevent a full analysis of all parts of this suggested rubric, but we will look at a couple of parts of it that merit special attention.

After the ringing of a bell, a flame is lit that represents the Black Flame. The phrase *Black Flame* entered first Satanic and then Setian discourse through a text transcribed in 1970 by Michael Aquino called *The Diabolicon*.[38] The Black Flame is the individual's particular manifestation of the Gift of Set; it is their personal source for magic and initiation, drawing from its source *beyond* the self, Set. Beyond this specifically Setian symbolism, all the cultural and semiotic associations we have with fire are in play as well (going all the way back to when humans first tamed fire and made it a critical tool in their survival and spread). The Black Flame evokes the uniqueness of Man the fire-wielder.

The invocation of Set follows in the basic rubric. The first line of the invocation functions as summary of the Setian approach to magic:

> *In the name of Set, the Prince of Darkness, I enter into the Realm of Creation to work my will upon the Universe.*[39]

The first thing to notice is the use of the power of naming, which we have seen in a variety of mythological and magical contexts. Beyond that, this functions as a performative utterance made possible through *pḥ-nṯr* or acting as Set within the context of the magician's actions and authority in the Working.

This passage utilizes several conceptual metaphors as well, tying the actions of the magician in the physical space where the Working is performed to the transcendental act of affecting the very fabric of the Universe.

The invocation ends with the line

> *Hear then this Doom which I pronounce, and beware the Ka which Comes into Being through that Art which is mine to command.*[40]

The *Ka*—which we looked at briefly in chapter 5—is *re*-created with each act of Greater Black Magic. This is the portion of the soul that is the repository of images of what is yet to be; it is created through ḥkꜣ (or *heka*) and sent out into the world to make those images real.* This is in effect another complex conceptual metaphor, giving a form and more importantly a name to the repository of the magician's desires for change.

In a semiotic sense, the *Ka* is a particular sign network that is sent out into the world. Food was left in the tombs of pharaohs to feed the *Ka*, as it can remain distinct and eternal *as long as it is properly nourished*. This is analogous to sustaining the sign network that is held together by the *Ka* through ensuring that other signs remain part of the network in order to support its coherence and meaning.

Another important semiotic feature to note in the base Setian ritual rubric is what Aquino termed the "Summoning of the Elements." This is not a reference to specific elements of any other mythical or magical tradition (e.g., the Greek earth, air, fire, water; the Germanic opposites of fire and ice; etc.). Rather, the Setian magician calls upon:

> the living creatures and inert elements whom/which he wishes to observe or control. He may do this by using their conventional names, or by invoking symbols of them in isolation or combination (gods, daemons, chemical or alchemical symbols, images, musical

---

*This is not to be confused with the magical technique of using a servitor—a mindless projection of the magician's desire created to perform a specific task. The *Ka*, an idea with deep historical roots in Egyptian magic and religion, is ultimately an aspect of the body-soul complex of the magician; thus, it has an awareness of all the thoughts and needs of the magician and maintains a connection to the magician even when sent forth to create some change within the world.

themes, or other media of description). He weaves around them the appropriate context of his subjective universe, thus creating what he wishes to Come Into Being.[41]

This is explicitly the construction of a semiotic web that includes the desire of the magician alongside the signs related to it, the combination of which will create a new vision of reality. This sign network is ultimately what the *Ka* carries forth into the phenomenal world to bring about the desires of the magician.

The Temple of Set began with an act of magical communication, and the hallmarks of communication and semiotics applied to magic that we have seen throughout this book find many examples within the writings and techniques of the Temple. Michael Aquino's interest in the origin and legacy of Enochian led him to engage in the experimentation that eventually resulted in a new approach to the Enochian language called the *Word of Set* (which also had a critical role in the founding of the Temple itself). Work with other systems and schools of magic continues to have an influence on the magic, philosophy, and religion of the Temple; its roots in the ideas of the *Word of Set* and the *Book of Coming Forth by Night* gave it a foundation for approaching magic through its own Aeonic lens with both implicit and explicit semiurgic ideas and techniques.

THE FOUNDATIONS OF CHAOS MAGIC

Sigil magic, especially the model and techniques pioneered by Austin Osman Spare, was a seminal influence on the techniques known as Chaos Magic, which first took shape in the UK in the 1970s. Chaos Magic (sometimes also written as Chaos Magick) is a loosely defined "current" that focuses on stripping magic down to its essentials and working with the malleability of belief as a magical tool in itself. Longtime chaos magician Dave Lee observes:

The core idea that the Chaos current grew from is that we are not stuck with a single belief about the world but that radically different beliefs about what is going on can be entertained within the same skull.[42]

The pioneers of Chaos Magic were not interested in continuing a particular tradition like the Hermetic Order of the Golden Dawn. Rather, more in line with their iconoclastic heroes they drew on the work of many idiosyncratic magicians who worked largely on their own (such as artist and occultist Austin Osman Spare and writer William S. Burroughs).

For them, magical techniques did not have validity due to their lineage or association with august schools of the Art. Instead, all that mattered was what *worked*—and only each individual could decide that.

Repopularization of Sigils

The work of Spare was a blueprint for many of the early Chaos Magic practitioners: Peter Carroll, Ray Sherwin, Lionel Snell (Ramsey Dukes), Dave Lee, and others. Due to Spare's importance to the current, sigils using variations on his method became one of their central magical techniques. The Chaos Magic approach to sigils was anti-ceremonial, in that it did not require special props, tools, or accoutrements *other* than the power of the spoken and written word (along with pen and paper). Spare-style sigils are one of the purest possible forms of semiurgy, with the partner in communication being the subconscious mind of the magician which—now conditioned by the sigil—will assist (rather than resist) in bringing about the stated desire.

Such sigils are newly created signs that are invested with symbolic meaning. Compare this with Jean Baudrillard's original conception of semiurgy as the creation of signs. As we have seen throughout this book, even when we reuse an existing sign, we are still recreating it through the meaning with which we invest it in the given context. Perhaps more than any other magical technique, sigils drive home the essential idea that working with semiotic codes *is* magic. Just as with magic, semiotics—through the manipulation of codes—works non-deterministically and outside of strict cause and effect to reorient a system of interconnected signs toward a new purpose. Manipulating signs and the relationships between them does not guarantee success, but instead makes certain outcomes more likely by making them more attractive (in the sense that they are more likely to attract potential interpreters who will derive a meaning analogous to the meaning the semiurgist invested into them).

While Spare had, through extensive experimentation, arrived at very specific techniques for creating and charging sigils, magicians within the Chaos current continued his penchant for experimentation and created even more idiosyncratic techniques based on what worked *for them*. In addition to being magical communication at its very core, sigil magic has only one rule: all that matters is what works.

Just as with mundane language, there is rarely only one way to communicate something effectively: if you get the point across, the communication is successful by any reasonable definition. Words only have meaning to the extent they are successful at evoking that meaning between the participants in a particular context; similarly, sigils have the meaning that is invested in them, and the only measure of success in communicating their intent is whether results are eventually perceived that are in line with the original intent behind the sigil.

The Malleability of Belief as Magical Semiosis

A key component of Chaos Magic is the magical diary: a record of experiments and experiences along with their results, failures, and observations. Writing desires into existence in the objective universe is something we have looked at in several different contexts so far, but in Chaos Magic this takes on even greater importance as "the magician's most essential and powerful tool."[43]

Beyond the semiurgic necessity of writing new ideas into existence in the material world, the diary is also a record that can be compared against—very important when models of reality are deliberately in flux. While the diary will always be imperfect—since intentionally or not we tend to color our interpretations of events in ways that are beneficial to us—nevertheless it can capture the signs and other parts of the semiotic codes that seem relevant to a given magical act. This is important when belief—the code(s) that we hold to be most applicable if not "true" at a particular time—is deliberately held to be malleable. We tend to treat the written word as somehow more accurate and/or permanent than the spoken word, and this use of the magical diary gives the Chaos Magician a way to craft their perception of the relevant sign networks—systems of belief—they are working with at any given time.

We looked at Austin Osman Spare's technique of *neither-neither* earlier in this chapter. This became one of the core tools within Chaos Magic alongside many other concepts from Spare. Sometimes it was referred to, especially in the earlier writings about Chaos Magic from Peter J. Carroll and Ray Sherwin, as *noninterest/nondisinterest* or *nonattachment/nondisinterest*.

The intent behind attainment of the neither-neither state is to change your relationship to the sign network that encompasses your magical goal. That is, an additional sign is attached to the network that draws attention away from the goal itself. As we saw with the work of Scott Shell and magical sign networks (see chap. 2), the most salient—significant, conspicuous, central—sign in the network dominates it and takes on an outsized influence on the overall meaning of the sign network. By moving the signs directly related to the magical goal to a more peripheral place in the network, they will still be present and working toward their desired end but are no longer the primary focus of attention, thus allowing them to work with less risk of being unconsciously sabotaged.

Organized Chaos

Chaos Magic by its nature tended to resist organization, although groups such as the Illuminates of Thanateros (IOT) and Thee Temple ov Psychick Youth (TOPY) did at times gather practitioners into loosely connected and mostly decentralized networks. The IOT was founded by Peter Carroll and Ray Sherwin in the late 1970s, with its structure and operations described in Carroll's early works *Liber Null* and *Psychonaut*. Thee Temple ov Psychick Youth, a loosely organized network of magicians created by musician and artist Genesis P-Orridge in 1981, was much more interested in working with media to spread ideas and subvert the mainstream through their own style of Chaos Magick.

THEE TEMPLE OV PSYCHICK YOUTH*

To talk about Thee Temple ov Psychick Youth (TOPY) and magickal communication, we first have to note their idiosyncratic spelling conventions that were an intentional subversion of mundane communication. TOPY were enamored with the magickal power of language and especially with *breaking* common patterns of thought that arise through the use of everyday language. The intent was to encourage really reading and thinking about the text instead of just reading it automatically. This was perhaps inspired by Crowley's intentional spelling of *magick*, but the extent to which TOPY used it became a distinctive style in its own right.

While only ever loosely organized (and never formally incorporated as a nonprofit despite occasional claims to the contrary), there *was* a sort of official way for someone to declare their affiliation with TOPY; see below for further discussion about that in the context of their methods of sigil magick.

TOPY especially emphasized the work of the well-known Beat Generation writer William S. Burroughs, who had his own idiosyn-

---

*For a recent first-hand account of the work of Thee Temple ov Psychick Youth, see Carl Abrahamsson's *Meetings with Remarkable Magicians: Life in the Occult Underground* (Inner Traditions, 2024). Abrahamsson created the Scandinavian branch of TOPY, and this later expanded into the branch for all of continental Europe.

cratic magical beliefs and techniques, and Brion Gysin, an artist who worked closely with Burroughs. One of the most significant of these practices was the *cut-up*, a form of collage that takes bits of pieces of media—pages from a magazine or newspaper, audio recordings, scraps of random writing, and so on—and recombines them to create new meaning out of the pieces. Sometimes a cut-up is deliberately shaped to highlight and recombine certain ideas, but it can also be partially or completely random—a sort of cosmic ransom note for reconfiguring the phenomenal world in completely new ways using the very pieces of a previous arrangement of reality. From the perspective of semiurgy discussed in this book, we can see that this practice both creates new signs and rearranges existing ones in novel ways. Burroughs himself was adamant that the cut-up was primarily a magical technique, not an artistic one, saying, "When you cut into the present, the future leaks out."[44]

Another fascinating quirk of TOPY's obsession with Burroughs was their embrace of the "23 enigma," attributed to him by Robert Anton Wilson (although Wilson was the one who popularized it). This enigma is the supposed tendency for the number 23 to show up when least expected. At one level this is just a manifestation for the general human tendency to find order in disorder and make patterns out of data. However, it is also a form of meaning-making, creating connections that are valid to the extent that they enable new relationships between signs. TOPY's use of the 23 enigma was more subtle than just looking for random occurrences of numbers to grab the attention:

> It is not so much that the number 23 is a "magical" number that does "tricks" for the person who invokes it, it is more that the number 23 reminds us of the inherent plasticity of our inherited reality and our potential to immerse our SELF in that quality to our own advantage and possible well-being. It represents a magical vision of life rather than a linear and existential one.[45]

One of the most famous applications of the number 23 in the TOPY universe was their approach to the regular creation of sigils.

What the central TOPY ritual consisted of, at least structurally, was that on the 23rd of each month, at 2300 hours, the dedicated adepts would perform a sigilising ritual in and/or on an artwork designed by themselves specifically for the desired goal. This piece of highly charged talismanic art was then sent in to a TOPY "Station" (bigger and more administrative headquarters than the Access Points). The idea was to "impose" or inspire self-discipline and regularity, to unite with other adepts in time, to initiate personal empirical research about ritual magick and, not forgetting, to honor the weird synchronistic concept of the number 23, as "inherited" from TOPY mentors William S. Burroughs and Brion Gysin.[46]

These sigils were sort of a modern equivalent to ancient curse tablets, where the intent of the sigil was enhanced by permanently sending it away from its creator into a numinous space. Collecting sigils in this way—so that they both connect the senders to a common goal but also put numerous examples in close proximity to enhance their effects—evokes Frazer's law of contagion. The design of each sigil has an indexical relationship to its creator, and the collected sigils feed off each other to create new combinations of signs from randomly connected elements. This is the same basic idea behind the magical use of cut-ups, where the sigils themselves effectively function as cut-ups of the original statement of intent.

Magicians working under the TOPY banner were keenly aware of the power of language and other semiotic codes: the power to persuade, to undermine, to rule, to rebel, to enchant. At times they were cynical:

Language is crucial. We judge and measure so much by it; yet language, to those who can articulate and manipulate it, is merely a game in itself, a word game, played to make their position stronger, to mask their greedy intentions.[47]

At other times, they were more optimistic, seeing language as a weapon that *anyone* can yield to transform reality for themselves and others:

> Chop it up, jumble it around, see what it really does, really says, expose it, reveal its strength, its weakness. We must change the language, the language of promises, contracts, manifestos, advertisements, deputations, mandates, formulas, boundaries, expectations, hopes, treaties, wars, education and justice.[48]

Quoting French intellectuals would have seemed out of character for the artistic British founders of TOPY, but there are clear echoes here of the demythologizing of Roland Barthes we discussed in chapter 3. Much like with a computer program, if you change the code, you change the behavior. The universality of language makes it especially ripe for using it as a tool for breaking down barriers and preconceptions while turning it in ways that literally speak (or write) into being new realities.

The concepts and techniques of Thee Temple ov Psychick Youth had many resemblances to the Chaos Magic current. However, TOPY's fixation on media and cultural reprogramming revealed an intuitive understanding of how to use semiotics to reconfigure reality and the perception of reality. Some of the central figures in TOPY have been hugely influential in the world of experimental music—groups such as Throbbing Gristle, Psychic TV, Coil—and this has created further outlets for perpetuating their ideas and practices long after TOPY itself had faded away.

FURTHER READING

Aleister Crowley and Thelema

Magick in Theory and Practice by Aleister Crowley

Overthrowing the Old Gods: Aleister Crowley and the Book of the Law by Don Webb

The Magick of Aleister Crowley: A Handbook of the Rituals of Thelema by Lon Milo DuQuette

Austin Osman Spare

Austin Osman Spare: The Occult Life of London's Legendary Artist by Phil Baker

Dark Spirits: The Magical Art of Rosaleen Norton and Austin Osman Spare by Nevill Drury

Ethos by Austin Osman Spare

Zos-Kia: An Introductory Essay on the Art and Sorcery of Austin Osman Spare by Gavin W. Semple

The Early Church of Satan (before 1975)

The Satanic Bible by Anton Szandor LaVey

The Satanic Rituals by Anton Szandor LaVey

The Church of Satan by Michael A. Aquino

The Temple of Set

The Temple of Set by Michael A. Aquino

Lords of the Left-Hand Path by Stephen E. Flowers

"The Left-Hand Path and Post-Satanism: The Temple of Set and the Evolution of Satanism" in *The Devil's Party: Satanism in Modernity*, edited by Per Faxneld and Jesper Petersen

Chaos Magic

Chaotopia! by Dave Lee

Condensed Chaos by Phil Hine

Liber Null and Psychonaut by Peter J. Carroll

Thee Temple ov Psychick Youth

Meetings with Remarkable Magicians by Carl Abrahamsson

The Magical World of William S. Burroughs by Matthew Levi Stevens

Thee Psychick Bible by Genesis P-Orridge

Enochian or Angelic Magic

Arguing with Angels: Enochian Magic and Modern Occulture by Egil Asprem

The Arch-Conjuror of England: John Dee by Glyn Parry

The Vision and the Voice by Aleister Crowley

Sigils

Practical Sigil Magic: Creating Personal Symbols for Success by Frater U∴D∴

Condensed Chaos by Phil Hine

Sigils, Ciphers and Scripts: History of Graphic Function of Magick Symbols by M. B. Jackson

CONCLUSION

Throughout this book, we have looked at semiurgy—or magical communication—through both ancient and modern semiotics, linguistics, and philosophy. The ideas, however, are timeless. We have seen how they are just as applicable to the execration texts of the Sixth Dynasty of ancient Egypt (beginning in the twenty-fourth century BCE) all the way to current, active modern schools of thought on magic. Any perspective that can illuminate the structures, concepts, and processes of magic across such an unfathomable span of time must be tapping into something that is at the very core of human cognition and experience.

Language and semiotics are incomprehensibly broad topics, and the last twenty years especially have seen ideas from these disciplines become more intertwined with magic. Many of the previously rigid boundaries between the various social sciences are becoming more fluid as researchers and theorists see the necessity of looking at the products of human experience in a holistic rather than a siloed way.

Semiotics shows us how seemingly separate parts of our worldview, behaviors, and thought processes are in fact deeply connected through complicated sign networks; Roland Barthes helped us to see how easily that can be used against us. Linguistics—which can be seen as a form of semiotics at its core—reveals why some types of communication are more effective than others, even if we follow all the "rules" of the language-games we play.

One of the most essential ideas in this book is that at a deep level semiotics is virtually indistinguishable from magic, working with constellations of signs that lead toward the desired outcomes in ways not strictly governed by cause and effect. The study of semiotics is the study of how ideas—and the symbols invoking those ideas—structure our perception of reality, create and maintain culture, enforce social norms, and even coerce us into acting contrary to our own interests.

If we could distill the central message of the book down to its essence, it would be this: finding the right signs and words to express what it is you really need is the key to working your Will on the universe.

THE WORDS AIM
THE ARROW

Don Webb

etween my elementary school and my home there was a gumball machine. Well, it was *almost* right between—let's allow for
about a half a block's deviation. It had huge, hard, sugary gumballs for
five cents (this was the sixties!). One day I was in my parents' bedroom
before school. Mom had laid her money next to her purse, both the
bills and the change for the vending machine. I filched a nickel. Who
would notice a nickel? I repeated my theft a few days later. My mom
sat me down one evening and said, "Honey, did you take money from
mommy's wallet?"

I answered honestly: "No."

I was waiting for the follow-up question, "Did you take money
off the dresser?" It never came. I understood that there was a world of
words and a world of facts. And what little power I had as a second
grader seemed to lie in that tiny gap between them.

When I was fourteen (1974), everybody read *Subliminal Seduction:
Are You Being Sexually Aroused by This Picture?* by Wilson Bryan Key,
which argued that the black magicians of Madison Avenue were making
(MAKING) you buy stuff by subtly putting the words SEX and FUCK

in the backgrounds of magazine ads and billboards. Well, it turned out that they had been—and they discovered that the process didn't work very well. The advertising industry was phasing it out before Key's book—but after the book became a bestseller, the process returned with great new vigor. The folks that bought the ads believed in it, and they paid for it. We all believed Key—initially, at least—so the question is: *Why?* In the processing of human sensory data, we intuit our split brain and we live with two minds, mainly working in sync. But that little gap between them gives us momma's nickels. We hide messages; we look for hidden messages—and if you are a magically sensitive person, you are stimulated by their presence. (By the way, the technique of subliminal seduction can still be spied in liquor ads, if you are really bored and own a good magnifying glass.)

The major occult schools of the English-speaking world are attracted to foreign and exotic words like iron filings to a magnet. Thelema, a Greek word meaning "desire; purpose; will" has its school. An Egyptian verb for "I/it has come into being"—*Xeper*—has many exponents. Followers of various flavors of the Golden Dawn intone "*Khabs am Pekht*" twice a year, thinking they are repeating an ancient Egyptian summary of Newtonian optics. Books on "Enochian" (the jargon Dr. Dee called "Adamical"), runes, ogham, hieroglyphs, bija mantras, and so forth sell like hotcakes—either because folks like you and I are mentally deficient OR because we live in the gap between words and things—and in that gap hidden, twisted, magical words are the lightning bolts between the clouds of meaning and the ground of the Real. There are three great grammars—the grammar of your language, which has rules derived by historical processes and psychological processes; the grammar of the objective universe, which has rules in mathematics (that sometimes seem contrary to common sense); and there is the hidden language of Magic, which can delude the weak-minded and empower those whose Will is contrary to the two other grammars.

Once upon a time, the Good Book (or at least *a* Good Book)

tells us there was a man named *Ḥănōk*, Hebrew for "Initiator." And IHVH so loved the guy that—of all humans—he did not kill him but took him to Heaven. In Heaven he learned that people who treated the Hebrews badly were in for deep shit—the book was written during an all-expenses-paid vacation that the Babylonian Empire was giving the Jews. He learned that devils were in for deep shit, and he also learned that the Watchers—the neutral angels who fought for neither God nor Satan, but enjoyed teaching cosmetics and magic to humans since Earth girls were easy—were also in for deep shit. How did he know that this was TRUE? Because IHVH let him learn the language of Angels, which could not be used to tell a lie, and was so powerful that whatever was said in it Became Real. Adam spoke this language before he got an apple stuck in his throat. Dr. John Dee and Edward Kelley managed to get the angels to reveal some of their lingo—and wrote it down. Dr. Dee also discovered that it made a great cipher to tell Queen Elizabeth about Spanish activities. (Incidentally, the word for "deception" in Dee's jargon was *Madrid*—one of those little Angel puns.)

Some British Freemasons loved the cipher magic of John Dee and decided to establish their own Order around it. Well, they didn't just say, "We think this is cool," they made up a story of a German Rosicrucian lodge. These "Rosicrucians" were implicated in some amazing hoaxes. These German Rosicrucians wrote down their instructions in ENGLISH (except for the "Enochian") in the cipher of Abbot Johannes Trithemius (not his real name)—and "found" the Cipher Manuscripts. So, Joke #1 ("Rosicrucians") + Joke #2 ("found documents") + Joke #3 ("German" magicians writing in English for our convenience) = the Golden Dawn and, later, the A∴A∴, OTO, Church of Satan, Temple of Set—and, finally, you reading this volume by the excellent Toby Chappell! Jokes, puns, stories—this is the world of Magick. It is both paper thin and infinitely powerful. It will fulfill your wildest dreams—even if that is just a gumball.

With such Magick as I might possess, I Setnakt MerynAumnRe

do bless and sanctify this collection of holy words, that it may lead you to discover the language of ultimate power and revelation that lies in the hidden depth of your own heart. So it is done. You owe me a gumball.

Ol sonf vorsg, goho Iad balt lansh calz vonpho.

DON WEBB is a prolific author of supernatural fiction as well as several works on left-hand path practice and philosophy, including *Mysteries of the Temple of Set, Energy Magick of the Vampyre,* and *How to Become a Modern Magus.*

APPENDIX A

WHY DO MAGICIANS WRITE FICTION?

Don Webb

Many modern occultists either base their mission on—or at least have a great deal of supernatural fiction in—their reading lists. It is not uncommon to see modern occultists perusing the works of Lovecraft, Chambers, Machen, or Blackwood. This practice leads us to two interested and related questions. Why would a magician (Machen, Blackwood, Fortune) write fiction (beyond the obvious reasons of amusement and remuneration)? Why would other magicians find their inspiration in fictive works?

A third question lies hidden in the first two: How is magic similar to the acts of reading and writing? I would like to take a look at the nature of magic as a communication system, answer the first two questions, give a few references for where important magical writing may be found today, and sound a warning call for its protection. This is a tiny rivulet, which I hope that others will take up as a new type of criticism. Like the dark streams that have never seen the light of the sun in the hills west of Arkham, I hope that this little rivulet may play an important role in the evolution of Life.

Mauss and other modernists attempted to reduce the power of

magic to a sociological context—the power of magic is equivalent to how society feels about the magician. This dreary attitude is still largely present in popular culture; however, postmodern theorists such as van Baal, Grambo, Flowers, and Tambiah have provided us with a semiotic theory of magic, which serves to illustrate both the practice of magic and its symbolic expression. Basically, the semiotic theory of magic is that man is able to effect communication with his universe and to think ascriptively (i.e., hidden meaning is ascribed to the phenomenon of the universe, and it becomes a partner in communication).

The semiotic theory postulates three elements: the magician seeking either a psychological change within him/herself or an environmental change; the message, which is cast in the form of culturally coded symbols; and the hidden "other side" of the universe. This goes beyond Frazer's notions of "sympathy" by elaborating not only a threefold process of sender–message–receiver, but actually proposes a willed volition to receive communication (in either the form of a revelation or an environmental change) back from the universe. Summing up this model of magic (after Flowers's *Runes and Magic: Magical Formulaic Elements in the Older Runic Tradition* [Lang 1986], 17):

```
subject ——————→ direct object ——————→ indirect object
(man)           (symbol-symbolized)        ("other reality")
                                                 │
                                                 ↓
indirect object ←———— (phenomenon) ←———— subject
(ultimate aim of operation)
```

Van Baal's model

This model suggests that, for the magician, the great secret is finding the correct mode of address—the method of communication that will produce the response from the hidden realm. This has always been intuited in the Mediterranean school of magic, as exemplified by choosing Hermes, god of communication, as its patron. For the magician operating in a traditional society, the method of communication is generally heavily determined—people know how to talk to the gods. But in modern and postmodern societies, the quest for the method of communication is ongoing.

The book ranks high as a sufficiently mysterious form of communication (video, movies, and the computer network are waiting in the wings). Who among us has not experienced that mysterious phenomenon of gleaning something from a piece of one's own writing long after it was written? And who among us has not experienced that mysterious process of "finding just the book we need" at a crucial time in our development? So, keeping in mind your own experiences of the Mystery of the written word, consider van Baal's description of the nature of a magical spell:

> The formula (spell) takes its origin from the discourse between man and his universe, in the case of a particular formula a discourse concerning a certain object and the fulfillment of a desire. In this discourse Man feels addressed or singled out by his universe, and he endeavors to address it in turn, trying to discover the kind of address to which his universe will be willing to answer, that is, willing to show itself communicable.
>
> The formula he finally discovers in answer to his quest is not really man's discovery but a gift, a revelation bestowed upon him by the universe. The formula is the outcome of an act of communication in which man's universe reveals to him the secret of how it should be addressed in this or that circumstance, a secret which is at the same time a revelation of its hidden essence in that particular field . . .[1]

Given the above, we may again ask: Why do magicians write fiction? It is not to provide an open communication of magic—it would be easier simply to write how-to books. The need to communicate with the hidden aspects of the universe of discourse is the magician's motive. Just as an Egyptian would stuff his letters to the dead in the crumbling tomb walls, the modern magician sends his or her message into the semiosphere. Dion Fortune didn't create her novels just as entertainment, but to actively Work the magic. By performing illustrative magic concerning the nature of initiation, of secret schools, et cetera, she actually received (from the Hidden parts of her own psyche) such information.

The simple act of visualization (i.e., daydreaming) is known to produce effects both psychological and environmental; how much greater an effect can be obtained through the writing and publishing of magical work? The precision of writing, editing, and rewriting, coupled with the aching wait for publication (with its inherent travails of lost manuscripts, marketing mistakes, and fraudulent publishers), creates an unbeatable combination of passion and precision.

These are the elements that effect any magical working. It is easy to get up passion for a particular end. We have all had that experience of needing to get that job, or make that meeting, and so forth, wherein our magical practice did pay off with the required miracle. But it is frankly hard to work up the passion required to achieve certain desired spiritual states. However, the test of publication will place the magician in the desire-filled mode necessary to achieve his or her spiritual goals.

Of particular interest in this model is a man who would have felt repulsed at the mere notion of placing him among magicians: H. P. Lovecraft. But he illustrates the case perfectly. Lovecraft, with his passions for astronomy and history, longed to be part of the vast forces of time. He longed to see the hidden essence of cosmology and history, which he felt would dissolve the details of the present like an acid.

With an entirely materialistic outlook, the practice of magic would've been absurd—but writing was another matter. His themes and topics were certainly not commercial (although there has been a good deal of money minted in his name). The desire to continue producing amateur fiction, or sticking with such fiction as could be only sold to the low-paying *Weird Tales*, shows that his need was a purely magical one. And it produces results. The plots of his stories often came to him in dreams.

Particularly noteworthy was the dream that led to the production of the prose-poem "Nyarlathotep," in which he found the Hermes of his pantheon. This communicator from the other side, with his swarthy Egyptian skin, resembles both the figure of Hermes-Thoth and the preternatural entity that Crowley contacted in 1904. Lovecraft knew his need for the cosmic feeling that his stories brought him, and throughout his letters and critical writings we see this need to evoke a mood repeated time and again. In fact, Lovecraft was sensitive enough to this process (even though his materialist attitude kept him from ever consciously expressing it) that many of his stories are about the desired result of receiving communication from the other side. Cthulhu sends dreams. The Fungi from Yuggoth take the seeker away on a cosmic quest, or at the very least whisper all the secrets of the cosmos via certain human appendages. The primordial ones communicate through their vast murals found in hidden Antarctica. In the most revelatory of all his work, *The Shadow Out of Time*, the hero not only sends a message to the other side (by writing in the library of the Great Race) but receives a revelation of finding the message deep below ground (i.e., in the unconscious) written in his own hand.

Having seen why magicians feel a need to use certain hidden or encoded communications such as fiction writing, we may now return to the question of why magicians need to read fiction. The simple reason of "inspiration" suffices, but it is to be noted that it is not the same sort of inspiration that one may glean from, say, a straightforward biography. Very little occult fiction provides a step-by-step account of ritual procedure, and those that do are among the most boring. One doesn't read *The White People* to find out the step-by-step ways of doing anything. Indeed, the operant material is generally described under only the broadest (and therefore most evocative) of terms. One may be tempted to invent the Aklo language, or to script out the Mao game, but the real purpose of occult literature is to allow the magician to receive communication from the "other side."

By the use of imagination and mood, the nature of that hidden realm is disclosed to us, although most often in a mysterious way. It would be difficult to provide a description of the shudder that hearing the cauldron spell from *Macbeth* first gave us. Crowley chose *Macbeth*, *The Tempest*, and *A Midsummer Night's Dream* for the reading list of the A∴ A∴ "as being interesting for the traditions treated." The objective realities of these traditions were very limited, but Crowley—who was nobody's fool—knew that the effect they had on the soul allowed something of the mysterious realm to be communicated. In short, reading works that illustrate actual magic brings closure to the diagram above, and enables the discerning magician to benefit from the illustrative work of others.

This is not a matter of simply receiving a message from the author—that simple act of decoding which we all do as readers—this is receiving an access point to the Unknown from the Unknown. The magician who manages such a feat in tandem with the act of fictional creation therefore achieves in this postmodern society a set of signs and symbols for communication with that unknown realm.

The task facing the modern occultist is to discover where the unknown is most active, or to put it in literary terms: Where are the new occult writers coming from, and in what arenas may they be found? As this quest is an intensely personal one, I can only give a few hints and recommendations. The works of Thomas Ligotti are universally praiseworthy and should be sought out. J. G. Ballard, who never once mentions anything overtly magical, is a great place to learn about stasis and rebirth. *Cities of the Red Night* by William S. Burroughs—with its masterful portrayal of the chthonic forces—should be in every magician's library, and the magical realism of Jorge Luis Borges and Gabriel García Márquez is not to be overlooked.

The late Fritz Leiber likewise crafted some places where a thing or two can be learned. As for magazines, *Elegia* provided a fairly high understanding of the magical process, cast in the Gothic idiom of the mid- to late 1990s.

If you desire to be part of this process, you must create, and you must also preserve by fighting off every attempt to suppress supernatural literature. The forces that produce writer's block within the self have their counterparts in the semiosphere—these mindless gray ones who remove books from school library shelves. If you are a knight who seeks the Grail of inspiration, or the magician who creates its brew—beware those gray dragons with dull eyes. There is no compromise with those who would limit our imagination. To sit back and allow them control of our libraries is a spiritual negligence that will take its toll on our hearts. Read! Write! Preserve!

MAGIA LOCI

Brenda Yagmin

This book is about semiurgy, honing our power of symbolic communication between our desires and the world in which they manifest. This appendix is about the way the World communicates with us—and how we can communicate back to it, shaping it to become a partner in delivering our desires to us.

Our immersion in the World is absolute, inescapable—we dream of places, even think of one place while existing in another. But the World is more malleable than we assume. Illusionists and stage magicians know this and manipulate objects to shift our perception of what's "real." Another type of magician—the kind seeking self-transformation—is likewise a master of the art of understanding just what is objective, what is subjective, and how to navigate and manipulate both. Magia Loci involves similar skill in working with places, for they are always both real and perceived.

The importance of place in magic is key. Every desire you have is contextualized by place. The person you want to become and the things you want to achieve will necessitate a change beyond attitude and daydreams: something real must change too. Transforming the self will—must—result in seeing the world in a different way, experiencing old places in a new light or expanding your physical horizons in tandem with your metaphysical horizons. Powerful magic often involves a place as a key element, whether it is the setting of a ritual or contextualizing the result—be it a new home, job, or experiences. As a methodology, Magia Loci shifts "place magic" from an aesthetic, supplementary force or consequence to being the anchor of the work.

We are able to assess the meaning of a place by rapidly taking in all bits of sensory information, which combine into an overall "feel." Feeding into this assessment is a blend of hardwired instinct, developed intuition, experiential sensations, and somatic pattern recognition—sensing where we are in the world and parsing it into a felt sense. Some shapes may trigger a physical response that cannot be suppressed: the sinuous line, the dominant mass, the sharp diagonal—symbols of ancient predators that our brains register in a flash. We subconsciously process angles that are slightly askew, which disturbs our expectations and can cause an eerie, mild distress. Cultural priming and past experiences deliver certainty about what should happen—say, in a hospital, the funeral parlor, an airplane, or when we enter the gym.

Despite such logic, you may feel that certain places have more to them than these explainable aspects—more than just shape, function, lore, and symbol, they have an essence or vibe of their own. Neil Gaiman, Alan Moore, H. P. Lovecraft, Fritz Leiber, and many others have written evocatively about places holding some vitality, some power—inexplicably reverberating with a purpose that eludes us and manipulates us to act in resonance with it. How and why? This is the fun part. Perhaps it is the Great Old Ones whose purpose is beyond our comprehension; or ancient occult rites repeated over the centuries; or fourth-dimensional activity by beings outside of our realm of perception; or a tangible resonance set off as the culmination of a million iterations set in motion by chance events eons ago or, paradoxically, by acts that have yet to occur.

Cities hold a particular fascination within place magic. Like humans, cities started as an anomaly, qualitatively different than all that had come before. Just like humans, who started out as a rather frail species in a hostile world, they now dominate the globe, evolving in tandem with us. They are thus a metasymbol of our species: non-natural, chaotic, somehow successful despite holding so many violent and destructive elements. And like us, cities have managed to function, grow, and endure through tragic cycles of destruction and rebirth. Urban symbols and urban magic draw their power from this conflict and dynamism.

Whether the cause or outcome of our evolution, civilization followed a logarithmic progression: from the first rare settlements, leaping with industrialization, rooting into permanence through imperialism, expanding through colonialism, and encompassing all with planetization. In myth, cities were created by the Gods, their design too grand, too complex to be a product of man; or, they had a patron god that kept the city vibrant—at least for a time. From the Industrial Revolution, the symbols of the gods—the temples and churches—were overtaken by skyscrapers and factories. Those symbols remain, even as power shifts from local to global, and slips from the real to the virtual.

If twentieth-century cities severed the connection between us and nature, the gods, and community (as is often decried), the twenty-first century is redefining those connections, along with the terms themselves: self, nature, gods, community. The burgeoning symbols of our age are the "Network" and "Fluidity," describing how we interact with our places, ourselves, and each other. The self is no longer defined by our job and religion, but by which app we are on and which Self we choose to share. Community isn't family and neighborhood, it's the one we forge for ourselves from the vast options that the internet and travel have opened to us. Nature can no longer be divorced from our touch— our building of civilization has affected every corner of the earth. As for Gods, they are Us—in our labs, creating new life forms, foods, diseases and cures, and artificial intelligence. Our realized interconnection with the World is something we work every day, along every line.

Let us look to urban fiction and fantasy to explore this connection. Sometimes, the city is the monstrous "other," feeding off us as we feed it, a creation out of our control and something with which we can no longer communicate. Sometimes mythic potential prevails, with cities evolving into sentient beings, or new life forms emerging from the mix of human angst and urban sludge (along with the advent of new magics to control these forms). In the most optimistic view, the city can serve as an advocate and co-conspirator in one's journey to Become, be it passive or active.

Magia Loci takes the optimistic view. We can shape the World to our advantage. The work is in learning to speak its language. We already have a master symbol book of what the World means and wants of us. It was created unconsciously, cribbed off the assumptions and experiences of those who had power in other ages. The definitions became concretized through your culture and upbringing, and your lived experiences. Your symbol book might say cities are exciting and "the place to be," but if you have a deep and unrealized need to be in the countryside, your belief is not serving you well.

The work of Magia Loci is using place to help you uncover your desires despite your current definitions. Place communicates in all those subtle physical ways as described above, but also in so many cultural, mythic, even metaphysical ways that it is most usefully cast as a magical art. It is also, importantly, a physical art. You've got to get off your ass and go to places—ones that you've never been to, some that you never liked, and all the ones you've always loved. Once you are immersed in them, let them "speak." See the signs. Take notes. Draw pictures. Feel the emotions that come up and live through the memories that surge. Go home. Do research. Note the synchronicities. Follow your instincts. Tell others about your places.

The last part is important: telling others. This is mythic work—you are creator, storyteller, world-builder. You are the one who makes it so! Communicating what you have seen and felt makes your experience visceral, from thoughts to reality. We are naturally adept at creating myths that exert influence in the real world, such as gods to rule over us or demons to blame for our troubles. When you speak the World into existence through the meaning you made, it becomes exactly what you need it to be.

Through even this simple practice of awareness, the World will begin to speak to you on your terms—in your language, as you have defined it. Do this even a few times, and you will start experiencing the World . . . differently. You'll notice new things about old places, learn to trust your gut about which way to turn at the crossroads, and find "hidden gems." The more you draw resonances to the surface—resonances between your deep-seated desires and the World as it is—and acknowledge them in the world of form, the clearer their symbolic importance will become. In this way, you create a World that is continually "working for you" rather than moving through someone else's world.

The outcomes go deeper. By becoming more adept at drawing out what is important to you from the World, you begin to shape your idea of Self that moves within it. To put it another way: you will be "transforming the magician," the real secret of magic.

BRENDA YAGMIN is the creator of the Urban Magic / Megapolisomancy blog *Magia Loci* (at the Magialoci website), which considers magical technologies stemming from our interaction with place, particularly the built environment. She lives in NYC and works with cultural, urban, and business anthropology.

GLOSSARY

arbitrariness: the lack of inherent connection between a word and its referent, with meaning being agreed upon by convention.

code: a set of conventions or rules for interpreting signs within a particular context. Also sometimes called a *semiotic code*.

coherence: a statement about whether meaning can be derived from a text. *See* text.

cohesion: the set of formal ties that exist within a text. *See* text.

conceptual domain: a set of ideas linked to a specific set of experiences; for example, all the objects, ideas, and processes related to taking a journey are part of a single conceptual domain.

conceptual metaphor: a particular type of metaphor that uses terms associated with a more concrete experience or concept (i.e., easier to perceive with the senses) to describe a more abstract experience or concept.

Firstness: the initial encounter with a sign, when we are drawn to it and struck by its potential but have not yet begun to interpret the sign. This is a feature of Peirce's typology of signs.

hyperstition: an aspiration within a culture that begins as a fantasy then takes root and spreads as it encourages work toward its ultimate realization.

icon: a type of sign in Peirce's typology of signs that resembles in some way the object to which it refers.

index: a type of sign in Peirce's typology of signs that points to the existence of something that is not present in the current place and/or time.

interpretant: the effect that a sign has on the mind that is attempting to interpret the sign. One of the three basic components of all signs in Peirce's typology of signs.

langue and *parole*: in Saussure's approach to linguistics, *langue* denotes the set of abstract rules (grammar, syntax, etc.) for a language; *parole* denotes the patterns of speech for an individual speaker of a language (including their conception of the meanings of the words they use).

law of contagion: in Frazer's view of magic, this is the principle that once an object has been in touch with another, a connection continues to exist between the objects and this connection can be used for magical purposes.

law of sympathy: in Frazer's view of magic, this is the principle that magic works with images or objects that are similar to the intended target or desired result of the magical operation.

linguistic community: a collection of language users who use language with similar norms and expectations (also called a *speech community*).

meme: a concept or behavior that is spread through human culture by imitation (a process called *memesis*).

metonymy: the use of some attribute or something closely associated with a concept or thing to substitute for the thing itself (e.g., using "the press" to refer to journalists).

object: the thing or concept to which a sign refers, in Peirce's typology of signs.

perceptual world: the inner world of the individual, including their worldview and experiences (as well as their self-image, which may or may not correspond to how others view them, as well as their hopes, desires, and fears).

performative utterance: a speech act that by the very fact of being spoken in the correct circumstances causes an immediate change in reality (such as a judge pronouncing a sentence or declaring that a marriage has occurred).

phaneron: the totality of signs present within the mind.

phenomenal world: the world outside the mind of the individual, including not only matter and physical laws but also the effects of other minds.

post-structuralism: a loosely defined intellectual movement that draws on structuralism's insights about the structures of thought that form the basis for culture, religion, and history, while rejecting structuralism's core contention that meaning is universal (instead of constructed, based on individual experience and perception). *See* structuralism.

representamen: the part of a sign that refers to or represents something else; this is the part of the sign that we encounter and then interpret. This is part of Peirce's typology of signs.

scientism: the belief that science and the scientific method are all that are necessary to discover truths about the world and its inhabitants.

Secondness: facts about a sign or the thing it references or refers to. Part of Peirce's typology of signs.

semiosis: the capacity for creating and interpreting signs.

semiotics: the study of the signs, including their creation and interpretation. Sometimes called *semiology*, in that case referring specifically to Saussure's theories of signs.

semiurgy: creating signs and using them to alter reality or the perception of reality. Coined by Jean Baudrillard and adopted in this book as an alternate term for magic emphasizing the use of signs as part of magic.

sigil: 1. an image created from a statement of intent, reducing the statement to a representation inspired by the shapes of its letters (one approach pioneered by A. O. Spare); 2. an abstract written sign standing for various demons, spirits, or other numinous beings (as in Agrippa's *De Occulta Philosophia* or the *Ars Goetia*).

sign: anything that stands for, refers to, represents, or evokes something else.

sign network: a collection of interrelated signs (also called a *semiotic web*).

signified: in Saussure's semiology, the object or concept to which a signifier refers.

signifier: in Saussure's semiology, the part of a sign that refers to something else.

source domain: in a conceptual metaphor, the conceptual domain that is drawn from in order to provide the vocabulary and viewpoint used as part of the metaphor.

speech act: an instance of spoken language that not only presents information but also requests or performs an action (such as "I'm cold; please close the window").

structuralism: an intellectual movement derived from Saussure's semiology, which holds that thought arises from pairs of opposing ideas ("up and down," "light and dark," etc.) projected onto the world to understand its structure and relationships. *See* post-structuralism.

symbol: a type of sign in Peirce's typology of signs that only has meaning according to culturally conditioned conventions.

syntagma: an ordered collection of signs that expresses more meaning than the individual signs can on their own.

target domain: in a conceptual metaphor, the conceptual domain that is made more concrete by comparison with the source domain.

text: any collection of signs (not limited to just written words).

Thirdness: In Peirce's typology of signs, our expectations about a sign and its meaning based on cultural convention or past experience.

Umwelt: the perceptual or subjective world that an organism models out of signs in its environment.

NOTES

CHAPTER 1.
WHAT DO LANGUAGE AND SEMIOTICS HAVE TO DO WITH MAGIC?

1. Everett, *How Language Began*, 60.
2. Webb, *How to Become a Modern Magus*, x.
3. Hawkins, *Mindstep to the Cosmos*, 2.
4. Everett, *How Language Began*, 60.
5. CCRU, *Writings 1997–2003*, 330.
6. Clarke, "Clarke's Third Law on UFO's," 255.
7. Dunn, *Magic, Power, Language, Symbol*, 10.

CHAPTER 2.
A SURVEY OF DIFFERENT MODELS OF MAGIC

1. Tylor, *Primitive Culture*, 101.
2. Sørensen, *A Cognitive Theory of Magic*, 115.
3. Sørensen, *A Cognitive Theory*, 15.
4. Davies, *Magic*, 22.
5. Lévi-Strauss, "The Sorcerer and His Magic," 187.
6. Grambo, "Models of Magic," 90.
7. Grambo, "Models of Magic," 94–95.
8. Tambiah, "The Magical Power of Words," 175.
9. Tambiah, "The Magical Power of Words," 182.
10. Wittgenstein, *The Mythology in Our Language*, 81.

11. Sørensen, *Theoretical and Empirical Investigations of Divination and Magic*, 216.

12. Wittgenstein, *The Mythology in Our Language*, 148.

13. Kuiper, "Religion, Symbols, and the Human Condition," 138.

14. Kuiper, "Religion, Symbols, and the Human Condition," 138.

15. Kuiper, "Religion, Symbols, and the Human Condition," 137.

16. Van Baal, *Symbols for Communication*, 263.

17. Sørensen, *A Cognitive Model of Magic*, 2.

18. Sørensen, *A Cognitive Model of Magic*, 3.

19. Dunn, *Magic, Power, Language, Symbol*, 6.

20. Chandler, *Semiotics*, 177.

21. Dunn, *Magic, Power, Language, Symbol*, 8.

22. Flowers, "How to Do Things with Runes," 66.

23. Flowers, "How to Do Things," 66.

24. Flowers, "How to Do Things," 70.

25. Antonsen, *A Concise Grammar of the Older Runic Inscriptions*, 36.

26. Flowers, "How to Do Things," 76

27. Ritner, *The Mechanics of Ancient Egyptian Magical Practice*, 214.

28. Flowers, "How to Do Things," 76.

29. Nöth, *Handbook of Semiotics*, 188.

30. Shell, *The Application of Peircean Semiotics to the Elder Futhark Tradition*, 39.

31. Shell, *The Application of Peircean Semiotics*, 39.

32. Peirce, *Collected Papers*, §8.213.

33. Shell, *The Application of Peircean Semiotics*, 80.

CHAPTER 3.
A BRIEF HISTORY OF SEMIOTICS

1. Quoted in Sebeok, *Signs*, 129.

2. Bennett, *Detotalization and Retroactivity*, 10.

3. Van Baal, *Symbols for Communication*, 263.

4. Barthes, "The rhetoric of the image," in *Image–Music–Text*, 48.

5. Chandler, *Semiotics*, 15.

6. Chandler, *Semiotics*, 17.

7. Chandler, *Semiotics*, 18.

8. Langer, *Philosophy in a New Key*, 60.

9. Peirce, "How to Make Our Ideas Clear."

10. Hardwick, *Semiotics and Significs*, 85–86.

11. Peirce Edition Project, ed., *The Essential Peirce*, 478.

12. Peirce, *Collected Papers*, §2.302.

13. Peirce, *Collected Papers*, §§1.524, 5.469.

14. Peirce, *Collected Papers*, §1.536.

15. Peirce, *Collected Papers*, §1.324.

16. Eco, *Foucault's Pendulum*, 365.

17. Peirce, *Collected Papers*, §1.169.

18. Peirce, *Collected Papers*, §1.257.

19. Peirce, *The Writings of Charles S. Peirce*, 324.

20. Peirce, *Collected Papers*, 324.

21. Peirce, *Collected Papers*, §8.213.

22. Lovecraft, "The Call of Cthulhu," in *Bloodcurdling Tales of Horror and the Macabre*, 76.

23. LaVey, *The Satanic Bible*, 127.

24. Eco, *A Theory of Semiotics*, 7.

25. Danesi, "Eco's Definition of Semiotics as the Discipline of Lying," in Thellefsen and Sørensen, eds., *Umberto Eco in His Own Words*, 21.

26. Eco, *Semiotics and the Philosophy of Language*, 26.

CHAPTER 4.
VIEWING MAGIC THROUGH
LINGUISTICS AND THE PHILOSOPHY OF LANGUAGE

1. Betz, *The Greek Magical Papyri*, 103.

2. The concept and the list are introduced in Hockett's article "The Origin of Speech" from *Scientific American* 203 (1960).

3. Burroughs, "Ten Years and a Billion Dollars," in *The Adding Machine*, 48.

4. Lakoff and Johnson, "Conceptual Metaphor in Everyday Language," 456.

5. Betz, *The Greek Magical Papyri*, 266.

6. Otto, *The Idea of the Holy*, 26.

7. Otto, *The Idea of the Holy*, 13.

8. Austin, *How to Do Things with Words*, 5.

9. Tambiah, "A Performative Approach to Ritual," 128.

10. Tambiah, "A Performative Approach," 128.

11. Tambiah, "A Performative Approach," 129.

12. LaVey, *The Satanic Rituals*, 118.

13. LaVey, *The Satanic Rituals*, 120.

14. LaVey, *The Satanic Rituals*, 124.

15. LaVey, *The Satanic Rituals*, 125.

16. Heidegger, "Letter on Humanism," in *Basic Writings*, 217.

17. Wittgenstein, *Philosophical Investigations*, §7 et passim.

CHAPTER 5.
LANGUAGE, MYTH, AND MAGIC

1. Miller, *The Poetry of Thought in Late Antiquity*, 241.

2. Te Velde, "The God Heka in Egyptian Mythology," 176.

3. Te Velde, "The God Heka," 184.

4. Faulkner, *The Ancient Egyptian Coffin Texts*, 1:199.

5. Te Velde, "The God Heka," 179.

6. Simek, *Dictionary of Northern Mythology*, 74.

7. Dalley, *Myths from Mesopotamia*, 233.

8. Dalley, *Myths from Mesopotamia*, 234–35.

9. Dalley, *Myths from Mesopotamia*, 235.

10. Jacobson, *The Treasures of Darkness*, 234.

11. Dalley, *Myths from Mesopotamia*, 235.

12. Sandars, *Poems of Heaven and Hell from Ancient Mesopotamia*, 36.

13. Dalley, *Myths from Mesopotamia*, 249–50.

14. Dalley, *Myths from Mesopotamia*, 274.

15. Chappell, *Infernal Geometry*, 86.

16. Lovecraft, "Nyarlathotep," in *The Dream Cycle of H. P. Lovecraft*, 52.

17. Stephenson, *Snow Crash*, 244.

18. Stephenson, *Snow Crash*, 296.

19. Stephenson, *Snow Crash*, 454.

20. Stephenson, *Snow Crash*, 455.

21. Stephenson, *Snow Crash*, 456.

CHAPTER 6.
MEDITERRANEAN MAGIC IN ANTIQUITY

1. Wilburn, *Materia Magica*, 72.

2. McCown, "The Ephesia Grammata in Popular Belief," 130–32.

3. Versnel, "The Poetics of the Magical Charm," 114.

4. Versnel, "The Poetics," 131.

5. Frankfurter, "The Magic of Writing in Mediterranean Antiquity," 630.

6. Frankfurter, "The Magic of Writing," 644.

7. Betz, *The Greek Magical Papyri*, 10.

8. Iversen, *The Myth of Egypt and Its Hieroglyphs in European Tradition*, 45.

9. Betz, *The Greek Magical Papyri*, 3.

10. Betz, *The Greek Magical Papyri*, 3.

11. Godwin, *The Mystery of the Seven Vowels*, 22.

12. Betz, *The Greek Magical Papyri*, 3.

13. Betz, *The Greek Magical Papyri*, 4.

14. Betz, *The Greek Magical Papyri*, 9.

15. Frankfurter, "Spell and Speech Act," 617.

16. Betz, *The Greek Magical Papyri*, 103.

17. Betz, *The Greek Magical Papyri*, 103.

18. Betz, *The Greek Magical Papyri*, 103.

19. Betz, *The Greek Magical Papyri*, 103.

20. Betz, *The Greek Magical Papyri*, 103.

21. Betz, *The Greek Magical Papyri*, 103.

22. Webb, *Seven Faces of Darkness*, 65.

23. Roblee, "Performing Circles in Ancient Egypt from Mehen to Ouroboros," 135.

24. Robinson, *The Nag Hammadi Library*, 296.

25. Robinson, *The Nag Hammadi Library*, 297.

26. Robinson, *The Nag Hammadi Library*, 297–98.

27. Robinson, *The Nag Hammadi Library*, 299.

28. Robinson, *The Nag Hammadi Library*, 300.

29. Robinson, *The Nag Hammadi Library*, 302.

30. Robinson, *The Nag Hammadi Library*, 302.

31. Robinson, *The Nag Hammadi Library*, 303.

32. Robinson, *The Nag Hammadi Library*, 321.

33. Bull, "Visionary Experience and Ritual Realism in the Ascent of the *Discourse on the Eighth and the Ninth*," 169.

34. Robinson, *The Nag Hammadi Library*, 322. In the extracts from this text presented here, the editor's quotation marks have been removed.

35. Robinson, *The Nag Hammadi Library*, 322.

36. Robinson, *The Nag Hammadi Library*, 322.

37. Robinson, *The Nag Hammadi Library*, 323.

38. Robinson, *The Nag Hammadi Library*, 323.

39. Robinson, *The Nag Hammadi Library*, 323.

40. Robinson, *The Nag Hammadi Library*, 324.

41. Bull, "Visionary Experience," 177.

42. Robinson, *The Nag Hammadi Library*, 324.

43. Robinson, *The Nag Hammadi Library*, 324.

44. Robinson, *The Nag Hammadi Library*, 326.

45. Robinson, *The Nag Hammadi Library*, 326.

46. Robinson, *The Nag Hammadi Library*, 326.

47. Gager, *Curse Tablets and Binding Spells from the Ancient World*, 4.

48. Gager, *Curse Tablets*, 7.

49. Gager, *Curse Tablets*, 89–90.

50. Gager, *Curse Tablets*, 89.

51. Gager, *Curse Tablets*, 89.

52. Ritner, *The Mechanics of Ancient Egyptian Magical Practice*, 142.

53. Ritner, *The Mechanics*, 144.

CHAPTER 7.
RUNES AND SEMIURGY

1. Flowers, *Runes and Magic*, 127.

2. Brown and Moynihan, *The Rune Poems*, 44 (trans. Moynihan).

3. Thorsson, *The Nine Doors of Midgard*, 3.

4. Brown and Moynihan, *The Rune Poems*, 10 (trans. Moynihan).

5. Elliot, *Runes*, 12.

6. Elliot, *Runes*, 82.

CHAPTER 8.
MODERN APPROACHES TO SEMIURGY

1. Spare, *Ethos*, 129.
2. Dunn, *Magic, Power, Language, Symbol*, 95.
3. Brann, "Trithemius, Johannes," 1135.
4. Asprem, *Arguing with Angels*, 50–51.
5. Owen, "The Sorcerer and His Apprentice," 106.
6. Eshelman, *Visions & Voices*, 61.
7. Owen, "The Sorcerer and His Apprentice," 123.
8. Crowley, *Magick in Theory and Practice*, 69.
9. Crowley, *Magick*, 265.
10. Betz, *The Greek Magical Papyri*, 103.
11. Crowley, *Magick*, 267.
12. Crowley, *Magick*, 267.
13. Drury, *Dark Spirits*, 141.
14. Carroll, *Liber Kaos*, 115.
15. Baker, *Austin Osman Spare*, 97.
16. LaVey, *The Satanic Bible*, 155.
17. LaVey, *The Satanic Bible*, 155.
18. LaVey, *The Satanic Bible*, 189.
19. DuQuette, *Enochian Vision Magick*, 203.
20. LaVey, *The Satanic Bible*, 192.
21. Aquino, "Charter of the Order of the Trapezoid," in *The Temple of Set*, 87.
22. LaVey, *The Satanic Bible*, 25.
23. LaVey, *The Satanic Bible*, 144.
24. LaVey, *The Satanic Bible*, 144.
25. LaVey, *The Satanic Bible*, 144.
26. Hawkins, *Mindsteps to the Cosmos*, 16.
27. Aquino, *The Temple of Set*, 20.
28. Aquino, *The Temple of Set*, 256.
29. Aquino, *The Temple of Set*, 256.
30. Aquino, "Contra Contra Templum," 2.
31. Aquino, *The Temple of Set*, 259.
32. Aquino, *The Temple of Set*, 19.
33. Aquino, *The Temple of Set*, 271.

34. DuQuette, *Enochian Vision Magick*, 201.
35. Aquino, *The Temple of Set*, 294.
36. Ritner, *The Mechanics of Ancient Egyptian Magical Practice*, 214.
37. Aquino, *The Temple of Set*, 18.
38. See Aquino, *The Church of Satan*, appendix 15.
39. Aquino, *The Temple of Set*, 216.
40. Aquino, *The Temple of Set*, 216.
41. Aquino, *The Temple of Set*, 217.
42. Lee, *Life Force*, 329.
43. Caroll, *Liber Null and Psychonaut*, 5.
44. Burroughs stated this in his essay "Origin and Theory of Tape Cut-Ups," which he read at the Naropa Institute in Boulder, Colorado in 1976. Recordings of the lecture can be found online.
45. P-Orridge, *Thee Psychick Bible*, 293.
46. P-Orridge, *Thee Psychick Bible*, 13. Punctuation modified.
47. P-Orridge, *Thee Psychick Bible*, 124.
48. P-Orridge, *Thee Psychick Bible*, 125.

APPENDIX A.
WHY DO MAGICIANS WRITE FICTION?

1. Van Baal, *Symbols for Communication*, 263.

BIBLIOGRAPHY

Abrahamsson, Carl. *Meetings with Remarkable Magicians: Life in the Occult Underground*. Rochester, VT: Inner Traditions, 2024.

———. *Occulture: The Unseen Forces That Drive Culture Forward*. Rochester, VT: Park Street Press, 2018.

Aquino, Michael A. *The Church of Satan*. N.p.: CreateSpace, 2013.

———. *The Temple of Set*. N.p.: CreateSpace, 2016.

———. "Contra Contra Templum." San Francisco: Privately published by the author, 2002.

Asprem, Egil. *Arguing With Angels: Enochian Magic and Modern Occulture*. Albany, NY: SUNY Press, 2012.

Austin, J. L. *How to Do Things with Words*. Cambridge, MA: Harvard University Press, 1962.

Baal, Jan van. *Symbols for Communication: An Introduction to the Anthropological Study of Religion*. Assen: Van Gorcum, 1971.

Baker, Phil. *Austin Osman Spare: The Occult Life of London's Legendary Artist*. Berkeley, CA: North Atlantic, 2014.

Barnes, Michael P. *Runes: A Handbook*. Martlesham, UK: Boydell, 2022.

Barthes, Roland. *Image—Music—Text*. New York: Hill and Wang, 1977.

———. *Mythologies*. New York: Hill and Wang, 2012.

Bennett, Tyler James. *Detotalization and Retroactivity: Black Pyramid Semiotics*. Tartu, Estonia: University of Tartu Press, 2021.

Betz, Hans Dieter, ed. *The Greek Magical Papyri in Translation*. Chicago: University of Chicago Press, 1992.

Bieser, Frederick. *German Idealism: The Struggle Against Subjectivism, 1781–1801*. Cambridge, MA: Harvard University Press, 2002.

Blackmore, Sue. *The Meme Machine*. Oxford, UK: Oxford University Press, 2000.

Brann, Noel L. "Trithemius, Johannes." In *Dictionary of Gnosis and Western Esotericism*, edited by Wouter J. Hanegraaff. Leiden: Brill, 2006. Pp. 1135–39.

Brown, P. D., and Michael Moynihan. *The Rune Poems: A Reawakened Tradition*. North Augusta, SC: Gilded Books, 2022.

Bull, Christian H. *The Tradition of Hermes Trismegistus*. Leiden: Brill, 2018.

Burroughs, William S. *The Adding Machine: Collected Essays*. London: Calder, 1985.

Campagna, Federico. *Technic and Magic: The Reconstruction of Reality*. London: Bloomsbury Academic, 2018.

Carroll, Peter J. *Liber Kaos: Chaos Magic for the Pandaemonaeon*. Second revised and expanded edition. Newburyport, MA: Weiser, 2023.

———. *Liber Null and Psychonaut: The Practice of Chaos Magic*. Newburyport, MA: Red Wheel/Weiser, 2022.

Casaubon, Meric. *A True and Faithful Relation of What Passed for Many Yeers between Dr. John Dee and Some Spirits*. London: Garthwait, 1659.

Cassirer, Ernst. *Language and Myth*. New York: Dover, 1953.

CCRU. *Writings 1997–2003*. Second edition. Falmouth, UK: Urbanomic, 2018.

Chandler, Daniel. *Semiotics: The Basics*. Third edition. New York: Routledge, 2017.

Chapman, Siobhan, and Christopher Routledge. *Key Thinkers in Linguistics and the Philosophy of Language*. Oxford, UK: Oxford University Press, 2005.

Chappell, Toby. *Infernal Geometry and the Left-Hand Path: The Magical System of the Nine Angles*. Rochester, VT: Inner Traditions, 2019.

Chomsky, Noam. *What Kind of Creatures Are We?* New York: Columbia University Press, 2016.

Clarke, Arthur C. "Clarke's Third Law on UFO's." *Science*, vol. 159, issue 3812 (19 Jan. 1968): 255.

Crowley, Aleister. *Magick in Theory and Practice*. New York: Dover, 1976.

———. *The Vision and the Voice*. New York: Weiser, 1972.

Dalley, Stephanie. *Myths from Mesopotamia: Creation, The Flood, Gilgamesh, and Others*. Oxford, UK: Oxford University Press, 2008.

Davies, Owen. *Magic: A Very Short Introduction*. Oxford, UK: Oxford University Press, 2012.

Drucker, Johanna. *Inventing the Alphabet*. Chicago: University of Chicago Press, 2022.

Drury, Nevill. *Dark Spirits: The Magical Art of Rosaleen Norton and Austin Osman Spare*. Muang, Thailand: Salamander and Sons, 2012.

Duncker, Dorthe. *The Reflexivity of Language and Linguistic Inquiry: Integrational Linguistics in Practice*. London: Routledge, 2019.

Dunn, Patrick. *Magic, Power, Language, Symbol: A Magician's Exploration of Linguistics*. Woodbury, MN: Llewellyn, 2008.

DuQuette, Lon Milo. *Enochian Vision Magick: A Practical Guide to the Magick of Dr. John Dee and Edward Kelley*. Newburyport, MA: Weiser, 2019.

———. *The Magick of Aleister Crowley*. Newburyport, MA: Weiser, 2022.

Eco, Umberto. *A Theory of Semiotics*. Bloomington, IN: Indiana University Press, 1976.

———. *The Limits of Interpretation*. Bloomington, IN: Indiana University Press, 1990.

———. *The Search for the Perfect Language*. Oxford, UK: Blackwell, 1995.

Elliot, Ralph W. V. *Runes: An Introduction*. Second edition. Manchester: Manchester University Press, 1989.

Eschelman, James A. *Visions & Voices: Aleister Crowley's Enochian Visions with Astrological & Qabalistic Commentary*. Los Angeles: College of Thelema, 2011.

Everett, Daniel. *How Language Began: The Story of Humanity's Greatest Invention*. London: Liveright, 2017.

Faxneld, Per, and Jesper Petersen, eds. *The Devil's Party: Satanism in Modernity*. Oxford, UK: Oxford University Press, 2012.

Fisch, Max. H., et al., eds. *Writings of Charles S. Peirce: A Chronological Edition, Volume I (1857-1866)*. Bloomington: Indiana University Press, 1982.

Flowers, Stephen E. *Hermetic Magic: The Postmodern Magical Papyrus of Abaris*. Boston: Weiser, 1995.

———. "How to Do Things with Runes: A Semiotic Approach to Operative Communication." In *Runes and Their Secrets*, edited by Marie Stoklund, et al. Copenhagen: Museum Tusculanum, 2006. Pp. 65–81.

———. *Lords of the Left-Hand Path*. Revised and expanded edition. Rochester, VT: Inner Traditions, 2012.

———. *Runes and Magic: Magical Formulaic Elements in the Older Runic Tradition*. Third Revised and Expanded Edition. Smithville, TX: Rûna-Raven, 2010.

Fowden, Garth. *The Egyptian Hermes*. Princeton, NJ: Princeton University Press, 1986.

Frankfurter, David. "The Magic of Writing in Mediterranean Antiquity," in *Guide to the Study of Ancient Magic*, edited by David Frankfurter. Leiden: Brill, 2019. Pp. 626–58.

———. "Spell and Speech Act: The Magic of the Spoken Word," in *Guide to the Study of Ancient Magic*, edited by David Frankfurter. Leiden: Brill, 2019. Pp. 608–25.

Frater U∴D∴. *Practical Sigil Magic*. Woodbury, MN: Llewellyn, 2012.

Fries, Jan. *Helrunar: A Manual of Rune Magick*. Oxford, UK: Mandrake of Oxford, 2006.

Gager, John G. *Curse Tablets and Binding Spells from the Ancient World*. Oxford: Oxford University Press, 1992.

Glucklich, Ariel. *The End of Magic*. Oxford: Oxford University Press, 1997.

Godwin, Joscelyn. *Mystery of the Seven Vowels in Theory and Practice*. Grand Rapids, MI: Phanes, 1991.

Grambo, Ronald. "Models of Magic: Some Preliminary Considerations." *Norveg* 18, 77–109.

Håkansson, Håkan. *Seeing the Word: John Dee and Renaissance Occultism*. Lund: Lunds Universitet, 2001.

Harris, Roy. *Introduction to Integrational Linguistics*. Oxford, UK: Elsevier Science, 1998.

———. *Language, Saussure, and Wittgenstein: How to Play Games with Words*. London: Routledge, 1988.

Hatab, Lawrence J. *Myth and Philosophy: A Contest of Truths*. La Salle, IL: Open Court, 1990.

Hawkes, Terence. *Structuralism and Semiotics*. Berkeley, CA: University of California Press, 1977.

Heidegger, Martin. *Basic Writings*. Edited by David Farrell Krell. Revised and expanded edition. New York: HarperCollins, 1993.

————. *Introduction to Metaphysics.* Translation by Gregory Fried and Richard Polt. New Haven: University of Connecticut Press, 2000.

————. *On the Way to Language.* San Francisco: Harper and Row, 1982.

Hine, Phil. *Condensed Chaos: An Introduction to Chaos Magic.* Tempe, AZ: Falcon, 2010.

Hockett, Charles F. "The Origin of Speech." *Scientific American* 203 (1960): 88–111.

Holdcraft, David. *Saussure: Signs, System, and Arbitrariness.* Cambridge: University of Cambridge Press, 1991.

Hoopes, James, ed. *Peirce on Signs.* Chapel Hill, NC: University of North Carolina Press, 1991.

Iversen, Erik. *The Myth of Egypt and Its Hieroglyphs in European Tradition.* Princeton: Princeton University Press, 1993.

Jackson, M. B. *Sigils, Ciphers and Scripts.* Somerset, UK: Green Magic, 2013.

Josephson-Storm, Jason. *The Myth of Disenchantment.* Chicago: University of Chicago Press, 2017.

Joshi, S. T. *The Rise and Fall of the Cthulhu Mythos.* Poplar Bluff, MO: Mythos, 2008.

Kaczinski, Richard. *Perdurabo: The Life of Aleister Crowley.* Berkeley, CA: North Atlantic, 2010.

Keller, Rudi. *A Theory of Linguistic Signs.* Oxford: Oxford University Press, 1998.

Kershaw, Kris. *The One-eyed God: Odin and the (Indo-)Germanic Männerbünde.* Washington, DC: Journal of Indo-European Studies, 2000.

Kroeger, Paul. *Analyzing Meaning.* Second edition. Berlin: Language Science, 2019.

Lakoff, George. *Women, Fire, and Dangerous Things: What Categories Reveal About the Mind.* Chicago: University of Chicago Press, 1987.

Lakoff, George, and Mark Johnson. *Metaphors We Live By.* Chicago: University of Chicago Press, 1980.

LaVey, Anton Szandor. *The Satanic Bible.* New York: Avon, 1969.

————. *The Satanic Rituals.* New York: Avon, 1972.

Lee, Dave. *Chaotopia! Sorcery and Ecstasy in the Fifth Aeon.* Oxford, UK: Mandrake of Oxford, 2006.

List, Guido von. *The Secret of the Runes.* Translated with commentary by Stephen E. Flowers. Rochester, VT: Destiny Books: 1988.

Lovecraft, H. P. *Bloodcurdling Tales of Horror and the Macabre: The Best of H. P. Lovecraft*. New York: Del Rey, 2002.

———. *The Dream Cycle of H. P. Lovecraft: Dreams of Terror and Death*. New York: Del Rey, 1995.

McCown, Chester C. "The Ephesia Grammata in Popular Belief." *Transactions and Proceedings of the American Philological Association* 54 (1923): 128–40.

Mercer, A. D. *Runa: The Wisdom of the Runes*. London: Troy, 2020.

Merrell, Floyd. *Semiosis in the Postmodern Age*. West Lafayette: Purdue University Press, 1995.

Miller, Patricia Cox. *The Poetry of Thought in Late Antiquity*. Burlington, VT: Ashgate, 2001.

Mirecki, Paul Allan, and Marvin W. Meyer. *Magic and Ritual in the Ancient World*. Leiden, Netherlands: Brill Academic Publishers, 2001.

Nöth, Winfried. *Handbook of Semiotics*. Bloomington: Indiana University Press, 1990.

Ostler, Nicholas. *Empires of the Word: A Language History of the World*. New York: Harper Collins, 2005.

Otto, Bernd-Christian, and Michael Strausberg, eds. *Defining Magic: A Reader*. London: Routledge, 2013.

Otto, Rudolf. *The Idea of the Holy*. Mansfield Center, CT: Martino Publishing, 2010.

Owen, Alex. "The Sorcerer and His Apprentice: Aleister Crowley and the Magical Exploration of Edwardian Subjectivity." *Journal of British Studies* 36.1 (January 1997): 99–133.

Parry, Glyn. *The Arch-conjuror of England, John Dee*. New Haven, CT: Yale University Press, 2011.

Peirce, Charles Sanders. *Collected Papers*. Cambridge, MA: Harvard University Press, 1932.

———. "How to Make Our Ideas Clear." *Popular Science Monthly* 12 (January 1878): 286–302.

Pollington, Stephen. *Runes: Literacy in the Germanic Iron Age*. Ely, UK: Anglo-Saxon Books, 2016.

P-Orridge, Genesis Breyer. *Thee Psychick Bible*. Port Townsend, WA: Feral House, 2010.

Rauch, Irmengard, and Gerald F. Carr, eds. *The Signifying Animal.* Bloomington, IN: Indiana University Press, 1980.

Ritner, Robert K. *The Mechanics of Ancient Egyptian Magical Practice.* Chicago: University of Chicago Press, 1993.

Robinson, James M., ed. *The Nag Hammadi Library.* San Francisco: Harper Collins, 1990.

Roblee, Mark. *"Greetings, I am an Immortal God!": Reading, Imagination, and Personal Divinity in Late Antiquity, 2nd–5th Centuries CE.* Dissertation. Amherst, MA: University of Massachusetts Amherst, 2019.

———. "Performing Circles in Ancient Egypt from Mehen to Ouroboros." *Preternature: Critical and Historical Studies on the Preternatural* 7.2 (2018): 133–53.

Sandars, N. K., trans. *Poems of Heaven and Hell from Ancient Mesopotamia.* London: Penguin, 1971.

Sapir, Edward. *Language.* New York: Harcourt, Brace, and Company, 1921.

Saussure, Ferdinand de. *Course in General Linguistics.* Translated by Roy Harris. Chicago: Open Court, 1983.

Schwaller de Lubicz, R. A. *Symbol and the Symbolic.* Rochester, VT: Inner Traditions, 1981.

Sebeok, Thomas A. *Signs: An Introduction.* Toronto: University of Toronto Press, 2001.

Segal, Robert A. *Myth: A Very Short Introduction.* Oxford: Oxford University Press, 2015.

Seifrid, Thomas. *The Word Made Self: Russian Writings on Language, 1860–1930.* Ithaca, NY: Cornell University Press, 2005.

Semple, Gavin W. *Zos-Kia: An Introductory Essay on the Art and Sorcery of Austin Osman Spare.* London: Fulgur, 1995.

Shell, Scott. *The Application of Peircean Semiotics to the Elder Futhark Tradition.* New York: Lang, 2023.

Sørensen, Jesper. *A Cognitive Theory of Magic.* Lanham, MD: AltaMira, 2007.

Spare, Austin Osman. *Ethos: The Magical Writings of Austin Osman Spare.* Edited by Frederick Carter. Thame, UK: I-H-O, 2001.

Steiner, George. *After Babel: Aspects of Language and Translation.* Oxford: Oxford University Press, 1975.

Stephenson, Neal. *Snow Crash.* New York: Del Ray, 1992.

Stern, David G. *Wittgenstein on Mind and Language*. Oxford: Oxford University Press, 1995.

Stevens, Matthew Levi. *The Magical World of William S. Burroughs*. Oxford, UK: Mandrake of Oxford, 2014.

Tambiah, Stanley J. *Culture, Thought, and Social Action*. Cambridge, MA: Harvard University Press, 1985.

———. *Magic, Science, Religion and the Scope of Rationality*. Cambridge, UK: Cambridge University Press, 1990.

———. "The Magical Power of Words." *Man*, n.s. 3.2 (June 1968): 175–208.

Taussig, Hal, Jared Calaway, Maia Kostritis, Colene Lillie, and Justin Lasser. *The Thunder: Perfect Mind: A New Translation and Introduction*. New York: Palgrave Macmillan, 2010.

Te Velde, Herman. "The God Heka in Egyptian Mythology." *Jaarbericht ex Oriente Lux* 21 (1974): 175–86.

Thellefsen, Torkild, and Bent Sørensen, eds. *Umberto Eco in His Own Words*. Berlin: De Gruyter, 2017.

Thorsson, Edred. *ALU: An Advanced Guide to Operative Runology*. San Francisco: Red Wheel/Weiser, 2012.

———. *The Big Book of Runes and Rune Magic*. Newburyport, MA: Weiser, 2018.

———. *The Nine Doors of Midgard: A Curriculum of Rune-work*. Fifth Revised and Expanded Edition. South Burlington, VT: The Rune-Gild, 2016.

———. *Rune Might: The Secret Practices of the German Rune Magicians*. Rochester, VT: Inner Traditions, 2018.

Versnel, H. S. "The Poetics of the Magical Charm: An Essay in the Power of Words" in *Magic and Ritual in the Ancient World*, edited by Paul Mirecki and Marvin Meyer. Leiden: Brill, 2002. Pp. 105–158.

Wallace, William. *The Catalpa Monographs: A Critical Survey of Austin Osman Spare*. London: Jerusalem, 2015.

Webb, Don. *How to Become a Modern Magus: A Manual for Magicians of All Schools*. Rochester, VT: Inner Traditions, 2023.

———. *Overthrowing the Old Gods: Aleister Crowley and the Book of the Law*. Rochester, VT: Inner Traditions, 2013.

———. *Seven Faces of Darkness: Practical Typhonian Magic*. Bastrop, TX: Lodestar, 1996.

Whorf, Benjamin Lee. *Language, Thought, and Reality*. Cambridge, MA: MIT Press, 1956.

Wilburn, Andrew T. *Materia Magica: The Archaeology of Magic in Roman Egypt, Cyprus, and Spain*. Ann Arbor: University of Michigan Press, 2012.

Wittgenstein, Ludwig. *Philosophical Investigations*. German text with English translation by G. E. M. Anscombe, P. M. S. Hacker, and Joachim Schulte. Fourth edition revised by P. M. S. Hacker and Joachim Schulte. Oxford: Wiley-Blackwell, 2009.

INDEX

absolute idealism, 97–98
acquiring an assistant daimon spell, 181–83
alphabet of desire, 258–60
Angelic Language, 247–48
Anglo-Saxon Futhorc, 221–22
anthropology
  British, magic and, 45–49
  development of, 44–45
  evolution of, 49–52
Aquino, Michael A. *See also* Temple of Set
  about, 265
  The Book of Coming Forth by Night, 266, 267–72, 278
  Dee and, 272–74
  Enochian Keys and, 272–73
  HarWer and, 269
  Word of Set, 266–67, 272–74, 278
Armanen runes. *See also* runes
  about, 230–31
  communicative features of, 234–36
  cycles, 236
  as ideographic, 239
  Kala and, 237–39
  key to, 238
  List's formula, 236–37
  Nazi rune imagery and, 232
  practices, 235

spells, 231–32, 236
system, 232–33
writings on, 234
articulation, 182
artificial intelligence (AI), 31, 303
Askr and Embla myth, 155
Austin, John Langshaw, 133–34
awareness, practice of, 305

Bacon, Roger, 73
barbarous names, 178–79, 183
Barthes, Roland, 108–10, 148, 170, 173, 285
Baudrillard, Jean, 11, 173, 270, 279
Being, 2, 90, 129, 138–40
bind runes, 228–30
biosemiotics, 103–5
Book of Shadows, 167–68
Book of Coming Forth by Night, The, (Aquino), 266, 267–72, 278
Brothers Grimm, 113–14
Bull, Christian, 197
Burroughs, William S., 123, 282–83, 299

Carroll, Peter J., 281, 282
categories, x, 59, 94, 96, 106, 124–25
Chaos Magic
  about, 278–79

magical diary, 280
malleability of belief and, 280–81
organized chaos, 281–82
sigils, 279–80
charaktêres, 179–80
Choronzon, 253
Church of Satan, 135, 260–65
Cipher Manuscript, 248–49
codes
  about, 60–61
  categories and, 125
  context and, 103
  finding altercations in, 107
  Firstness and, 90
  magic and, 107–8
  perception and, 61
  sharing and ownership of, 84
  use of, 84
Cognitive Linguistics, 125–26
cognitive science, 58–59
coherence, 3, 27, 76–77, 80, 100,
    109–10, 152–53, 250, 277
cohesion, 27, 76–77, 250
cohesiveness, 3, 100
coincidence intensifiers, 21–22
Come Into Being, 273, 277–78
communication
  action of, 132
  language and, 2–3
  magical, 2, 3, 32, 38
  mundane, 11, 26, 101, 131, 240, 282
  occurrence of, 2
  operative, 4–5, 63, 212
  signs and, 27
  SMR model of, 29–32
  symbolic, 36–39
community, 37, 77–78, 142–43, 303
conceptual metaphors
  about, 126, 216

examples, 127–28, 192, 198, 199–201
  mapping and, 128
  processing, 128
  rituals and, 250
  sequence of, 189–90
  use of, 183, 252, 276–77
conceptual models, 31–32, 42, 104–5
context
  about, 78
  codes and, 103
  creating and influencing, 131
  importance of, 25, 102
  in magical communication, 131
  practitioners and, 11–12
  SMR model and, 31
contextualization, 131
conventional signs, 6
Course in General Linguistics
    (Saussure), 74–75
critical period, 16
Crowley, Aleister
  about, 251
  Choronzon and, 253
  Liber Samekh and, 254–57
  preparation statement and, 256
  reading list, 299
  ritual setting, 255–56
  scrying, 253
  Thelema and, 251–57
  The Vision and the Voice, 251–53
cultural evolution, 20
cultural transmission
  about, 6, 17, 52
  codes and, 120
  functioning of, 17–18
  principle of, 120, 123
culture
  categories of, 13
  conceptual artifacts of, 122

ethical, 13
ethnic, 13
language and, 17–18
linguistic, 17–18, 44
magic and, 56
material, 13
mythology and, 158
perspectives of, 68
universal patterns of, 59
curses, 70, 203–5, 228
curse tablets (*defixiones*)
about, 153, 203
connection, 205
magic as communication and, 204
Set-Typhon and, 205
use of, 204
Cybernetic Culture Research Unit
(CCRU), 19

Dasein, 138–40
Dee, John, 242, 246–48, 252, 269,
272–74
default, the, 107
descriptive meaning, 140–41
design features of language
about, 118
cultural transmission, 120, 123
duality of patterning, 119, 120–21
features, 118–20
learnability, 120, 122
prevarication, 120, 121
reflexivity, 120, 121–22
diachronic linguistics, 115
dialectical materialism, 45
Die Elektrischen Vorspiele (The
Electrical Preludes), 135–37
*Discourse on the Eighth and Ninth,
The*, 196–203
disenchantment, 41, 49, 55

displacement, 6, 16, 121
duality of patterning, 119, 120–21
Dunn, Patrick, 38, 60–61, 247
Durkheim, Émile, 48–49
dymythologizing, 108–9

Eco, Umberto, 105–8
Egill's Saga, 220
Egyptian magic, 206
ek erilaR formula, 64–65
Elder Futhark. *See also* Futharks
about, 214, 216
inscriptions, 63–65
names, 224
staves, 217
system, 217–18
emergent complexity, 80–81
Enki, 168–70
Enochian Keys, 260–61, 272
Enochian magic
about, 242–43
Angelic Language, 247–48
Cipher Manuscript and, 248–49
"Enochiana" history and, 247
Golden Dawn and, 248–51,
252
origins of, 246–48
Enuma Eliš
about, 159–60
Anu-power and, 163
divine speech, 198
Ea and, 161–62, 163
Lahmu and Lahamu and, 161
Marduk and, 162–65
Mummu and, 161
Tablet of Destinies and, 163–65
title origin, 160
ephesia grammata, 177–78, 184
ethical culture, 13

ethnic culture, 13
Everett, Daniel, 12, 18
execration texts, 205–7
expressive meaning, 140–41
externalization, 194

"family resemblances," 143
Father, the, 197–99, 201–2
fehu, 88, 215, 216
felicity conditions, 133
Fichte, J. G., 92, 94–96, 193
fiction, 39–40
Firstness, 88, 89, 90–91, 92, 104
fixed code and fixed rules, 30
Flowers, Stephen E., 10, 61–65, 211
frame of reference, 5, 51–52, 53, 57.
    See also context
Frazer, James, 46–48, 101–2, 273
Futharks. *See also* runes
    about, 213
    Anglo-Saxon Futhorc, 221–22
    Elder Futhark, 214, 216, 217–18, 224
    semiotics and metaphor in, 215–22
    Younger Futhark, 218–21

Geist, 97–98
German idealism, 92–98
gods, Lovecraftian, 22–24
Golden Dawn, 242, 247–52, 254,
    260, 279
Gospel of John, 157–58
Grambo, Ronald, 52–54
Greater Black Magic (GBM), 274–75,
    277
Great Old Ones, 22–24, 40, 301–5
Greek Magical Papyri (PGM)
    about, 153, 157, 176
    acquiring an assistant daimon spell,
    181–83

barbarous names and, 178–79, 183
charaktêres and, 179–80
ephesia grammata and, 177–78, 184
history and collection, 176
memory spell, 184–85
spells, 180–90
Grimm, Jacob and Wilhelm, 113–14

Harris, Roy, 130–31
Headless One, 117, 186–90, 254, 256
Headless Ritual. *See also* Greek
    Magical Papyri (PGM); spells
    about, 185–86
    communication with the Headless
    One, 188–89
    Headless One manifestation, 190
    invocation of *Aképhalos*, 186–87
    invocation success, 190
    paired opposites, 187–88
    preparation instructions, 187
    summoning the Headless One,
    187–88
Hegel, W. F., 92, 97–98
Heidegger, Martin, 137–40
heka, 151–53
Hermes, 65, 150, 153–54, 167,
    175–76
Hermes-Thoth, 154, 298
Hermes Trismegistus, 150, 154, 176,
    196–97, 201–2
Hockett, Charles, 118–22, 194–95
Homo genus, 12–13
Hubert, Henri, 49
hyperstitions
    about, 18–20
    beginning of, 20
    coincidence intensifiers, 21–22
    commonality of, 21
    cultural evolution and, 20

functioning of, 21
recognition of, 20

icons. *See also* signs
about, 6, 47, 87, 101, 128
Firstness and, 90
runes, 101
use of, 68
idealism
about, 92–93
absolute, 97–98
German, 92–98
subjective, 94–96
transcendental, 93–94
"ignorance is childhood," 199
Illuminates of Thanateros (IOT), 281
indexes, 48, 87–88
indirect object, 57
*Infernal Geometry and the Left-Hand
Path* (Chappell), 22, 245, 266
infinite semiosis, 27–28, 61, 87, 99
information hazard, 168
integrational linguistics, 129–32

Jakobson, Roman, 29–31, 66
Johnson, Mark, 125–26

ka, 152–53, 277
Kala, 237–39
Kant, Immanuel, 92, 93–94
Kelley, Edward, 242, 246–47, 269
Key, Wilson Bryan, 290–91
Kia, 257–58
knowledge
esoteric, reverence for, 202
initiation into, 196–97
as prerequisite, 199
transmission of, 197
Kragehul spear shaft, 229

Lakoff, George, 125–26
Land, Nick, 21
language
about, 6, 11
acquisition of, 16–18
in adding precision, 18
in altering connections/categories,
124
as collection of signs, 25
concept externalization in, 145
culture and, 17–18
design features of, 16–17, 118–22
hyperstition and, 18–24
as living phenomenon, 143–44
magic of, in modern creations, 165–71
mental capability for, 12
mythology and, 149, 159–65
philosophy of, 132–40
in ritual, 55
in spreading memes, 123
transmission and transformation of,
17–18
use of, 11
as virus, 122–25
when did it begin, 12–14
why did it begin, 14–16
word deployment, 129
language-games, 141–42
langue/parole, 75–79, 115–16
LaVey, Anton
about, 135–36, 260
Church of Satan, 260–65
communication techniques, 265
Enochian Keys and, 260–61
Invocation of Satan, 264
Law of the Trapezoid, 261–62
Nine Satanic Statements, 263
performative utterances and, 265
ritual style, 262–63

law of contagion, 47–48, 102, 185
law of magical semiosis, 67–68
law of similarity, 101, 273
law of sympathy, 47, 49, 67, 69, 128, 180, 295
Law of the Trapezoid, 261–62
lead, 204
learnability, 120, 122
Lee, Dave, 278
Leiber, Fritz, 299–300
Lesser Black Magic (LBM), 274, 275
Lévi-Strauss, Claude, 51–52
Liber Samekh (Crowley), 254–57
linguistic communities, 142–43
linguistic culture, 13, 17–18, 44
linguistics
    about, 7, 112
    cognitive, 125
    development of, 43–44
    diachronic, 115
    integrational, 129–32
    magic and, 8–9
    modern, beginnings of, 113–18
    synchronic, 115
linguistic turn, 133
List, Guido von, 230–39
Locke, John, 73–74
Lovecraft, H. P., 19, 22–24, 40, 100, 165–67, 297–98
lying, 106–7

Magia Loci, 301–5
magic
    about, 4, 32–33, 34
    alternative solutions, 50
    change and, 4
    cities and, 302–3
    cognitive models of, 58–60
    as communication, 2, 3, 38

as conceptual model, 34
fictional, 39–42
importance of, 301–2
power of, 294–95
runes and, 210–12
science and, 1
secret of, 15
semiotic view, 38
sigil, 131–32
sympathetic, 47
magical communication. *See also* communication
    Shell's approach to, 70
    within Temple of Set, 274–78
    van Baal model, 57–58
magical fiction, 39–42
magical link, 271
magical semiosis, 66–68, 206. *See also* semiosis
magical techniques, 15
magical theories, ix–x
magical thinking
    about, 32–33
    defaults as, 34
    as mindset, 33
    in shifting frame of reference, 51–52
    sympathetic magic, 47
    Umwelt and, 105
Malinowski, Bronisław, 50–51, 56
mapping, 128, 249
material culture, 13
Mauss, Marcel, 49
meaning
    ancient alphabets and, 215
    descriptive, 140–41
    expressive, 140–41
    rituals and, 84
    semiotics and, 62

signs and, 25–27, 28
as social phenomenon, 77–78
symbolic means and, 49
symbols and, 57
syntagma, 116–17
of words, 56
meaning is use, 78, 84
Mediterranean magic, 176, 183, 193
memes
about, 14
coevolution of, 15
humans and, 17
language in spreading, 123
magic and, 15–16
as secondary replicator, 14–15
memory spell, 184–85
Mercury, 154–55
metaphors, 125, 215–22. *See also*
conceptual metaphors
metonymy, 47
Miller, Patricia Cox, 147
models
cognitive, 58–60
conceptual, 31–32, 42, 104–5
Flowers, 63–65
Grambo, 52–54
for magical communication, 32
runes and, 61–62
SMR, 29–31
Tambiah, 54–56
mudras, 235
mundane communication, 11, 26,
101, 131, 240, 282
mutual intelligibility, 64
mythology
about, 148–49
Babylonian creation myth,
159–65
language and, 149, 159–65

neomythology and, 166
Sumerian roots, 167–71

Nag Hammadi library
about, 191
Discourse on the Eighth and Ninth,
The, 196–203
protecting, 203
The Thunder, Perfect Mind, 191–96
naming, 194–96
nam-shub, 168–70
Necronomicon, 166, 167–68
neither-neither, 258, 259, 281
neomythology, 166, 262–63
Neuburg, Victor, 252, 253
noninterest/nondisinterest, 281
Nöth, Winfried, 66–67
Nyarlathotep, 166–67, 298

Odin
about, 65, 155
Askr and Embla myth and, 155–56
etymology, 223
Mediterranean gods of
communication and, 156–57
rune poems and, 225
runes and, 70, 222–23
speech and, 225
operative communication, 4–5, 63, 212
opposites, 187–88, 192
organization, this book, 7–8
Otto, Rudolf, 129, 145

paradigm and syntagma, 79–81, 116
Peirce, Charles Sanders
about, 6, 27, 74, 85
as father of pragmatism, 85–86
German idealism and, 98
the phaneron and, 98–101

pragmatism, 158
Scott Shell and, 68
semiotics as fundamental core and, 86
semiurgy and, 101–3
signs and, 86–92
Pentagram of Set, 271
perceptual world, 34–35
performative utterances
about, 54, 133
constitutive, 134, 135
as language model, 137
operative communication and, 4
regulative, 134–35
phaneron, the, 35, 98–101
pleroma, 200–201
Poetic Edda, 222–23
pragmatism, 85–86, 158
prevarication, 120, 121
productivity, 16, 119

reflexivity
about, 6, 17, 120, 139
language and, 121–22
semiosis and, 158
this book as example, 17
use of, 202
representamen, 87
ritual
about, 54
language in, 55
meaning and, 84
as mythic narrative, 81
signs and conceptual metaphors
and, 250
ritual space, 83–84
ritual work, 84
Rosicrucians, 292
rune formulas
about, 211

association of, 211–12
runemaster formulas, 226,
227
runestave repetition, 226, 228
types of, 211, 226
runemaster formulas, 226, 227
rune poems, 224–25
runes
about, 209–10
Anglo-Saxon Futhorc, 221–22
Armanen, 230–39
blind, 228–30
Elder Futhark, 215, 216, 217–18
historical and linguistic roots of,
212–15
iconic signs of, 101
magic and, 62–65, 210–12
mythic origins, 222–23
names of, 214–15, 237
other alphabetic systems and, 213–15
syntagmatic uses of, 227
as system of operative
communication, 212
types of, 213
use of, 210
working with, 55–56
Younger Futhark, 218–21
Runes and Magic (Flowers), 63
runestaves, 213, 226, 228

Satanic Bible, The (LaVey), 263
Satanic Rituals, The (LaVey), 262–63
Saussure, Ferdinand de
about, 52, 74–75
dichotomies, 115–16
langue/parole and, 75–79, 115–16
linguistic sign and, 81
paradigm/syntagma and, 79, 116
signifier and signified and, 81–84, 114

speech circuit, 78
structural linguistics and, 114–15
Science of Knowledge, 95
scientism, 1, 32, 41
secondary replicator, 14–15
Secondness, 88, 89, 91, 92, 104
seed words, 237–39
Self, 94, 305
semiology, 5, 25, 52, 83, 85, 308
semiosis
    about, 5, 24, 35, 73
    communication and, 27
    Firstness and Secondness and, 104
    infinite, 27–28, 61, 87, 99
    magical, acts of, 66–67, 206
    magical, law of, 67–68
    physiology behind, 103
    reading a text and, 76
    reflexivity and, 158
semiotic chain, 27
semiotic codes. *See* codes
semiotic model, 53–54, 56
semiotics
    about, 5, 24
    biosemiotics and, 103–5
    conclusion, 288–89
    core concepts of, 10
    development of, 73–74
    in Futharks, 215–22
    infinite semiosis and, 27–28
    linguistics and, 10–11
    meaning and, 62
    Peircean, 85–103
    perspectives on, 103–11
    structural, 74–85
    use of, 2
semiotic theory, x, 295
semiotic webs
    about, 25

altering, 36, 37, 41–42
creation of, 100–101, 106
magicians and, 53
signs of, 38
sketching out, 38
in use, 206
semiurgy
    about, 11, 81, 173, 242
    coherence and, 100
    emergent complexity and, 81
    Firstness and, 90
    language and, 132, 144
    of LaVeyan satanism, 263–64
    modern approaches to, 242–85
    Peirce and, 101–3
    practice of, 145
    runes and, 209–40
    theories of, 106
sender-message-receiver (SMR) model, 29–31, 66
sense and referent, 141
Set-Typhon, 154, 180, 189, 205
Shell, Scott, 61–62, 67–71, 206
sigils
    about, 131, 243
    Austin Osman Spare and, 244–46
    charging methods, 245–46
    creation of, 131–32, 245
    evolution of, 242–46
    functioning of, 243
    repopularization of, 279–80
    roots, 243–44
    TOPY and, 284
signals, 57
signifier and signified, 81–84
sign networks, 25, 81, 118, 141, 188.
    See also semiotic webs
signs. *See also* semiotics; symbols
    about, 24–25, 86–87

accumulated experience of, 89–92
actionable interpretation of, 28
categories of, 87–89
communication and, 27
creation of, 270
cultural origin and content of, 107
existing, interrelating with, 26
Firstness and, 88, 89, 90–91, 92
functions, 107
interpretation of, 26, 36
interrelations between, 109–10
lying and, 106–7
meaning, 25–27, 28
parts of, 86
Peirce and, 86–103
qualities of, 88–89
rituals and, 250
Secondness and, 88, 89, 91, 92
text, 76–77
Thirdness and, 88–89, 91, 92
as vehicles for conception, 83
similarity, 64, 101, 273
Snow Crash (Stephenson), 168, 170
Sørensen, Jesper, 59–60
source domains, 128, 216
Spare, Austin Osman
  about, 242
  alphabet of desire, 258–60
  Kia and, 257–58
  neither-neither and, 258, 259, 281
  sigils, 280
speech acts, 133
speech community, 37, 77–78
spells
  about, 180
  for acquiring an assistant daimon,
    181–83
  Armanen runes, 231–32, 236
  description of nature of, 296

"Headless Ritual," 185–90
language and, 130
memory, 184–85
from PGM, 180–90
preparation instructions, 187
Spencer, Herbert, 45
staves, 210, 226
storytelling, 149–50
structuralism, 25, 51, 52
subjective idealism, 94–95
Sumerian language, 167–71
summons, 96, 163
superstition, 19–20
symbolic communication, 36–39
symbolic means, 4, 5, 49, 51, 83, 105
symbolist magic, 49
symbols
  about, 6, 35, 57, 88
  as arbitrary, 36
  characteristics of, 36–37
  as culturally coded, 37
  framework for, 60–61
  key concepts, 6
  meaning and, 7, 57
  use of, 57
  words, 49
sympathetic magic, 47
synchronic linguistics, 115
syntagma
  about, 53, 116
  analysis, 116–18
  full meaning of, 116
  paradigm and, 79–81, 116
  use of, 182–83

Tablet of Destinies, 163–65
Tambiah, Stanley, 54–56, 134–35
target domain, 128
telementation, 29–30

Temple of Set. *See also* Aquino,
  Michael A.
  about, 266
  Black Flame, 276
  Gift of Set, 269
  Greater Black Magic (GBM),
    274–75, 277
  invocation of Set, 276–77
  Lesser Black Magic (LBM), 274, 275
  magical communication within,
    274–78
  Pentagram of Set, 271
  Setian rubric, 275–76
text, 76–77
Thee Temple of Psychick Youth
  (TOPY), 282–83
Thelema, 251, 254–57
Thirdness, 88–89, 91, 92
Thoth. *See also* Hermes-Thoth
  about, 150
  heka and, 151–53
  Hermes and, 175–76
  influence of, 150–51
  language and, 151
  reflexivity and, 202
Thunder, Perfect Mind, The,
  191–96
Tolkien, J. R. R., 209
Tower of Babel myth, 169–70
transcendental idealism, 93–94

transcendent word, 158
"truth is a mirror," 201
Tylor, E. B., 46, 48

Uexküll, Jakob von, 103–5
Umwelt, 35, 68, 103–5

van Baal, Jan, 56–58, 78, 295–96
visualization, 131, 297
voces magicae, 177–78, 182, 189

Webb, Don, 5, 15, 190, 290–93,
  294–300
Weber, Max, 49–50, 55
Weltanschauung, 68–69
Westcott, W. W., 248–49
Wittgenstein, Ludwig, 78, 103,
  140–44
Word, 157–59
Word of Set (Aquino), 266–67,
  272–74, 278
word(s)
  kernel, 237
  meaning and, 215
  seed, 237–39
  self-creation through, 193
  transmission of, 200

Yagmin, Brenda, 301–5
Younger Futhark, 218–21